Paul + Meg,

May this work contribute to
the blessing of a new,
colorful, + multifaith
tomorrow. Thank you
for your work in social
transformation.

Ed Jennings

9/5/17

Teaching for a Multifaith World

Teaching for a Multifaith World

Edited by
ELEAZAR S. FERNANDEZ

PICKWICK *Publications* • Eugene, Oregon

TEACHING FOR A MULTIFAITH WORLD

Copyright © 2017 Wipf and Stock. All rights reserved. Except for brief quotations in critical publications or reviews, no part of this book may be reproduced in any manner without prior written permission from the publisher. Write: Permissions, Wipf and Stock Publishers, 199 W. 8th Ave., Suite 3, Eugene, OR 97401.

Pickwick Publications
An Imprint of Wipf and Stock Publishers
199 W. 8th Ave., Suite 3
Eugene, OR 97401

www.wipfandstock.com

PAPERBACK ISBN: 978-1-4982-3974-5
HARDCOVER ISBN: 978-1-4982-3976-9
EBOOK ISBN: 978-1-4982-3975-2

Cataloging-in-Publication data:

Names: Fernandez, Eleazar S., editor.

Title: Teaching for a multifaith world / edited by Eleazar S. Fernandez.

Description: Eugene, OR: Pickwick Publications, 2017 | Includes bibliographical references.

Identifiers: ISBN: 978-1-4982-3974-5 (paperback). | ISBN: 978-1-4982-3976-9 (hardcover). | ISBN: 978-1-4982-3975-2 (ebook).

Subjects: Multiculturalism—Religious aspects | Religious education.

Classification: BV1471.3 T15 2017 (print) | BV1471.3 (ebook).

Manufactured in the U.S.A.   05/04/17

Scripture quotations come from the New Revised Standard Version Bible, copyright 1989, Division of Christian Education of the National Council of Churches of Christ in the United States of America. Used by permission. All rights reserved.

Contents

Contributors

Justus N. Baird is Dean of Auburn Theological Seminary in New York. He oversees education programs that help build multifaith movements for social justice. Prior to becoming Dean in 2012, he directed Auburn's multifaith work for five years. Rabbi Baird was ordained at Hebrew Union College–Jewish Institute of Religion where he studied as a Wexner Graduate Fellow. He received a B.S. from Rice University and holds a certificate in Strategic Human Resource Management from Harvard Business School. As an educational entrepreneur he co-founded Questia.com (1999), a successful and far-reaching academic online library, and Yerusha (2009), an experimental approach to Jewish supplementary school. Some of his recent writings include *Israel and the Diaspora: Two Foci of a Single Ellipse*; *Faith, Money, and Politics* (remarks given at a Congressional Briefing on June 11, 2014, and featured on Congress Blog "The Hill"); *Free Speech Just Got More Expensive*; and *Multifaith Education in American Theological Schools: Looking Back, Looking Ahead*, in *Teaching Theology and Religion* 16:4.

Eleazar S. Fernandez is Professor of Constructive Theology at United Theological Seminary of the Twin Cities, New Brighton, Minnesota. Some of his published works include *Teaching for a Culturally Diverse and Racially Just World*; *Burning Center, Porous Borders: The Church in a Globalized World*; *New Overtures: Asian North American Theology*; *Reimagining the Human*; *Realizing the America of Our Hearts*; *A Dream Unfinished*; and *Toward a Theology of Struggle*. He is also President of Union Theological Seminary, Philippines.

Ruben L. F. Habito is Professor of World Religions and Spirituality and Director of Spiritual Formation at Perkins School of Theology at Southern Methodist University, Dallas, Texas. Some of his works include *Zen and the Spiritual Exercises: Paths of Awakening and Transformation*; *The Gospel* *among Religions: Christian Ministry, Theology, and Spirituality in a Multi-faith World* (co-edited with David R. Brockman); *Vida Zen, Vida Divina: Un Dialogo entre Budismo Zen y Cristianismo,* (Spanish edition of *Living Zen, Loving God*); *Healing Breath: Zen for Buddhists and Christians in a Wounded World,* 3rd ed., rev.; and *Experiencing Buddhism: Ways of Wisdom and Compassion.*

Mary E. Hess is Professor of Educational Leadership and Chair of the Leadership Division at Luther Seminary, St. Paul, Minnesota. Hess joined the Luther Seminary faculty in July of 2000. She received her B.A. in American Studies in 1985 from Yale University in New Haven, Connecticut, and her M.T.S. degree in 1992 from Harvard University in Cambridge, Massachusetts. In 1998, she received her Ph.D. in religion and education from Boston College in Chestnut Hill, Massachusetts. Her most recent publications include: *Teaching Reflectively in Theological Contexts: Promises and Contradictions,* and *Engaging Technology in Theological Education: All that We Can't Leave Behind.*

Robert A. Hunt is Director of Global Theological Education, Professor of Inter-religious Relations and Christian Mission, and Director of the Center for Evangelism and Missional Church Studies at Perkins School of Theology at Southern Methodist University, Dallas, Texas. Among his professional distinctions are: President, Association of Professors in Mission (2008–2009); Board of Scholars, *Journal of Inter-Religious Dialogue*; Leadership Team, *Christianity in Southeast Asia Research Project,* Center for the Study of Christianity in Southeast Asia. Some of his writings include, "Christian Identity in a Pluralistic World," in *Missiology,* Vol. 36, Spring 2009; "Reforming American Views of Muslims: A View from the Trenches," in *World Christianity in Muslim Encounter,* Vol. 2 (ed. Stephen R. Goodwin), and *Continuum Religious Studies.*

Cindi Beth Johnson is Director for Arts, Faith, and Culture at United Theological Seminary of the Twin Cities, New Brighton, Minnesota. Johnson is an ordained minister in the Evangelical Lutheran Church in America, and a Board member and secretary of the Society for Arts in Religion and Theological Studies (SARTS), an academic society. Some of her works include, "Messengers of Jazz," in *Visual Theology: Forming and Transforming the Community through the Arts,* edited by Robin M. Jensen and Kimberly Vrudny, and "Exploring Caravaggio's Calling of Saint Matthew," in *Seasons of the Spirit Congregational Life Resource for Pentecost 1.* Johnson's essay was written with the invaluable assistance of Dr. Jann Cather Weaver, Associate

Professor Emerita of Worship, and Theology and the Arts, United Theological Seminary of the Twin Cities.

Sheryl A. Kujawa-Holbrook is Vice President for Academic Affairs, Dean of the Faculty, and Professor of Practical Theology and Religious Education at Claremont School of Theology, California. A priest of the Episcopal Diocese of Los Angeles, she is an educator, trainer, writer, and retreat and conference leader. She is a member of the boards of the *Journal of Inter-Religious Dialogue* and the Kaleidoscope Institute, and review editor for *Anglican and Episcopal History*. Her recent publications and achievements include: *Pilgrimage—The Sacred Art: Journey to the Center of the Heart*; Interfaith Grant Recipient from The Center for the Study of Jewish-Christian-Muslim Relations at Merrimack College; *God Beyond Borders: Congregations Building Interfaith Community*; *Seeing God in Each Other*; and *A House of Prayer for All Peoples: Congregations Building Multiracial Community*.

Lucinda Mosher is Faculty Associate in Interfaith Studies at Hartford Seminary, Connecticut, where she teaches courses on chaplaincy, Christian-Muslim relations, and comparative theology. She was the founding instructor for the annual Worldviews Seminar, an innovative introduction to America's religious diversity held at The University of Michigan-Dearborn 2002–2012. She is the author of the Faith in the Neighborhood series from Seabury Books, co-editor of the Building Bridges Seminar series (on Christian-Muslim dialogical scripture study and comparative theology) from Georgetown University Press, and guest editor of a Teaching Theology and Religion special issue on Multifaith Theological Education. As an interreligious relations consultant, her clients have included Auburn Seminary's Center for Multifaith Education, SCUPE (Seminary Consortium on Urban Pastoral Education), Trinity Institute, Unity Productions Foundation, and National Disaster Interfaiths Network.

Jennifer Peace is Associate Professor of Interfaith Studies, Co-director of the Center for Interreligious and Communal Leadership Education (CIRCLE) at Andover Newton Theological School, Newton Centre, Massachusetts. Prof. Peace is the founding co-chair of the Interreligious and Interfaith Studies group at the American Academy of Religions, launched in 2013. Author of numerous articles and essays on interfaith cooperation, Prof. Peace has been an interfaith organizer and educator since the 1990s. Prof. Peace co-edited *My Neighbor's Faith: Stories of Interreligious Encounter,*

Growth, and Transformation. Currently she is a series editor for a new Palgrave Macmillan book series on interreligious and interfaith studies.

Shanta Premawardhana is the President of SCUPE, an organization based in Chicago that provides leadership education for pluralism, teaching people of faith to break down barriers that divide human communities and build bridges of hope. Previously, he was the director of Interreligious Dialogue and Cooperation at the World Council of Churches in Geneva, Switzerland. Originally from Sri Lanka, he is a long-time urban pastor and leader in congregation-based community organizing and an expert in interreligious dialogue. His Ph.D. in Religion is from Northwestern University in Evanston, Illinois.

Daniel S. Schipani is Professor of Pastoral Care and Counseling at Anabaptist Mennonite Biblical Seminary, Elkhart, Indiana. He received his PhD from Princeton Theological Seminary, Princeton, New Jersey. His works include: *Nuevos Caminos en Psicología Pastoral* (editor); *Interfaith Spiritual Care: Understandings and Practices* (co-editor); *Spiritual Caregiving in the Hospital: Windows to Chaplaincy Ministry* (co-editor); *Mennonite Perspectives on Pastoral Counseling* (editor); *Through the Eyes of Another: Intercultural Reading of the Bible* (co-editor); and *Multifaith Views in Spiritual Care* (editor).

Acknowledgments

THE EVOLUTION OF MY awareness and concern for interfaith relation has been slow even as it has been consistently deepening and expanding. It would be difficult to trace a well-marked beginning, but there are some events that I can identify. My formal introduction to the subject was during my student days at Princeton Theological Seminary in a class taught by M. M. Thomas (1985). A few years later, I encountered Aloysius Pieris who was then a Visiting Professor at Vanderbilt University when I was doing my PhD studies. My encounter with these two scholars jumpstarted my interest and when I submitted a list of courses (1993) to teach at United Theological Seminary of the Twin Cities, theology of religions was one of them. From then on I continued teaching theologies of religions. As the years progressed, my understanding and approach continued to evolve and expand as well as experienced shift: from an overemphasis on the study of various theologies of religions to a more integrative and practical aspect, which is interfaith practices. My justice-immersion courses, both local (Minnesota and Hawaii) and international (Philippines and Israel-Palestine), included interfaith encounters. Issues of migration and interfaith got intertwined in these courses. In the past couple of years, the matter of interfaith kept coming back even as I was focusing on Christianity in my course on Global Christianities.

At the risk of forgetting some, my journey into interfaith has been enriched by institutions and faith communities and by individuals whom I encountered along the way. I am grateful for the opportunity to serve on the Interfaith Relations Commission (IRC) of the National Council of Christian Churches in the U.S.A. My interaction with members of the IRC and its work on interfaith has helped sharpen my thoughts on the subject. Working with Christians in relation to the issue of interfaith, I realized, is as complex and challenging as dealing with people of other faiths. I recall the long conversation we had on christology and salvation. Although it was not easy, the experience was rewarding and empowering.

Another institution that contributed to the making of this project is The Association of Theological Schools in the United States and Canada (ATS); I am especially glad to have worked on its project on Christian Hospitality and Pastoral Practices in a Multifaith Society. I am grateful, in particular, for Stephen Graham for inviting me to take part in the project and for the grant money for United Theological Seminary of the Twin Cities to support Christian interreligious hospitality initiatives. My essay on multifaith competencies evolved out of my involvement in the ATS Christian Hospitality project.

My gratitude goes as well to United Theological Seminary of the Twin Cities for supporting my work and giving me the freedom to write and publish. I could not have done this without the generosity of United through the understanding and encouragement of our Vice President for Academic Affairs and Dean, Sharon Tan, former President Barbara Holmes, and President Lewis Zeidner.

Now let me take the opportunity to express my appreciation to significant individuals who helped make this project possible. My appreciation goes to the essay contributors: Justus Baird, Ruben L. F. Habito, Mary Hess, Robert Hunt, Cindi Beth Johnson, Sheryl Kujawa-Holbrook, Lucinda Mosher, Jennifer Peace, Shanta Premawardhana, and Daniel S. Schipani. It was a delight to receive their enthusiasm on the project and an honor to have these scholars contribute essays for this volume.

A writer or editor cannot make significant progress on a project without individuals providing various forms of support. Gail Anderson has been of immense help in connecting me to leaders of other religious faith traditions. Cathy Pino and Brian Braskich, both former students of mine, helped in the editing and formatting of this manuscript. I am thankful in particular to Cathy for her diligence and care in preparing the whole document until its final submission to the publisher, and to Kristen Soltvedt Rinaldi for her help with proofreading.

Finally, my gratitude goes to my wife, Jo, for the much-needed support in the writing and editing of this book. As writers and editors know, birthing a book project entails enormous focus and sacrifice. I could not have done this without the generous encouragement and support of my wife.

Eleazar S. Fernandez
Long flight: Tokyo, Narita to Minneapolis, MSP
Fridley, Minnesota
July 2016

Introduction
Multifaith Education Matters

INTERCONNECTIONS, DIVERSITY, AND SHARED vulnerabilities and hopes characterize our highly globalized world. The increasing mobility and accelerated migration of people, especially the current refugee crisis, has only heightened this awareness. This phenomenon, in turn, has created new realities and, without a doubt, new challenges. Migration has changed the ethnic and cultural landscape of many places that were once relatively homogenous. This is the case with my neighborhood in the northern suburbs of Minneapolis, Minnesota. Personally, it has made me feel more at home even while far away from my country of origin (Philippines). It was a great delight when I started seeing the Global Food section at the local Cub Foods grocery store. Today I can go to the seafood section and get the more affordable fresh tilapia fillet. That was unheard of fifteen or so years ago. There is also the Global Market, Mercado Central, and Somali Mall at Lake and Eat Street (Nicollet Avenue). When my family arrived in Minnesota in 1993, there was Pannekoeken (Scandinavian restaurant) along Central Avenue, Columbia Heights. I still remember the bread that puffs up and deflates rapidly, which people sprinkle with powdered sugar. Then Pannekoeken gave way to Jang Won, a Korean restaurant, which then gave way to Udupi, and then to Nala Pak, both Indian vegetarian restaurants. What a change, from "Nordeast" to "Far East." On the opposite side of the street is a Chow Mein restaurant that used to be Kentucky Fried Chicken. And, about twenty-five meters away is the Jerusalem Market, where one can get Mediterranean food.

Something more, however, complexified the diversity of the place. Not only has the ethnic and cultural landscape changed but also, more specifically, the religious landscape. Temples, mosques, and *gurdwaras* are sprouting up along with Christian churches of various ethnicities and theological persuasions. This phenomenon of increasing ethnic and religious diversity is observable not only in the large urban areas or cities of the world but also in the rural areas, particularly where agribusiness factories are present. These agribusiness factories are drawing workers of varied ethnicity and religious beliefs from around the world. One place that comes to mind is southwestern Minnesota, an immersion site for a course (Globalization at our Doorstep) I teach regularly at United Theological Seminary of the Twin Cities. The demise of the family farm and the presence of agribusiness companies or, more particularly, food processing plants in this region, have drawn newcomers (migrants and immigrants, including Somalis, Hmong, Laotians, Cambodians, Karens [from Myanmar], Vietnamese, Guatemalans, and Mexicans) into towns and cities such as Worthington, Willmar, Marshall, Tracy, Lynd, Madelia, Mountain Lake, St. James, and Montevideo.[1] The presence of these newcomers has changed the demographics and socio-cultural-religious landscape of the place and, of course, has brought attendant challenges.

The religious landscape of my immediate neighborhood has changed. The influx of Somalis and Bosnians in Minnesota, for example, has increased the number of Muslims in the area, and their presence is slowly changing the landscape. The Islamic Center of Minnesota is in the neighborhood where I live. Earlier, the coming of refugees from East Asia (Vietnamese, Hmong, Lao, and Cambodians) following the fall of Saigon contributed to the rise of Buddhist presence in the area. More recently, Hindus have made their presence more visible with the construction of a huge temple in Maple Grove. And, not far away, is the Wheel of Dharma, a Tibetan monastery. With some Christian congregations folding, some formerly Christian places are now places of worship or meditation for Muslims, Buddhists, Jews, Hindus, and Sikhs.

What is happening in my neighborhood is a microcosm of what is happening throughout the U.S. and other places in the world. Newcomers have changed the religious demographics of many places. Among the largest non-Christian religions in the United States today are Islam, Judaism, Buddhism, and Hinduism. The Council on American Islamic Relations reports that there are seven million Muslims in the United States, a figure almost comparable to the Jewish population.[2] Rising from a cornfield along the interstate outside Toledo, Ohio, is a mosque. Breaking stereotypes, a Buddhist temple rises in Salt Lake City, Utah, a place associated with the Church of Latter Day Saints (Mormonism). Hillside Terrace, in Fremont, California,

---

1. See Amato, *To Call It Home.*

2. The numbers are contested. The estimates range between 2 million and as many as 11 million. See Haddad, *Not Quite American?*, 1–2.

has become Gurdwara Road. Diana Eck notes that along New Hampshire Avenue, just beyond the beltway of Washington, D.C., USA, there is a stretch of road a few miles long that passes the new Cambodian Buddhist temple, the Ukrainian Orthodox Church, the Muslim Community Center with its new copper-domed mosque, and the new Gujarati Hindu Temple as well as new dimensions of America's Christian landscape: Hispanic Pentecostal, Vietnamese Catholic, and Korean evangelical congregations sharing facilities with more traditional English-speaking "mainline" churches.[3]

The major cities of Europe have also experienced dramatic change in religious landscape. France, according to the Pew Research Center, has the highest Religious Diversity Index (RDI) in Europe.[4] Besides Christianity, the two largest religious groups are the religiously unaffiliated and Islam. In the United Kingdom, the city of Birmingham is one of the largest Muslim cities outside of the Middle East. It has more than fifty mosques. The central mosque in the city is known to be the largest in Europe outside Istanbul. Muslims constitute nearly 20 percent of Birmingham's population.[5] Not surprisingly, because of its colonial ties with India, it also has a large number of Sikh. Shifting from the U.K. to Germany: while Christians are still the majority, the number of Muslims is increasing. Meanwhile, the Jewish population has a sizeable presence, particularly in cities like Berlin, Frankfort, and Munich. The Buddhist population of the country is mostly immigrants from Asia.

In spite of the increasing diversity in Europe, however, Asia continues to have the highest religious diversity. According to the Pew Research Center, of the twelve top religiously diverse countries in the world, six are in Asia. The rest are in Africa (five countries) and Latin America (Suriname).

While those in the global North or West may consider encounters with people of other faiths a "newly discovered reality," this is not the case for many in other parts of the world. Rather, for them, it is a "recovery" of what they already are.[6] It is a recovery of a more religiously pluralistic context that has characterized Asia and Africa, which Christian colonizers and evangelists attempted to silence. Speaking in particular of India, Stanley Samartha asserts: "Thus to talk about the 'emergence' or the 'discovery' of religious pluralism in India is like taking a beehive to a sugar[cane] plantation."[7]

3. Eck, *A New Religious America*, 187. Also, Sernau, *Bound*, especially chapter 7: "Metro Sprawl: The Making of the Global City."

4. Pew Research Center: Religion and Public Life, "Global Religious Diversity" (April 4, 2014).

5. Thangaraj, *The Common Task*, 21.

6. See Samartha, *One Christ, Many Religions*, 8.

7. Ibid.

With religious diversity as a context, encounters between people of various faiths are becoming more and more common. Connections between people of various religious convictions happen either through direct face-to-face encounter or through cyberspace. These encounters happen in a wide variety of places, such as schools, workplaces, hospitals, grocery stores, department stores, restaurants, gyms, parks, public rallies, and military and prison facilities. When I go to the bank and department stores to transact business, there is a variety of ethnicities and beliefs represented by the bank tellers and cashiers. When I go to buy *halal* or *kosher* meat, I meet people of other religious faiths. And, a few meters away from my residence is the house of Belkar, a Sikh from India who has become a friend. On some occasions I have invited him to our church and the seminary where I teach and, in return, he also has invited me to visit the Sikh's *gurdwara*. When I prepared food for my daughter's graduation party, I was made aware that I needed to prepare food for her Muslim friends, which was quite a challenge because Filipinos like to prepare *lechon* (whole roasted suckling pig) for special occasions.

HOW ARE WE RESPONDING TO
OUR RELIGIOUSLY DIVERSE WORLD?

The world and its diversity of various types have come to our doorsteps. Indeed, we are living in a religiously diverse world. Religious diversity is our reality. This is a statement of fact. It would be incredulous to deny this fact. "Religious diversity is as much a reality as bio-diversity," says Jay Rock.[8] However, beyond recognizing this as a fact, which in itself is not always easy, I believe it is also a statement of principle, that is, a reality to be embraced because that is who we are.

Yet, we know that embracing our diversity in general and religious diversity in particular has been a challenge. There are several responses to our religious diversity challenge. Our society is awash in superficial responses to the matter. The modernist-secularist privatizing of religious faith has made us ignorant of the role of religion and, sadly, at our peril. While religious diversity is easily acknowledged, our secular and privatized world has made it possible for people to avoid engaging with people of different religions, partly because it is relatively easy for people to live with each other without reference to their religious identities. There is also the toleration—a non-engaging niceness—that borders on indifference.

8. Jay Rock, Christian Theological Approaches to Religious Diversity, September 10, 2009. Email response to Interfaith Relations Commission, Theology Caucus Group.

There are also those who continue to live in denial about this reality or run away from it. A study by Robert Putnam, author of *American Grace*, is very revealing of this common reaction.[9] Perhaps contrary to our expectations, the increasing ethnic and religious diversity has triggered social isolation and, in more diverse communities, people trust their neighbors less. They put up walls or retreat to their private spaces.

A private space is important: It is, as Parker J. Palmer puts it, a "sanctuary for people we know and trust, not an arena where we meet the stranger as stranger."[10] Yet, there is an irony that we should not fail to notice, an irony found in the Latin root from which the word "private" is derived: *prevare*, which means "to deprive" or "to be deprived of." Imagine depriving oneself of the richness of the encounter and the potential for growth and transformation in an ethnically-culturally diverse and multifaith context. It is not a surprise that the Greek word for a strictly private person is *idiotes*, from which we derive the term "idiot," someone who does or says something stupid.[11]

Isolation or retreat to one's private space where one slowly becomes an *idiot* is only one expression of reactive behavior. Fundamentalism, which is basically reactive, is on the rise. At its heart fundamentalism is a "reaction" to perceived threats. Religious fundamentalism, in particular, does not stand by itself, but is intertwined with economic, ethnic, and nationalist interests. Religious fundamentalism may yield support for or ride with ethno-nationalism. While there is no direct correlation between fundamentalism and violent extremism, when the right mixture of fundamentalist markers and context come into play, fundamentalism can easily slide into the slippery slope of violent extremism.

Our global village is witnessing a clash of fundamentalisms or a clash of barbarisms. A world of clashing fundamentalisms and barbarisms is our context, and it is intensifying every day. This is the kind of global village where we are called to live out our faith both as individuals and faith communities. We need to move past superficial and harmful religious stereotypes and reactive fundamentalisms. The reality of our highly globalized and religiously diverse global village calls for a serious, respectful, thoughtful, and creative response to the issue of religious diversity. Beyond the practical reality of learning to live together in a religiously diverse world, we people of faith need to respond to the challenge of religious diversity in accord with our faith convictions. This requires nothing but in-depth examination of

9. Putnam, *American Grace*, 291.

10. Palmer, *Healing the Heart of Democracy*, 92.

11. Ibid., 95.

our deeply-held theological views, a genuine desire to encounter believers of other faiths with respect, and a humble posture of bearing witness to the faith. Serious engagement with people of other faiths does not require that we abandon our deeply cherished convictions. Far from it. Instead, it involves the commitment to engage believers of other faiths—with our deep commitments.

How shall we educate our faith communities so that they can practice hospitality in the world of many faiths? How are we to prepare religious leaders who are capable of leading congregations and communities in the practice of hospitality in a multifaith context? How are we to equip religious leaders in the practice of ministry in interfaith settings? What curriculum design, educational programs, and pedagogies shall we pursue to lead and minister effectively in multifaith settings? These are the larger questions that frame this particular project. What does a competent religious leader for a multifaith context look like? What qualities and competencies must he or she possess?

While there are many books about theologies of religions and inter-faith relations, I have yet to see a single book that deals comprehensively with how we educate or form individuals so they are better equipped to lead and serve our multifaith world. This book is intended to address such a concern, particularly with its focus on curriculum, pedagogy, and institutional supports. It is hoped that this project not only leads to greater understanding, but also encourages educational institutions to develop curricula and programs that equip leaders to minister in a multifaith world.

DESCRIPTION OF THE BOOK PROJECT

This book project, excluding the Introduction, has twelve chapters. Chapter 1 takes a critical account of interfaith works, identifies critical crossroads, and offers general proposals on the direction we need to take and on how we may move forward to create a more religiously hospitable society. What direction shall our theological formation take to prepare men and women for leadership and ministry in a multifaith context?

After this general overview and assessment (Chapter 1), the rest of the book project comprises eleven chapters. Chapter 2 presents important competencies that one needs to have and develop in a multifaith context. The next chapters (Chapters 3 and 4) address the topic of seminary curriculum and interfaith matters. How shall we design a curriculum in such a way that interfaith relations become part of formation? How shall we integrate interfaith concerns in a curriculum so that they will not remain peripheral or optional?

Following the two chapters on curriculum are the two chapters (Chapters 5 and 6) on pedagogy. What pedagogical principles and skills shall we adopt and adapt for teaching interfaith competencies? Are there pedagogical strategies that would work best for a curriculum that is geared toward developing multifaith competencies?

Chapters 7, 8, 9, 10, 11, and 12 explore and articulate the intersection of interfaith and spiritual formation (Chapter 7), pastoral care (Chapter 8), chaplaincy (Chapter 9), public ministry (Chapter 10), arts (Chapter 11), and congregational studies and vitality (Chapter 12). How shall we do spiritual formation in the world of many faiths? How shall we do pastoral care in a multifaith setting? What do students need to learn and what skills do they need to acquire for pastoral care in the presence of followers of other faiths? What training should teachers of pastoral care have? How shall we prepare chaplains (schools, hospitals, military establishments, prisons, etc.)? How does a multifaith context shape the work of chaplains? How shall we pursue public ministry in a religiously plural setting? What content knowledge shall we need to have? What strategies and skills must we learn? How are we to relate arts and interfaith? Where are the creative intersections in these two areas of studies? And, finally, how shall we relate multifaith reality and congregational studies? Do multifaith matters have a place in the identity and mission of congregations? How do interfaith concerns find a place in the lives of congregations seeking vitality?

BRIEFS FROM ESSAY CONTRIBUTIONS

Robert Hunt's essay, "Our Journey in Multifaith Education," presents in a sharp and stark way the challenge of our multifaith context to the global community in general, and to the way we do religious education in our churches and in theological formation centers in particular. Hunt contends that, in a highly contentious environment in which religion plays multiple roles and supports various sentiments, a robust response must involve a new conceptualization of religion in a religiously pluralistic context. He contends, further, that both content and pedagogy of our formation programs must address the various roles of religions in the areas of identity formation, social transformation, and political engagement. Taking these multiple aspects can, however, only go deep and far if they are integrated, and if learning moves beyond easy "acceptance" of diversity and comprehension of information toward "understanding," which can only happen through encounters between religiously committed and socio-politically located and imbricated human beings.

The next essay is "Competencies for a Multifaith Context" by Eleazar S. Fernandez. After saying that multifaith competencies must include the categories of attitude, content, and skills, or awareness, knowledge, and skills, he proceeds to name and articulate seventeen competencies namely: (1) awareness and understanding of our religiously plural setting; (2) proper understanding of the place and role of religion in society and in the formation of identity; (3) functional understanding of the interlocking relationships of various social identities; (4) distinguishing religious beliefs from cultural and ethnic customs or practices; (5) understanding other religious traditions on their own terms; (6) interpathic way of understanding and relating; (7) respecting and celebrating differences, (8) an enlarged identity: cosmopolitan heart; (9) the religious stranger as a subject-companion in meaning-making and world-making; (10) being at home in one's house; (11) reaching out and being open by going deep; (12) expressing one's deep convictions with honesty, respect, and openness; (13) hospitality: receptivity, space, and presence; (14) building trust, solidarity, shared ministry, and interfaith actions; (15) establishing ethical norms in a multifaith context; (16) spiritual self-care; and (17) living the questions.

Mary Hess' essay, "Designing Curricular Approaches for Interfaith Competency, or, Why Does Learning How to Live in a 'Community of Communities' Matter?" addresses the issue of curriculum design for developing leaders in a multifaith context. Instead of focusing on the content (or a list of courses) of a curriculum (explicit, implicit, and null) that supports what she calls "interfaith competency," Hess focuses on forms of knowing that a curriculum will *uncover* and *strengthen*. She makes the point that *how* we teach (pedagogy) is a better predictor of what is learned than *what* is taught. With this point, Hess articulates the shifts in a "new culture of learning" that favors learning-based approaches, fluidity and change, and openness to diversity, which provides an opening for multifaith theological education. In the remaining parts of her essay, Hess delved into the practical aspects, providing guidelines on how theological formation centers may develop the content of their curriculum for interfaith competency. Not offering a one-size-fits-all curriculum template, Hess says that if a school's implicit curriculum is known to strongly support multifaith education, the content of the curriculum is more likely to flow naturally. However, in settings in which interfaith competency is professed as important, but is ephemeral in practice, then the curriculum must have courses that integrate the explicit and implicit curricula around interfaith competency. Other curricula configurations may be adopted depending on the curricular context of the school.

Another essay on curriculum is by Jennifer Peace, "Religious Self, Religious Other: Coformation as a Model for Interreligious Education." Peace asks the question: What does adequate preparation for the next generation of religious leaders and educators look like given the complex multireligious-contexts where our graduates will serve? Her answer: design a curriculum to move from a model of religious formation to a model of interreligious *coformation*. Her involvement in the CIRCLE program provides a test case for the relevance and effectiveness of *coformation*. Peace makes the assertion that we cannot form religious leaders and educators in mono-religious isolation. In contrast to the dominant world religions paradigm, which is basically learning *about*, *coformation* makes learning *with* (*not simply about*) the norm. Religious literacy, which is commonly understood as learning *about*, is not enough. Moving beyond religious literacy, Peace contends that *coformation* does not remain content in the safe haven of sameness—a common default, which, when examined carefully belies a discomfort with, if not fear of difference. A competent religious leader in a multifaith world must be able to embrace and live comfortably with irreducible differences because that is who we are, and in our differences and multi-dimensionality lay our richness, says Peace. A healthy embrace of our rich diversity and differences is not a threat to our common humanity; it deepens our understanding and practice of our shared humanity.

As the title of her essay suggests, "Beyond World Religions: Pedagogical Principles and Practices for the Encouragement of Interfaith Hospitality and Collaboration," Lucinda Mosher, while acknowledging the gains of the past, calls us to move beyond *comparative religions* approach. Knowledge *about* other religions is a good beginning regardless of motivations (e.g., conversion of the religious other or for effective interfaith social action), but the formation of religious leaders with heart and skills for interfaith hospitality demands more. Having said this, Mosher devotes the rest of her essay to articulating models and methods of multifaith education, which she believes are effective in forming competent religious leaders for a multifaith world. What competencies in general and knowledge and skills in particular should we be cultivating in our students, which would enable them to lead their communities in elegant practice of interfaith hospitality and collaboration? In response to her own question, Mosher names eight attributes that education for leadership in a multifaith context must have. These eight attributes include: (1) a faith-based rationale that sees interfaith hospitality and cooperation as acts of faithfulness; (2) appreciative knowledge of one's own religion; (3) adoption of experiential learning; (4) taking a phenomenological approach—allowing each religion to be appreciated on its own terms; (5) encouraging understanding of each religion's own multiplicity of expressions; (6) encouraging both formal and functional comparison-making, paired with an attitude of delighting in the differences; (7) taking a dialogical approach; and (8) teaching concrete skills and strategies for facilitating interfaith hospitality and collaboration.

Pursuing the subject of pedagogy in his essay, "Pursuing and Teaching Justice in Multifaith Contexts," Justus Baird deals with the interweaving of justice and multifaith concerns, particularly in the context of educating faith-based leaders and faith-based movements in a multifaith world. Before proceeding further in articulating this interweaving and their mutual impingement, Baird makes the critical point which one can only miss at a great cost: "There is no approach to cross-faith learning or engagement that can completely ignore issues like race, inequality, sexuality, and gender." Moreover, he makes the claim that social justice offers an important setting for multifaith learning. After asserting these fundamental points, Baird clarifies the nature of faith-based organizing, which is not simply organizing people of faith but helping them dig into their religious traditions as foundational for social justice work, and pursues matters related to pedagogy. The rest of the essay finds Baird wrestling with and responding to the questions: How does multifaith justice work influence multifaith education and, conversely, how does multifaith education influence multifaith justice work? What pedagogical wisdom can inspire social justice work in a multifaith setting? And, what are the competencies that one needs to have to do justice work in a multifaith context? Finally, he brings to our attention the competencies that one may acquire as a result of doing social justice in an interfaith setting.

Ruben L. F. Habito's essay, "Spiritual Formation in a Multifaith World," responds to the challenge that our multifaith context poses in relation to spiritual formation. What does a multifaith context have to offer in spiritual formation? What difference does it make in spiritual formation? Habito answers these questions by starting with a working definition of spirituality, which, in its most fundamental sense, is about that deepest center of the human being opening up and reaching out to the transcendent dimension. With this transcultural and trans-religious definition, Habito explores how spirituality plays out in various religious traditions. How is this seeking and reaching out to the transcendent finding expressions in the major religious traditions: Islam, Hinduism, Buddhism, Judaism, and Christianity? After articulating the multiple expressions of spirituality in the major religious traditions, Habito focuses his attention on Christianity and how Christians, particularly their religious leaders, must address other religious faiths with the purpose of developing a viable theological framework for a multifaith setting. With a viable framework that enables a faithful Christian to be open and engaging, one may discover in the interfaith encounter the richness of his or her tradition, and grow deeper in one's spiritual life. At the end of his essay, Habito identifies some pedagogical practices to help pave the way for such a spiritual journey of discovery and transformation to happen.

Shifting to the subject of pastoral and spiritual care, Daniel Schipani's essay, "Pastoral and Spiritual Care in Multifaith Contexts," has two parts: First, he articulates a tri-dimensional anthropological model (embodied, animated, spiritual self) that views humans as inherently spiritual creatures; second, he offers some guidelines for the holistic formation of interfaith caregivers. Humans, for Schipani, are human beings only because they are spiritual beings. With that as an entry, Schipani proceeds to articulate what this spiritual being is in an interdisciplinary way, critically situating the human being within a complex and highly textured context, and mindfully explaining the interactive dynamics of the spiritual, psychological, and bodily in a person's life. This dynamic spirit searches for meaning, seeks out relationship to others including the Divine, and orients itself in relation to a purpose.

Taking these expressions of the spirit, a wholesome spiritual self, for Schipani, would manifest hope (purpose), faith (meaning), and love (communion). What could be more transcendent-universal than these three-dimensions? Yet, these transcendent-universal dimensions of the spiritual self are only so because they find expressions in various particularities. Schipani makes it imperative that we recognize that the human spirit expresses itself in specific socio-cultural and religious contexts, and manifests itself in various spiritualities. Given our multifaith context, spiritual care givers must have competencies that address the needs of the care receiver as an embodied psychological and spiritual self. The rest of his essay articulates the competencies that caregivers in a multifaith context must develop.

Lucinda Mosher's "Chaplaincy Education Meets Multifaith Literacy Development: Strategies for Teaching Models and Methods of Spiritual Caregiving in Multifaith Contexts," introduces the field of chaplaincy and the challenges that chaplains are facing as well as the competences, trainings, and the resources that they need to develop and acquire to function effectively. Given the multifaith context that most chaplains serve (hospitals, schools, military facilities, counseling clinics, etc.), the chaplains' training must involve multireligious literacy development. Multireligious literacy is important not only for chaplains to offer spiritual care with sensitivity to multireligious constituency, but also to be aware that, in moments of crisis, affected individuals and communities will draw from their own religious traditions to sustain them. In addition to the *Common Standards for Professional Chaplaincy* that have been widely accepted by the profession, and which fall into four categories (theology of pastoral care; identity and conduct; applied pastoral skills; and professional skills), Mosher introduces multireligious literacy inventory and interfaith literacy inventory as necessary for chaplains to serve effectively in their multifaith settings. Moreover, Mosher cites resources that are useful for chaplains and chaplains in training for a world that has become religiously diverse.

From the opening to the closing lines of his essay, "Public Ministry in a World of Many Faiths," Shanta Premawardhana argues for the centrality of marginality as a hermeneutical starting point for doing public theology and the ending point by which a public theology is judged to be at its best. Does this public theology take seriously the plight of the marginalized or those who are dying before their time in its articulation, and does this public theology make itself accountable to them—for their liberation and wellbeing? When it does, the how, the what, and the direction of public theology will be different. It will start from where the suffering people are—their struggles and hopes—and its content and direction will be to heal the wounded and bring wellbeing to all, especially the disenfranchised.

The marginalized in our society are leading social change, but is the church listening? Either our preaching and theologies are not effective or our preaching and theologies support unjust policies and practices. Premawardhana ventures to say that our failure is *not in spite of* but, most often the case, *because of* our theology. For the most part, our public theology has been effective in supporting unjust policies and practices. So, we must liberate theology from its elitist captivity in order that it can help break the theological backbone of dehumanizing practices, and he cites a few examples of this kind of liberation.

The immensity and complexity of our social challenges cannot, however, be addressed singlehandedly by a single religious group, much more so in a globalized and multifaith world. So, contends Premawardhana, we must acknowledge that Christians, even as we give our best, do not have all or the best answers. There are times when other religious traditions and believers of other faiths have better answers than us. Or, that we arrive at better and more comprehensive answers if we work together and integrate our answers. Premawardhana cites some examples from other religious traditions that can contribute to the wellbeing of our shared lives.

In "Letting Arts Lead: The Role of Arts in Interfaith Dialogue," Cindi Beth Johnson explores the relevance of the arts for our multifaith world, particularly in developing interfaith competency. But before arts can become a crucial companion in developing interfaith competency, they must be allowed to lead—not simply used as illustration—so they can fully express their distinctive and inherent power. After this initial assertion, Johnson proceeds by articulating the power of the arts to tap our ways of knowing and connects the insights she has articulated to the subject of interfaith engagement. Johnson identifies three characteristics of the arts that are significant for interfaith encounter and for developing interfaith competency, namely (1) mystery, (2) polyvalency, and (3) transformative power. Mystery is at home with the arts; the arts are at home with mystery. The arts, says Johnson, have the ability to house and hold together "mysterious difference" and polyvalent truths, which are helpful in developing multifaith competencies. Moreover, the arts have transformative capacity that transgresses rigid polarities and deepens one's connections with the wider world without overlooking distinctive differences. These are characteristics that are helpful in building bridges in a multifaith world. In the remaining part of her essay, Johnson offers concrete examples or ways in which the arts can be used effectively in interfaith education including pedagogy, resources, and community partnerships.

The final essay by Sheryl A. Kujawa-Holbrook, "The Sacrament of Human Life: Cultivating Intentional Interreligious Learning in Congregations," calls us to the task of cultivating interreligious learning among congregations. This task, she contends, must be rooted in the understanding that interreligious learning is central to the mission of the church if it is not to be considered an add-on, which is quite a prevalent understanding and practice. Kujawa-Holbrook cites Pentecost as offering a vision for congregations engaged in interreligious learning. It is a vision in which individuals and communities grow in self-understanding and learn to dwell together while fully recognizing and celebrating differences. As to be expected in any grand vision, the Pentecost vision is demanding: It demands "courageous border crossing" and active engagement with people of other living faiths, ethnicities, and traditions. It demands as well, says Kujawa-Holbrook, "the creation of intentional communities where people can be affirmed in their own religious, social, and cultural identities, and at the same time creatively transformed through authentic engagement with others." Beyond calling congregations to engage in interreligious learning and identifying vision, Kujawa-Holbrook provides guidelines and suggests practices that congregations may adopt and adapt. Furthermore, she suggests some ways for congregations to cultivate interreligious learning.

ACTIVE HOPING IN A THREATENING WORLD:
MAKING A DIFFERENCE

As I was about to close this Introduction, a series of disturbing and heart-wrenching events around the world came onto the scene within a short period of time. On June 12, 2016, at about 2:00 in the morning in Orlando, Florida, sounds of excitement and laughter suddenly turned into staccatos of gunfire, screams of those who were trying to flee for their dear lives, and desperate cries for help. In the aftermath, about forty-nine people were killed, and several others wounded. What was previously a site of life bursting at the seams with excitement became a place of carnage and death. Crying, wailing, and mourning followed, then the jeremiads.

Not long after, while the world was still reeling from the tragedy, terror struck again: in Dhaka (Bangladesh), killing about twenty-one (July 1, 2016); [12] Baghdad (Iraq), killing more than 215 (July 3, 2016);[13] and, most recently, in Nice (France), killing about eighty four and wounding about 200 (July 14, 2016).[14]

Aghast, I realize more than ever that the world that I am living in is becoming more and more dangerous, and that I cannot fully isolate myself from my neighbors and insulate myself from the threats. It appears that civilization, instead of moving toward progress and greater openness, is moving toward building more walls. In the face of perceived threats, it appears that hearts are constricting and moral imagination shrinking. It is difficult not to see the world in this way and to dwell differently.

Yet I must. *We* must. We must think, dwell, and act differently, if we are to avoid the clash of fundamentalisms and barbarisms. This project is an attempt to bear witness to my struggle to hope amidst the sea of hopelessness, and to my belief that we still can make a difference and that another world is possible. We have to believe it: another world *is* possible.

Yes, another world is possible, but it does not come by itself. It comes with our participation: from those of us who have caught the vision and have become one with the vision. Another world is possible when we have made the resolve to help midwife its coming. How shall we help midwife its coming?

We can help midwife its coming by doing what we can, whenever we can, and wherever we can, and by joining the group of what John Paul

12. http://edition.cnn.com/2016/07/03/asia/bangladesh-isis-al-qaeda/index.html.

13. http://edition.cnn.com/2016/07/04/middleeast/baghdad-car-bombs/index.html.

14. http://www.usmagazine.com/celebrity-news/news/isis-claims-responsibility-for-nice-terrorist-attack-w429515.

Lederach calls the "critical yeasts." Without "critical yeast," there would be no "critical mass," which is commonly understood in terms of numbers. When we think of bread baking, the largest part of the common ingredients is the flour. The flour is the mass. In contrast to the flour, the yeast is among the smallest. Yet it is this smallest ingredient, the yeast, that is "critical" for making the mass grow. The yeast, the smallest ingredient, when mixed correctly with other ingredients, and when the right environment is provided, is the only ingredient that has the capacity and power to help others grow. If we want to create sustainable movements for change, we need to form the "critical yeasts." Mass movements have no enduring power without the leavening presence of "critical yeasts." We need the presence of "critical yeasts" to help mass movements realize their dreams.

Beyond dreaming our individual dreams and rooting these dreams in the hard facts of our contexts, we must dream in community. I remember John Lennon's song: "You may say that I'm a dreamer, but I'm not the only one." We must weave our dreams together. Moreover, we must walk our dreams together. We need to create safe places for people to dream and walk in community. The "critical mass" for which we have been waiting would remain a farfetched reality unless and until we are attentive to our "critical connections."

One may say that I am *only one*, but here is a response from Edward Everett Hale: "I am only one, but *still I am one*. I cannot do everything, but still I can do something; and because I cannot do everything, I will not refuse to do the something that I can do."[15] Pursuing to interpret Hale's words: Yes, I am only one, but I am not nothing. I am still one, a significant one. As one being I can do something. My being one and my acting as one are my entry points and contributions to the wider and complex world.

Yet, even as I am one, it does not mean that I am alone. Being one and being alone are not the same. I am *one* among *many*. Even more, I *am many*; *I am a multitude.* I am one only because I am many. It is through this inextricable relation to the many that I am one. Just like the whitecap of the waves of the ocean, I belong to the ocean as I belong to the people, to the multitude. Embracing my oneness with the multitude while fully conscious of my self-agency, I refuse to act alone. Rather, I seek companionship (*cum + panis* = "bread sharers") and conspiracy (*con + spirar* = "breath sharers") with others in order to make waves, a movement. I refer to an African proverb, which says that if we want to go fast, we must go alone; but if we want to go far, we must go together. The distinctive and significant ones must go together in order to go far. Moreover, as one, though not alone, and as many,

15. Hale, "Lend a Hand," emphasis supplied.

I refuse not to do something just because I cannot do everything. After all, I am not called to do everything, but called to do something—to sew my piece into the quilt of our global agenda.

This project is one such piece, a collection of pieces that the essay writers of this volume have sewn into the quilt of our global agenda. It is our hope and prayer that this work makes a distinctive contribution into our common dream of a world that is truly hospitable to all.

BIBLIOGRAPHY

Amato, Joseph. *To Call It Home: The New Immigrants of Southwestern Minnesota.* Marshall, MN: Crossing, 1996.

Eck, Diana. *A New Religious America: How a "Christian Country" Has Become the World's Most Religiously Diverse Nation.* San Francisco: HarperSanFrancisco, 2001.

Hale, Edward Everett. "Lend a Hand." In *Masterpieces of Religious Verse,* edited by James Dalton Morrison, 416. New York: Harper & Brothers, 1948.

Palmer, Parker J. *Healing the Heart of Democracy: The Courage to Create a Politics Worthy of the Human Spirit.* San Francisco: Jossey-Bass, 2011.

Putnam, Robert, and David Campbell. *American Grace: How Religion Divides and Unites Us.* New York: Simon & Schuster, 2010.

Samartha, Stanley. *One Christ, Many Religions: Toward a Revised Christology.* Maryknoll, NY: Orbis, 1991.

Sernau, Scott. *Bound: Living in the Globalized World.* Hartfold, CT: Kumarian, 2000.

Thangaraj, M. Thomas. *The Common Task: A Theology of Christian Mission.* Nashville: Abingdon, 1999.

Yazbeck Haddad, Yvonne. *Not Quite American? The Shaping of Arab and Muslim Identity in the United States.* Waco, TX: Baylor University Press, 2004.

1

Our Journey in Multifaith Education

—Robert Hunt

AMERICANS ARE ILLITERATE WHEN it comes to religion. This reality is brought home to me semester after semester in the first few weeks of the general introduction to World Religions that I teach to Master's level students in theology and liberal arts. The majority of my students will have completed an undergraduate education without ever studying about Muslims, Hindus, Buddhists, Jews, Jains, Taoists, or their respective communal beliefs and practices. And the majority will have no knowledge, or only a distorted knowledge, of Christian denominations other than their own. We don't need to rely on anecdotal evidence for this illiteracy. Research by the Pew Charitable Trusts confirms my observations and Stephen Prothero has offered convincing documentation in his book *Religious Literacy: What Every American Needs to Know—And Doesn't.*

Prothero and others have shown the reasons for this lack of knowledge. Public schools from the 1960s onward found it easier, and less likely to result in litigation, to teach nothing about religion than to try to address all religions equally. The introduction to the Pew Forum report on "Religion in the Public Schools" articulates the problem clearly: "Nearly a half-century after the Supreme Court issued its landmark ruling striking down school-sponsored prayer, Americans continue to fight over the place of religion in public schools. Indeed, the classroom has become one of the most important battlegrounds in the broader conflict over religion's role in public life."[1]

---

1. Pew, "Religion in the Public Schools," 1.

Despite the observation that religion is becoming more visible in University settings, university curricula have been pressed to provide professional development in what are assumed to be a-religious professional cultures, if not necessarily social environments. This is particularly the case as public and not-for-profit universities compete for students with vocationally oriented profit making universities, leading to what Larry Shinn calls "a false choice."[2]

If the only need in American education were to introduce knowledge of the various religions to rising generations of young Americans, the solution to illiteracy would be relatively easy. It would reside in minor changes in school curricula and history textbooks reflecting both the role of different religions in shaping human history and the diversity of a changing religious environment today. Churches, civil organizations, businesses, and others could offer opportunities for their constituents to learn about religion. And, in fact, many of them do. This author speaks on an average more than once a week to groups outside the university seeking knowledge of non-Christian religions, and these include Rotary Clubs, Sunday school classes, private companies, NGOs, retirement homes, and even some government bodies. Yet these encounters, if somewhat enlightening to the participants, may fail to really engage the most urgent and vexing questions about religion because these questions are not understood to be properly "religious."

Perhaps the leading candidate as a question unaddressed by traditional knowledge of religions is why and how religion motivates intense and often contradictory political movements. To take a contemporary example: How is it that Islam motivates the brutality of ISIS? On the other hand, how is it that Islam also motivates the recent *Marakkash Declaration on the Rights of Religious Minorities in Predominantly Muslim Majority Communities* calling for full civil rights for religious minorities? Both groups justify their beliefs and behaviors by reference to the Qur'an and Muhammad's treaty with the tribes resident in Yathrib (Medina), yet they have opposite intentions and effects. We could also ask how it is that the constellation of religious teaching called Hinduism inspires wide ranging acceptance of the legitimacy of all religions as paths to the Divine, yet also inspires Hindu nationalism that has violently oppressed non-Hindu religious minorities in India. How is it that Judaism inspires Israeli Jewish settlers to attack and seek to displace their Arab neighbors while also inspiring Jewish movements that seek to guarantee Palestinian rights?

Closely related to this is the question of how religion motivates sectarian conflict of the kind between Shi'ites and Sunnis in Iraq and Pakistan,

2. Shinn, "Liberal Education," 6–10.

Catholics and Protestants in North Ireland, or less violently but as vigorously between nationalist and religious Zionists in Israel. Why is it that groups which share nearly identical beliefs, rituals, and ethics wish to destroy or marginalize one another?

For the public to answer such questions, or engage in a reasonable discourse around them, requires an understanding of how religion shapes both personal and communal identities and then both asserts and defends them in the larger society. This, in turn, requires an understanding that religion is fundamentally concerned with the distribution and use of political power, even when this is not an overtly religious goal. Older anthropological understandings of religion centered on meaning resonate with those for whom religion gives life meaning. Yet even the structures of meaning to which Clifford Geertz refers in his definition of religion require, in a modern multireligiouss context, a stalwart defense at the very least, if they are not to dissipate entirely.

While multireligious social contexts have existed for millennia, the particular social space created by modernity and shaped into more or less coherent units with the rise of the nation-state is fundamentally different from that of the pre-modern world. First, in this new social space, earlier communal boundaries are breeched continually by the state and its claims upon all its citizens. From the time of the American Revolution political philosophers have discussed how a liberal democracy can respond. Yet, as John Rawls has noted before his death, the complexities of liberalism are vastly increased when there exist a plurality of irreconcilable doctrines. In the sphere of religion, the rise of the Federal Religious Freedom Restoration Act (1992) and its state analogues has brought sharply into focus the role of religion and religious freedom in public discourse. Whether this legislation has actually succeeded as either an expression of public discourse or a means of protecting religious freedom remains hotly debated.[3] Regardless of the outcome of those debates, no public understanding of religion will be adequate if it does not address the tension between the demands of religious freedom and those of the common good.

Nor can it be adequate without understanding how broad characterizations of American culture as "Christian" or "Judeo-Christian" distort our understanding of religious pluralism. The recent work of Kevin Kruse, *One Nation Under God*, traces the creation of "Christian" America by the concerted effort of a group of American industrialists and their Christian clergy allies to oppose "godless" communism. But regardless of our ability to trace the genealogy of the myth it retains its force in the public consciousness

3. Hamilton, *God vs. the Gavel.*

until that myth is exposed with a more far-reaching and factual account of religious pluralism.

The very fact that these debates rage as this essay is being written suggests that the envisioning of religions as relatively stable voluntary associations is no longer useful. In contemporary America individual actions that were previously unimaginable or severely limited, such as withdrawing to join another religious community or engaging in religiously forbidden social partnerships, become possible. We are experiencing what Charles Taylor calls a "super-nova" (sic) of religious choice, one that makes the realm of religion one of vast personal agency and deep communal threat.[4]

Or as Mike Rynkiewich points out in his *Soul, Self, and Society; a Postmodern Anthropology*, we cannot characterize society in terms of distinct, unchanging cultures within which humans construct the meaning of being a human self. Kinship systems, class structures, ethnicity, political systems, and economic structures are all changing, and with them the choices individuals and groups make concerning their religious identity.

This is the case because modern social structures are built around a fundamentally different understanding of the human person than is found in non-modern societies. As Taylor so carefully explicated in his recent work, *A Secular Age,* those persons who dwell in a modern worldview, that pioneered and inhabited primarily by Europeans and their cultural descendants, no longer live within the "great chain of being" that in non-modern societies gave individuals and communities their distinctive identity and sense of dignity and purpose. Instead, individuals are thrown into a process of self-creation in which there are inevitable winners and losers, not merely in hierarchical status, but in the possession of any dignity and purpose at all. In its most extreme form a modern human identity is reduced to being a consumer whose worth is based entirely on the acquisition of material goods.

It is small wonder that religious communities whose members have been the losers in this process are attracted to movements that defend or promise to defend the vestiges of meaning and purpose they possessed in the old order, and try to recreate it as best they can. A failure to understand this will be a failure to understand the multireligious world in which we all live. A quotation from a recent talk given by the Orthodox Rabbi Hanan Schlesinger aptly demonstrates this aspect of contemporary religion:

> What that means is that for committed Jews of modernity, Jewish survival becomes the biggest game in town. To be a Jew in modernity means to abhor and to do battle against public

4. Taylor, *A Secular Age,* 300.

enemy number one—assimilation of Jews into the American melting pot! Almost all means are kosher in our personal and communal efforts to maintain Jewish identity and to prevent Jews from jettisoning their sense of identity as Jews.[5]

Finally, as Abigail Green, Vincent Viaene, and the contributors to their volume, *Religious Internationals in the Modern World: Globalization and Faith Communities since 1750* convincingly show, in the modern era, there has been a significant reimagining of religious communions from being universal to being international. Put another way, religious groups such as Jews, Catholics, Protestants, and Muslims have integrated both their self-understanding and structures into the international order, a shift from being universal religions to being international religions.

Yet this shift has not been universally embraced or possibly even fully understood. The result is significant tension between universal claims that rise above all social orders and claims that are captured into and limited by the international order. Catholics, Jews, Muslims, Hindus, Buddhists, and such Protestant movements as were always suspicious of the nation-state as a natural home for religion, continue to experience this tension, whether in the question of how community members who disobey both state and religious laws should be sanctioned or in the question of whether missionaries obedient to the mandate of their faith should obey state laws that forbid their mission.

Lacking an understanding of the factors shaping religious life results in a lack of understanding of how and why religious groups and individuals behave in the ways they do in a multireligious society. No study of creeds, rituals, and structures will explicate the behavior and self-understanding of these religious communities in contemporary society. Yet the knowledge sought by both Christian groups and others remains based on a construct of religion and religious belonging and identity still rooted in modern Christian self-understandings.

The most typical knowledge of non-Christian religions sought by my students is of religious beliefs, followed by an understanding of religious rituals, ethical principles, structures of authority, and almost inevitably, how the religion teaches that people are "saved." Only with regard to Islam are there questions about politics and power, and even these questions are pitched in terms of how belief shapes political structures. This kind of knowledge does not provide answers to the most urgent public questions about religion and may be more misleading than informative.

---

5 Faiths in Conversation Dialogue, March 29, 2016, Temple Adat Chevarim, Plano, Texas.

Thus, we need different approaches to education about religions and religious difference, and they have been emerging. As I look at a shelf of textbooks dedicated to teaching a general world religions course to undergraduate students I find, from the earliest (*The World's Religion* by Houston Smith) to the most recent (*Introducing World Religions,* by Charles Farhadian), almost all have refrained at an overt level from simply shoehorning non-Christian religions into a Christian framework. What they have done instead, with greater or lesser intentionality, is to use what might be called a "religious studies" approach to understanding religion.

One of the most recent, *Introduction to World Religions* by Fortress Press (2005), even has an opening chapter introducing the student to the evolution of religious studies through the advent of critical theory and the questioning of whether "religion" is even a valid category for the study of human experience. Yet even this textbook reverts in the sections on individual religions to sacred writings, beliefs, worship and festivals, and such other behaviors as may be particularly relevant to the religion at hand (Law for Islam, Family and Society for Judaism.) Other textbooks (such as Oxford's *World Religions Today,* 2006) approach each religion through its history and both explicate and place sacred writings, beliefs, worship, ethics, etc. in that context. What both, and the others I have reviewed, have in common is the objectification of both how religion is known and the knowledge of world religions itself, perhaps under the constant pressure by accrediting agencies (certainly felt at my institution) for quantifiable goals and thus measurable results.

Engaging religion simply cannot take place through a textbook, however careful in its deployment of the latest of religious studies perspectives or colorful, diverse, and animated its presentations of the behavior of the followers of the various religions. Engagement and understanding of living religious traditions cannot take place through encounters with objects, especially humans presented as objects. It requires first an actual encounter between religious people, and secondly an initial awareness of the social, cultural, and historical situation that influences the self-understandings, motivations, and behaviors of all religious people.

From the standpoint of designing pedagogical approaches to teach an understanding of our complex multireligious society at least three things emerge as critical. The first is that the roots of its complexity in the multidimensional changes being wrought by the now continual engagement of modern and non-modern societies be exposed. Traditional linear presentations of an evolution from pre-modernity to modernity to post-modernity are inadequate to understand the context of a multireligious society.

Secondly, emergent forms of interaction between still-evolving nation states and religious communities, changes in the structure of both personal and communal identity, and shifts and contestations between universal, global, and international self-understandings are basic to understanding the nature and function of religion and of the forces shaping inter-religious engagement.

These, in turn, need to be explored in the context of inter-religious dialogue so that students at any level grasp that religious engagement is engagement between human beings in all their diversity. Theory shouldn't merely be illustrated by case studies, but interrogated and made complex by relationships with religious people in all their particularities. Put more strongly, one can never understand Islam without talking to Muslims. And their idiosyncrasies will reveal both the limitations of any characterization of Islam and the necessity of the broadest possible dialogue to make such characterizations as useful as they are necessary.

Along the path to first discovering the diversity of religions and cultures in the world, Christians have demonized, romanticized, subjugated, assimilated, objectified, and sometimes subsumed religions and religious identities. The impulse toward these methods of comprehending, but not necessarily understanding, non-Christian religions remains. Yet as not only the cultures of the West, but cultures world-wide become more acutely diverse it appears that only multiple forms of engagement, informed by a recognition of our complex social evolution, will become the means by which a diverse religious society can emerge whose members all feel a sense of ownership and commitment to the whole.

BIBLIOGRAPHY

Dowley, Tim, and Christopher Partridge, eds. *Introduction to World Religions.* 2nd ed. Minneapolis: Fortress, 2013.

Esposito, John L., et al. *World Religions Today.* New York: Oxford University Press, 2006.

Farhadian, Charles. *Introducing World Religions.* Grand Rapids: Baker Academic, 2015.

Geertz, Clifford. "Religion as a Cultural System." In *Interpretation of Cultures: Selected Essays,* 87–125. New York: Basic, 1973.

Gomez, Edmund, et al. "Introduction: Religion, Business, and Contestation in Malaysia and Singapore." *Pacific Affairs* 88/2 (2015) 153–71.

Green, Abigail, and Vincent Viane, eds. *Religious Internationals in the Modern World: Globalization and Faith Communities since 1750.* New York: Palgrave McMillan, 2012.

Hamilton, Marci A. *God vs. the Gavel: Religion and the Rule of Law.* Cambridge: Cambridge University Press, 2005.

Jacobsen, Douglas, and Rhonda H. Jacobsen. *No Longer Invisible: Religion in University Education*. New York: Oxford University Press, 2012.

Kruse, Kevin Michael. *One Nation under God: How Corporate America Invented Christian America*. New York: Basic, 2015.

"Marrakesh Declaration: Executive Summary of the Marrakesh Declaration on the Rights of Religious Minorities in Predominantly Muslim Majority Communities." (Jan. 25–27, 2016). http://www.marrakeshdeclaration.org/marrakesh-declaration.html.

Prothero, Stephen. *Religious Literacy: What Every American Needs to Know—And Doesn't*. New York: HarperCollins, 2008.

Rawls, John. *Political Liberalism*. New York: Columbia University Press, 1993.

"Religion in the Public Schools." Washington, DC: Pew Research Center, 2007. http://www.pewforum.org/files/2007/05/religion-public-schools.pdf.

Rynkiewich, Michael. *Soul, Self, and Society: A Postmodern Anthropology for Mission in a Postcolonial World*. Eugene, OR: Cascade Books, 2011.

Shinn, Larry. "Liberal Education vs. Professional Education: The False Choice." *Trusteeship Magazine* 22 (January/February 2014) 6–10.

Smith, Huston. *The World's Religion*. New York: HarperCollins, 1991.

Taylor, Charles. *A Secular Age*. Cambridge: Belknap Press of Harvard University Press, 2007.

"U.S. Religious Knowledge Survey: Executive Summary." Washington, DC: Pew Research Center, 2010. http://www.pewforum.org/2010/09/28/u-s-religious-knowledge-survey/.

Wood, Graeme. "What ISIS Really Wants." *Atlantic Monthly* 315/2 (2015) 78.

2

Multifaith Context and Competencies

— Eleazar S. Fernandez

THE SOCIAL ENVIRONMENT OF my younger years did not prepare me well for living with a hospitable heart in relation to people of other faiths. In many instances, the atmosphere nurtured prejudice against people of other faiths, particularly Muslims. A stage performance that I loved to watch as a young boy during barrio fiestas such as the *moro-moro*, I later realized, was a reenactment of the *Reconquista*, which represents the capture of a city in the Iberian Peninsula by the Moors and the subsequent re-conquest by Christians. And often, though it may have been only a social device that parents used to prevent children from wandering, we were told not to get close to the ocean because the *Moros* (identified as pirates) might snatch and kill us. Additionally, in some instances parents would say, "the *Moros* are coming," in an attempt to quiet a crying child. We grew up learning to distrust and fear Muslims.[1]

Relationships among Christians, however, were not cordial either. Public debates on certain doctrines were common. Knowing how to de-bate was deemed important if a pastor was to defend his or her flock. I am glad I learned it, and it served its purpose. Fortunately, as my theological education progressed, I was exposed to a different and, I believe, better way of living together with people of other faiths. I was exposed to interfaith dialogue, which, as Yossi Klein Halevi puts it, is "the true spiritual adventure

1. "Moro" is one of the terms used in the Philippines to refer to Muslims.

of our time."[2] I chose to participate in this spiritual adventure, and in this adventure I have learned and continue learning to witness with passion to what God in Jesus the Christ has done in my life, while at the same time remaining open to the claims of others. The pages that follow are my evolving thoughts on competencies that citizens in general and religious leaders in particular need for a multifaith world. In this attempt to articulate religious competencies, I have asked the questions: What does a competent religious leader in a multifaith context look like? What qualities and competences must he or she possess?

In order to cover all possible major and significant points, I operate on the understanding that competencies must include these three categories: (1) attitude, (2) content, and (3) skills. Other versions of these three categories include (1) being, (2) knowing, and (3) doing; or (1) awareness, (2) knowledge, and (3) skills.[3] I agree with Daniel Schipani that competencies must address the matter of who we are, what we know, and what we do.[4] People are interested in what we know only when they know that we care. If they sense a dissonance between what we know and what we do, they will not take us seriously. Without moral integrity, competencies would simply be a matter of appropriate or right techniques. Conversely, moral integrity without techniques (skills) does not contribute much to the specific needs of individuals and communities. We need an integrated view of these three categories as we think about competencies in general and of competencies for multifaith education in particular. Let me now proceed with identifying and articulating these competencies.

1. AWARENESS AND UNDERSTANDING OF OUR RELIGIOUSLY PLURAL SETTING

Awareness and understanding of the growing religious pluralism and its challenges is a critical basic competency for multifaith contexts. Religious diversity is our reality. If we have not taken this seriously, then we must be living in our own small bubble. Knowledge of religious traditions other than our own is crucial for dwelling together in our shared space. This competency calls for basic interfaith literacy, which, sadly, is still low even as the world has become increasingly multifaith. This is particularly true in North America. Its record in multifaith literacy is dismal. Worse, not only do common people not know much about other religions, they often get the

2. Halevi, "A Coming Together," 7.

3. Schipani, "Pastoral and Spiritual Care."

4. Ibid.

distorted stereotype of other religious traditions through the media. Generally speaking, it appears that those in the dominant religious tradition in North America (Christianity) do not have much motivation to learn from other religious traditions. After all, as the dominant group, Christians can continue to live in their Christian bubble, although this may be not the case for long.

Teaching people about other religious traditions is a step in multifaith literacy, but it is not sufficient. If multifaith literacy were simply about teaching individuals the content of other religious traditions, it would be much easier to address. This would require minor changes in school's curricula. Multifaith literacy, however, demands more than learning the content, beliefs, and rituals of other religious traditions. It requires, contends Robert Hunt in his essay in this volume, encounter of flesh-and-blood believers of various faiths in their day-to-day life in society.[5] When this happens, an opportunity for a deeper understanding is opened.

2. PROPER UNDERSTANDING OF THE PLACE AND ROLE OF RELIGION IN SOCIETY AND IN THE FORMATION OF IDENTITY

Encounter with people of various faiths is a step in the right direction, but something more is needed. Beyond the actual encounter of people of various faiths, there must be a proper understanding of the place and role of religion in society and in the formation of people's identity. Religion is not separate from the rest of the factors that make up a society; it is an integral part of the entire social fabric. Religion cannot be understood properly apart from its unity with the rest of the social forces that mutually influence and shape each other.

An example may be useful to illumine the point mentioned above. It may be misleading to speak of "religious conflicts"; after all, religion, contrary to the Western secular mindset that has given birth to religion as an academic discipline, cannot be separated from the totality of life. If I continue to speak of "religious conflicts," it is primarily to highlight the crucial role of religion in many global conflicts and not to isolate it from the complex web of social relations. It may be a critical triggering factor in some conflicts, but it is hardly the sole factor. "Rarely is religion the principal cause of conflict," argues David Smock, "even when the opposing groups, such as Protestants and Catholics in Northern Ireland, are differentiated

5. Hunt, "Our Journey."

by religious identities. But religion is nevertheless a contributing factor to conflict in places as widely scattered as Northern Ireland, the Middle East, the Balkans, Sudan, Indonesia, and Kashmir."[6]

In his essay Hunt speaks of the need for an awareness of the social, cultural, and historical situation that informs and shapes the self-understandings, motivations, commitments, and behaviors of religious people. The formation of religious identity cannot be isolated from the cultural and political context of a person's location and community of belonging. Understanding this is crucial if we are to make sense of the different motivations and actions of believers within the same tradition and believers of different religious traditions.

The rise of religiously-motivated militantism should wake us up to the reality of the interweaving of religious identity and the larger socio-political dynamics. When predatory capitalism invades, destroys, and consumes a nation in pursuit of the bottom line, and traditional anchors of identity and belonging are threatened, what is left of the disempowered people? In situations like this it is not a surprise that people gravitate around religion as one of the remaining bastions against the forces of predatory capitalism. Also, it is not a surprise that religious identity can be disastrously wedded to militant-fundamentalist politics.

A competent person in a multifaith context must understand the importance of the role that religion plays in the interweaving of various social issues. This competency is especially important for religious leaders.

3. FUNCTIONAL UNDERSTANDING OF THE INTERLOCKING RELATIONSHIPS OF VARIOUS SOCIAL IDENTITIES

This third competency pursues further and refines the points of the second competency. Sheryl Kujawa-Holbrook makes a strong point—and I agree—that "[w]ithout functional understanding of the interlocking relationships between social identities of race, ethnicity, and culture, there is no foundation upon which to build greater interreligious understanding."[7] Religious identity is but one of the many dimensions of culture that constitute the identity or social profile of people, yet it is a significant one. What is important for this third competency is the understanding that it interacts

---

6. Smock, *Interfaith Dialogue*, 3.

7. Kujawa-Holbrook, *God Beyond Borders*, xxxi.

with other forms in an interlocking non-additive framework. What is this interlocking non-additive framework?

Although I did not include religious identity in my work, *Reimagining the Human*, I made the point that we need not only see the various identity markers in relation to one another, we also need to see their interlocking relationship in a non-additive fashion.[8] I am not simply advocating the addition of one, such as religious identity, into the mix, as if one were separate from and external to the rest, or one is experienced as separate from another. Following this thinking, a Black Muslim woman, for example, is not Black from Monday to Thursday and Muslim on Friday: she is a Black Muslim woman seven days a week. An individual experiences all the categories of identity simultaneously even as one or a combination would play a prominent role in certain circumstances. An interlocking-non-additive framework claims that the configuration of a person's experience of a specific identity marker is influenced by the extent to which one is affected by other forms of identity. Focusing on religion, this is to say that a person experiences religious identity in relation to other categories of identity. Hence, a competent person in a multifaith context must see religious identity within these interlocking dynamics.

4. DISTINGUISHING RELIGIOUS BELIEFS FROM CULTURAL AND ETHNIC CUSTOMS OR PRACTICES

In the previous competency, the interweaving of religion with other phenomena was highlighted. This fourth competency emphasizes the distinction. In her essay, Kujawa-Holbrook stresses the need to differentiate religious traditions or religious teachings with cultural and/or ethnic customs and the importance of not making comparisons without a proper understanding of the distinctions. Without proper understanding of the distinctions we cannot make right comparisons. When we are oblivious of the distinctions, we make comparisons that betray truth. Without proper understanding of the distinctions, any interpretation and comparison misses the mark and the consequences may be serious. Often, we make comparisons to put down or discredit another to support our point of view, if not our prejudices. In the end we violate the integrity of each.

The differences and the conflicts among those within the same religious tradition should wake us up to the realization that there is no generic and essentialized Christianity, Islam, Hinduism, Judaism, and Buddhism, although there are common and fundamental elements within each

8. Fernandez, *Reimagining the Human*. 31–52.

tradition. Each religious tradition has evolved over time under various circumstances producing various expressions. Thus, we cannot simply speak of Christianity, but of Christianities; likewise, we must speak of Islams, Judaisms, and Buddhisms. This is much more so when we speak about people or the believers/followers of each religious tradition. There is no generic and essentialized Christian, Muslim, Jew, Buddhist, and Hindu. There is Iraqi-Sunni Muslim, Iraqi-Shia Muslim, or a Syrian-Sunni Muslim, Syrian-Shia Muslim, and a finer distinction, Syrian Shia-Alawite Muslim. Encounters among adherents of the same religious tradition are not always easy as we commonly think. There are times when it is much easier to relate with people outside of one's faith tradition. Commonality and shared tradition do not always produce goodwill. The conflictive history of the children of Abrahamic faith (Christianity, Islam, and Judaism) is a painful example.

5. UNDERSTANDING OTHER RELIGIOUS TRADITIONS ON THEIR OWN TERMS

We must strive as much as possible to learn the religious worlds of others. Recognizing the limits of what we can know, we need to develop attitudinal openness. Having an appreciative understanding of other religious traditions fosters such openness. As much as we would like others to have an appreciative understanding of our own religious traditions, we also must learn to have an appreciative understanding of other religious traditions. As much as we would like others to recognize that our religious tradition makes sense and that it matters to us, we also must learn to recognize that other religious traditions make sense to believers of other faiths and matter to them.

Adopting a posture of appreciative understanding changes the way we see and relate with those unfamiliar to us. It does not mean that we turn off our critical minds and be oblivious to the questionable side of religion. It calls out the best in us as our fundamental posture as we relate to people of different religious traditions. This fundamental posture prepares us to listen attentively and differently to what others may have to teach. When we assume this posture, we lower the level of our prejudices and attune our ears to listen to what others have to say. This may elicit a response of appreciative understanding, which could then lead to deeper understanding and relationship.

Appreciative understanding leads to the ability to relate to and understand other religious traditions on their own terms. We must recognize and understand that each religious tradition has its own worldview and inner coherence. Though we may not fully understand the worldview and inner coherence of other religious traditions from the outside, this does not diminish the importance of approaching other religious faiths on their own terms. This approach recognizes the inherent integrity of other faiths.

It is a constant temptation to view and relate to other religions on our own terms. After all, we interpret and act on others and the world based on our understanding. Understanding others on their own terms requires self-discipline and intentionality. It requires exposing and knowing our assumptions and not letting them shape the way we understand and relate to others. We must develop the ability, following Robert Kegan, to distinguish between the assumptions that we hold and the assumptions that hold us.[9] All of us have assumptions that *we hold*, but these assumptions need not *hold us*. It is important that we state or expose our assumptions so that our assumptions can be carefully examined, corrected, or validated. Stating our assumptions is a way of exposing the risk of having these ideas hold us or constrain us from seeing other points of view. When we do, we allow others to speak. The ability to articulate other views faithfully even when we disagree is a mark of intelligence and integrity. If we cannot articulate about and present others on their own terms, how can we expect others to do the same for us? We need this kind of competency.

6. INTERPATHIC WAY OF UNDERSTANDING AND RELATING

This sixth competency deepens the point of the previous competency. If an individual wants to see or understand others on their own terms, empathy is very useful. In empathy a person puts himself or herself in the place of the other, which enables him or her to see the world from the other's location and perspective. She or he enters the world of the other not to conquer and manipulate, but to experience what it is like to see and feel the world from the other. Relating this to the matter of religious traditions, Michael Kinnamon speaks of empathy as a capacity "that enables leaders to see from inside a tradition not their own." How would we know that such empathy is happening? We know that empathy is happening, continues Kinnamon, "when others recognize themselves in what you say about them."[10]

Eunjoo Mary Kim extends the point of empathy through the term "interpathy." Interpathy pursues the point we have made about empathy by expanding the boundaries of what is considered other. Empathy, says Kim,

9. Heifetz and Linsky, *Leadership on the Line*, 234.

10. Kinnamon, *Can a Renewal Movement be Renewed?*, 138.

presupposes that "people share common linguistic and cultural assumptions" while in interpathy people "attempt to 'enter the other's world of assumptions, beliefs, and values and temporarily take them as one's own.'" In interpathy there is the "'voluntary experiencing of a separate other without the reassuring epistemological floor of common cultural assumptions.'"[11] Having extended the boundaries of what is considered other, "[interpathic] capacity involves two abilities: the ability to see as others see, and the ability to see ourselves as others see us." In developing the sensibility of interpathy, our understanding of the world is not only broadened, we also grow in the understanding of ourselves by having the eyes to see ourselves "through the eyes of the other."[12]

Interpathy is a useful competency for living in a multifaith world. Interpathic ability would be useful especially for those who are promoting interfaith understanding and cooperation. It should be cultivated as one of the essential competencies of a religious leader. Educational learning opportunities must be provided to cultivate this competency.

7. RESPECTING AND CELEBRATING DIFFERENCES

Driven to establish goodwill and cooperation, it is a common and constant temptation to rush toward establishing sameness while muting difference. Riding high with good intentions, sameness fails to understand that authentic religious understanding and cooperation, following Kujawa-Holbrook, "is not built on denying the reality or importance of differences, but rather on the acknowledgement of difference and the commitment to build relationships with that recognition as given."[13] And, contrary to common understanding, "the denial of differences," continues Kujawa-Holbrook, "actually becomes an impediment to interreligious learning."[14] The common default of sameness, as pointed out by Jennifer Peace in her essay, actually belies the assumption that difference is abnormal and, therefore, threatening. While affirming our shared humanity and the many aspects that we share in common, Peace's approach dives deep into the irreducible differences and claims that a competent interfaith person must be one who safeguards and celebrates differences.

---

11. Kim, 70, quoting David Augsburger's *Pastoral Counseling across Culture* in *Preaching in an Age of Globalization*.

12. Kim, *Preaching*, 70–71.

13. Kujawa-Holbrook, *God Beyond Borders*, xxxiii.

14. Ibid.

More than making the argument that difference is normal or that authentic cooperation is not built on the denial of differences, we must have a positive articulation of difference. In *The Dignity of Difference,* Jonathan Sacks makes the point that "difference does not diminish; it enlarges the sphere of human possibilities."[15] Difference enlarges our humanity. "This is not the cosmopolitanism of those who belong nowhere," Sacks contends, "but the deep human understanding that passes between people who, knowing how important their attachments are to them, understand how deeply someone else's different attachments matter to them also."[16] Sacks continues, "[o]nly when we realize the danger of wishing that everyone should be the same—the same faith on the one hand; the same McWorld on the other—will we prevent the clash of civilizations, born of the sense of threat and fear." Given all the conflicts in the world, he sees this as "our last best hope."[17]

Can we make this shift in understanding difference? Relativism is helpless; toleration is not sufficient. If we are to find a powerful force that can help us make the shift that is equal to the challenge, it must come, argues Sacks, from our great religious traditions because there is nothing powerful enough to help us make this shift short of a religious mandate that the transcendent God is the creator of diversity and that God commands us to honor diversity. Hence, Sacks drives home the point that it is only when "we understand the God-given, world-enhancing dignity of difference" that "we will learn to live with diversity."[18]

8. AN ENLARGED IDENTITY: COSMOPOLITAN HEART

Identity is a relational concept. It acquires its form, as mentioned earlier, through social interaction. This is true of Christian identity in particular. When religious diversity and difference is perceived as a threat, identity takes the form of being "over against." This is a very common response. One adopts an identity that is set in opposition to the other. We have witnessed the ugly consequences of this identity formation: fragmentation, the reassertion of virulent nationalism, the rise of militant religious fundamentalism, and global confrontation or what others call the "clash of civilizations," "clash of fundamentalisms," and "clash of barbarisms."[19]

15. Sacks, *The Dignity of Difference,* 201.

16. Ibid., 201–2.

17. Ibid., 209.

18. Ibid.

19. Huntington, *The Clash of Civilizations*; Ali, *The Clash of Fundamentalisms*;

"A pain that is not transformed is transferred," Richard Rohr so aptly says.[20] The pained or wounded may develop what Marc Gopin describes as "negative identity," or an identity that has emerged out of one's own experience of being a stranger, particularly when the experience is negative. As he puts it, "If the rule of deep identity of the stranger is 'love your neighbor as you love yourself' (Lv 19:18), then the rule of superficial identity or negative identity is 'do unto others what they have done unto you, or before they do it unto you again.'"[21]

People of our multifaith context need to develop a different kind of identity, an identity understood not as over-against or in opposition to but in right connection to or in right relationship with the whole. It is not an identity that rises or falls by being dogmatically right, for we are greater than being right. "We want supremacy, but that is not what we really need. What we really need," contends Samir Selmanovic, "is to learn to be a part of the whole."[22]

What we really need is a sense of belonging in which our distinctive difference is respected and taken seriously as our contribution to the whole, not taken as a threat. When a society has learned to honor and respect the dignity of difference of its members, the whole is enriched. The whole that is enriched also enriches the members, and vice versa. When this happens the humanity of all is enriched and enlarged. We become cosmopolitan by heart. "Cosmopolitans," explains Kwame Anthony Appiah, "think that there are many values worth living by and that you cannot live by all of them. So we hope and expect that different people and different societies will embody different values."[23] A cosmopolitan person is one who has learned to embrace diversity and difference. She or he is at home with mixture and actively engages in conversation across difference. A cosmopolitan does not assert homogeneity or universality as the starting point for engagement. A critical starting point for the engagement is the recognition of the commonalities that people share. These commonalities that people share, for Appiah, "do not need to be universal; all they need to be is what these particular people have in common. Once we have found enough we share, there is a further possibility that we will be able to enjoy discovering things we do not yet share. That is one of the payoffs of cosmopolitan curiosity."[24]

Achcar. *The Clash of Barbarisms.*

20. Rohr, cited in Yoder, *The Little Book of Trauma Healing*, 30.
21. Gopin, "The Heart of the Stranger," 17.
22. Selmanovic, *It's Really All about God*, 170.
23. Appiah, *Cosmopolitanism*, 114.
24. Ibid., 97.

9. THE RELIGIOUS STRANGER AS A SUBJECT-COMPANION IN MEANING-MAKING AND WORLD-MAKING

The stranger is a prime symbol of difference. If we follow this line of thought, which we should, then how we treat the stranger in our midst becomes the litmus test of how far we have learned to embrace the dignity of difference. The concept of stranger is so central in monotheistic religions that the stranger is a classic Other, which is also a classic metaphor for the presence of the Divine. That is to say, the Divine has chosen the encounter with the Other or the real flesh and blood other as a condition for the Divine-human encounter. Put differently, how we see and relate to the stranger is the litmus test of our faith or to any claim of having encountered the Divine. Marc Gopin puts it clearly and powerfully:

> [T]here is no person of greater concern in the Bible than the stranger who is with us but not with us, whom we know but do not know, who is a source of great mystery and yet ancestral familiarity, whose treatment by us is ultimately a litmus test of whether we and our culture have succeeded or not in the eyes of God, and whose experience is essentially a yardstick of our moral stature.[25]

With the above caveat, we must pursue the project of reclaiming the importance of the category of stranger. Only through the stranger, not outside it, can we experience salvation. Outside of the stranger there is no salvation. This is not to say that the stranger is a means for our salvation; rather, it is to say that our very own salvation is bound with the stranger. The stranger/alien is crucial for our liberation from our narrow worldviews, stereotypes, and prejudices; we need more doses of the unfamiliar, the strange, and the discomforting to help us move into different ways of thinking, dwelling, and acting. "When God visits us through the other," writes Selmanovic, "we are awakened and begin to feel what we could not feel before, we see what we could not see before, and we think what we could not think before. In the presence of the other, everything changes."[26]

Recovering the importance of the category of the stranger in the context of our multifaith world demands that we give integrity to the religious others in our midst by recognizing what we owe them. When we do so, we can recognize and honor their subjecthood, which is the only way they can become our subject-companions in our meaning-making and

25. Gopin, "The Heart of the Stranger," 6.

26. Selmanovic, *It's Really All about God*, 261.

world-making. When we do so, we have allowed them to speak to us as subjects of their own right. In the words of Raimon Panikkar, we must learn to "see our [religious] neighbor not only as some*thing* else, but as an *alius/alia*, as some*one* else—not only as an object of observance or cognition, but as another source of intelligibility, and an independent subject of our categories."[27]

When we see the religious strangers or others in our midst as subjects, we treat them differently. We treat their difference or strangeness differently. Instead of dissolving and assimilating the strange when it is found useful or rejecting it when it is perceived as threatening, we treat difference differently by allowing it to present for what it is. When we do this, to our surprise, the strange or the stranger may become a blessing. The strange or the stranger can then, following Raúl Fornet-Betancourt, fully represent "the exteriority that widens the frontiers of our understanding." And, in allowing this to happen, "we discover a new world": we are "born again."[28]

When we have gained a positive view of the other, they become subjects and our hermeneutic companions, helping us see the wider world and ourselves better. We cannot understand religious others without their cooperation as subjects. To understand them we must learn to understand together (*convivencia*) with them as subjects. And in our *convivencia* of interpretation, we also come to understand ourselves better and deeper. Moreover, we understand our connections and shared context and challenges better. The world would not be as fearsome as it seems, because we have the gift of the other. "We have," in the words of Margaret Wheatley, "each other's curiosity, wisdom, and courage. And we have Life, whose great ordering powers, if we choose to work with them, will make us even more curious, wise, and courageous."[29]

10. BEING AT HOME IN ONE'S HOUSE

"You, estranged from yourself, short-sighted turtle looking for home,
be home to yourself."[30]

Are we at home with ourselves? Are we wishing to be someone else or somewhere else? Are we at home in our own house? Or, do we loathe being in our

---

27. Panikkar, *Cultural Disarmament*, 36.

28. Fornet-Betancourt, "Hermeneutics and Politics of Strangers," 218.

29. Wheatley, *Leadership and the New Science*, 193.

30. Norita Dittberner-Jax, quoted in Hering, *Writing to Wake the Soul*, 64; emphasis added.

house because it is constraining or stifling us? Are we running away from our house because we no longer feel that it fits us? "Some of us were raised in faith traditions that fit us about as well as a glass slipper meant for someone else's foot," says Karen Hering. And "[w]e know too well the pain of trying to walk in a faith that contradicts who we are, whom we love, what we know, or what we do and do not trust. . . If faith is truly a matter of trust, it requires a better fit with our inner self and soul."[31]

It is only when we find a slipper or house that fits our desires that we can feel at home. It is only when we find a fit between our religious house and who are and what we care about that we can speak of being at home or say that we have found a home. What does this being at home mean? One way of speaking about finding home is finding one's place in the world or in the scheme of things. "To be at home," says Kujawa-Holbrook, "is to have a place in the scheme of life—a place where we are comfortable; know that we belong; can be who we are; and can honor, protect, and create what we truly love."[32] When our habitation or dwelling place reflects fitness with our spirit, we can say that we are at home or we have found a home, even as we are always on the way.

Finding our voice is another way of speaking about finding home. Finding home is another way of saying that we have found our voice or our place. Only those who have found their voice (home) as well as know its range and compass can understand the need of others to claim their voice. As in vocational clarity, "[i]nability to know and claim one's own voice. . . results in and produces confusion."[33] Confusion begets confusion. Confusion in one's self leads to confusion in one's dealing with others. It will have bearings on how we treat others.

People who can appreciate others are those who understand the depth of their own religious traditions. They are in a better position to assume the posture of "hospitable presence" and to help create a "hospitable space" if they are at home with their inner voice and deep convictions. Because they are at home with themselves, they can be more respectful of others' inner voices.

11. REACHING OUT AND BEING OPEN BY GOING DEEP

Related to or as an extension of the previous point, if we want to reach out we must go deep. If we want to fly high and far, we must be deeply rooted.

31. Hering, *Writing to Wake the Soul*, 64–65.

32. Kujawa-Holbrook, *Pilgrimage*, 152.

33. Hunter, *Desert Hearts*, 36.

Only those who are deeply rooted can fly high and far. This is true of faith and spirituality. The outward journey of a pilgrim (Latin: *peregrinus*— "stranger") is as much, or even more so, an inward journey into one's very depth of being. The ultimate measure of pilgrimage is not the physical distance that is covered, but the journey within until one discovers one's self, feeling rooted and at home and attuned to life. As Kujawa-Holbrook puts it, "[t]he *inward journey* of pilgrimage takes us to those places where we feel *a sense of rootedness,* even if we find ourselves physically in a strange and faraway place."[34]

I am reminded of William Blake's poem: "To see a World in a Grain of Sand / And Heaven in a Wild Flower / Hold Infinity in the palm of your hand / And Eternity in an hour. . . ."[35] If we want to see the world, we must see it in a grain of sand. If we want to taste eternity, we must taste it in an hour. Going deep and going far are not contradictory. Being mindful of the particular is not a distraction to embracing the universal. If we want to address the universal, we must go deeper into the particular, that is, to our religious tradition. Particularity is not the same as exclusivism; it is our entry point to the universal. Any claim to the universal without recognition of the particular context of its utterance needs to be suspected.

There is no path to universal values and connections except through the particular faith traditions in which we belong. It is in and through the depths of our religious tradition that we must see its openness. If we cannot find it there, then it is a matter that we must take seriously. Perhaps, as we go deeper we will arrive at the affirmation that we are open to other faiths because we are faithful to our religious heritage.[36] Deep religiosity is not the opposite of openness. A Christian in a multifaith context, in particular, must be able to say with confidence that he or she is open *not in spite of* but *because of* his or her Christian faith. To put it differently, a Christian must be able to say, "I am open because I am Christian." After all, the central message of the Christian narrative is not God's exclusivity but God's radical love and hospitality. And, as I articulated elsewhere, "Christians must witness to God's radical comma where exclusivism has put a period. Moreover, they must proclaim God's radical openness with the passion and excitement of an exclamation point."[37]

34. Kujawa-Holbrook, *Pilgrimage,* 150. Emphasis supplied.

35. Blake, *"Auguries of Innocence,"* stanza 1.

36. Cobb, *Transforming Christianity,* 60.

37. Fernandez, *Burning Center,* 316.

12. EXPRESSING ONE'S DEEP CONVICTIONS WITH HONESTY, RESPECT, AND OPENNESS

Interfaith interaction in a multifaith context does not require that we must leave our deep theological convictions behind; neither does it mean that every participant must agree. It does not mean tolerating one another, for the idea of toleration already means that one has won and others have lost. It is, as Harvard's Pluralism Project puts it, the "energetic engagement with diversity, active seeking of understanding across lines of difference," and an "encounter of commitments."[38] It does not require that everyone at the table has to agree, but it does require a "commitment to being at the table—with one's commitments."[39]

If religious encounter is an encounter of commitments, a competent religious person must not only be at home in her or his religious identity and knowledgeable about her or his tradition; she or he must also know how to engage in passionate conversations with honesty, respect, and openness. A religious person in a multifaith context must be competent to do this. Part of this person's training must be about attentive listening and active speaking. There are those who speak because they have something to say; there are those who speak because they must say something. It is not always easy to distinguish one from the other. The quality of our speech is dependent on the quality of our listening. Only those who listen well are worthy of being listened to. With attentive listening, we have gained the right to speak. But beyond this right to speak, we must learn to speak with the strength of conviction without putting others down. Moreover, we must have the ability to ask honest questions and offer honest answers. Lastly, we must learn how to get unstuck from stuck conversations.

13. HOSPITALITY: RECEPTIVITY, SPACE, AND PRESENCE

Hospitality in common parlance is basically about warm welcome and excellent reception. In the world of business, particularly the tourism industry, hospitality is about fine dining, accommodation, and professionalized service; and, of course, it is only for those who can afford it. While hospitality as warm welcome and excellent reception is to be welcomed, we need to go deeper when we consider it as a competency in a multifaith context. Here

38. See Harvard Pluralism Project at Harvard University.
39. Ibid.

I would like to propose two aspects of hospitality: receptivity and space and presence.

Hospitality of Receiving

While hospitality is often equated with giving, it is but one side of the coin. Giving is a virtue that needs to be encouraged. But this virtue, when not examined critically, may undermine other equally important virtues. The virtue of hospitality as giving can easily turn into the vice of power and privilege. It can reinforce the dominant position and lead to the disempowerment of others. We must always be on guard when we are motivated "to do something good," for we may be serving our own needs in "doing something good." In matters of religious faiths, it can find expressions in religious arrogance, closed-mindedness, and imposition.

Hospitality is also about the ability to receive the gift of the other. It means making ourselves receptive to what others bring: who they are, their concerns and ideas, and their hopes. They may have something that we need; yet, this is difficult to acknowledge when we live as if we are sufficient. This is true in matters of religion. If we have all the religious truths, then there is no need for what religious others bring. A change in perspective must happen: Being in need is part of what it means to be perfect.

A much needed virtue or competency of religious leaders in a religiously plural context is the hospitality of receiving. Being able to receive, especially the gifts from religious others or strangers, is a competency.

Hospitable Space and Presence

I have found Henri Nouwen's distinction of the German and Dutch word for hospitality insightful: the German *Gastfreundschaft* emphasizes "friendship" with the guest, whereas the Dutch *gastvrijheid* emphasizes "freedom" of the guest. Integrating and re-appropriating these two distinct emphases, Nouwen speaks of hospitality as "offering a friendship without binding [freedom] the guest and freedom without leaving him alone [friendship]." In this notion, hospitality is primarily a "creation of a free space" where the stranger can be at home and be a friend instead of a threat or an enemy.[40]

Hospitality transforms strangers into friends, but the stranger embraced as a friend is allowed free space. Hospitality is about creating a space for others to breathe, find their own voice, sing their own songs, and dance

40 Nouwen, *Reaching Out*, 51. Words in brackets supplied.

their own dances. It is about creating a space where strangers can be who they are in their strangeness. Conformity to our views, expectations, and practices should not be the basis of our hospitality. "*Freedom*," for Marjorie Thompson, "is the medium of human exchange in true hospitality."[41] Along with the creation of free space for the guest or stranger, hospitality is also about our openness and humility: it is about receiving the gifts of the strangers, and about opening ourselves so we can truly listen and learn from strangers.

Given the aura of symbolisms that surrounds religious leaders, it is a challenge to create this hospitable space, but it is something that must be pursued. An open and hospitable space must be cultivated in which we not only teach but learn, receive instead of give, and submit or yield instead of being always in control. Religious leaders in a multifaith context must have the ability to create hospitable space where others are free to express and explore their own faith. This is a "fearless space"—a space in which a person is at home in one's faith in an interfaith context. Competent ministers in a multifaith setting must be able to provide this hospitable space.

Intertwined with hospitable space is hospitable presence. Hospitable space does not just happen by itself; it is created. How do we create this hospitable space? Religious leaders can play an important role in the creation of hospitable space by their hospitable presence. They must constantly reflect on the kind of presence they are creating. How are they presenting themselves to the people they are encountering or ministering to, such as in a hospital or military facilities setting, whose religious faiths are different from theirs? Encounter with people of other faiths can be more complex when the encounter happens in a hospital setting or in a moment of health crisis.

14. BUILDING TRUST, SOLIDARITY, SHARED MINISTRY, AND INTERFAITH ACTIONS

The ability to build trust and respect in relation to religious others is an important competency in a religiously plural context. This is basic before we can proceed further. Trust and respect are the foundations of lasting and healthy relationship. To use a building metaphor, they provide the internal support in a well-built house. Without this support, relationships cannot stand; they will crumble. Relationship can sprout, grow, and thrive only in the spirit of trust and respect. The actions of each must build and nourish trust. Trust cannot be demanded; it is earned. One earns the trust of others

41. Thompson, *Soul Feast*, 134. Emphasis in the original.

by being trustworthy. Without this element of trust, which is nurtured by tested and proven commitments, it is really difficult to do much more.

Reinforcing the foundation of trust is solidarity. We are in this life together. If the destiny and hopes of one are connected with the other, then the fundamental mode and posture of our relationship is solidarity. When a form of support is requested and extended, the support is given/received on the basis of solidarity with the other. Other than this, a support can easily turn into power over the receiver. Solidarity on the other hand, subverts this temptation. In the act of solidarity, we accompany the other in the journey of life and its challenges. Accompaniment is best expressed in the mode of solidarity. The companion does not solve the issues and do the walking for the other, but walks with the other/partner, knowing fully that their pains and joys are intertwined.

Building on trust and solidarity, religious leaders in a multifaith context must have the ability to work together with believers of other religious faiths to advance common community concerns.

15. ESTABLISHING ETHICAL NORMS IN A MULTIFAITH CONTEXT

Religious diversity and our work for interfaith relations must be subjected to a rigorous test not only in relation to our deeply held theological views but also in the face of another pressing and, in many cases, matter-of-life-and-death challenge: the challenge of being open to religious diversity while taking a firm stand and acting against diversities—oftentimes couched in the language of "religious" diversity—that are life-negating, idolatrous, and demonic. What shape does the pursuit of interfaith relations take in the face of moral challenge? What norm/norms shall interfaith relations embrace so it may have a clear guide in the face of a serious moral challenge? What theological views may be helpful in sorting out the moral challenge?

Kinnamon identifies moral challenge as one of the difficult aspects that must be addressed in a multifaith setting especially by those committed to interfaith openness and dialogue. This is the challenge, in the words of Kinnamon, "of being both open to legitimate diversity and firmly opposed to those diversities, including some called 'religious,' that are demonic."[42] Kinnamon asks: "If one belief is really as good as the next, then how do we say no to Qur'an-burning congregations or religious practices that demean women or advocates of religiously based terrorism with sufficient

---

42. Kinnamon, *Can a Renewal Movement be Renewed?*, 104.

conviction?"[43] Openness does not mean live and let live. Openness to differences takes a moral stand in the face of evil. Sachs is emphatic on this point: "We must withhold the robe of sanctity when it is sought as a cloak for violence and bloodshed. If faith is enlisted in the cause of war, there must be an equal and opposite counter-voice in the name of peace. If religion is not part of the solution, it will certainly be part of the problem."[44]

Hospital chaplaincy, for example, provides a rich context for moral decision-making. Ethical/moral norms play a crucial role in making informed decisions along with other factors, such as religious and cultural beliefs, health and life, medical practices, and policies. While the religious world of the patient and his or her family, for example, is listened to and respected, there are larger norms that play significantly in making complex ethical decisions. Even if there are medical consensus and mandated legal policies, the space is wide for making ethical deliberations. "A professional chaplain must develop skills in the ethical dimensions of care, advocating for folks who are working to apply their guiding principles to complex health care decisions," says Helen Wells O'Brien.[45]

16. SPIRITUAL SELF-CARE

We cannot relate well to people of other faiths as faithful believers if we are not spiritually grounded in our religious life. We cannot relate well to people of other faiths as faithful believers and understand the depth of their spirituality if we are spiritually shallow. If we do not give much value to the care of our spiritual life, we cannot give the same to others. When we are spiritually empty, we cannot give what we do not have. Conversely, we cannot receive well because it requires spiritual receptivity or readiness to welcome the spiritual gift of others.

Building and nurturing interfaith relation is not an easy job; it is demanding; it requires so much of us. Surely, there are many challenges to be faced, and it is easy to get overwhelmed and frustrated, and to experience burn out. We have known many who are burning with passion in the pursuit of their vocation and the work of social transformation, but have not been able to sustain this passion in the long run. They have succumbed to "compassion fatigue" and burnout. "People can exhaust themselves," warns Howard Rice, "by ceaselessly doing good. Activity as an end in itself can

43. Ibid.

44. Sachs, *The Dignity of Difference*, 105.

45. Presentation made at a faculty retreat, United Theological Seminary of the Twin Cities.

drain us of our vitality. Some have found themselves depleted by work for social justice and have retreated into a highly privatized form of spirituality, reacting their way into a spirituality of retreat."[46] Burnout is more than being tired from being busy. Burnout is giving what we do not have; it is giving when our wellspring has dried up. It is giving or doing when the act has not nourished us back.

We must prepare for the long haul by sustaining ourselves spiritually. Self-care is not selfishness. It is an essential practice for nourishing our lives and the vocation to which we are committed. Self-care is a holy act; it is a spiritual act. We do it not only for ourselves but because we are committed to give ourselves for the long haul. When we give our best to a vocation that calls us, such as interfaith works, we may experience burn out. We may continue to be busy, but we can be spiritually dry. Hence, cultivating our spiritual life must be intentional. In addition to regular retreats and set-aside practices, it is important that we see and experience spirituality in the mundane, the banal, and the ordinary, if we are to prevent burnout, numbing, and bitterness. It is in this sense that the notion of integral or holistic spirituality can offer a particular contribution.

Caring or nourishing ourselves spiritually for the long haul is no doubt both individual and communal. Gaelic speakers have another custom associated with *grieshog,* or the "preservation of coals." Besides burying hot embers in a heap of ash to preserve the fire for the next day's peat fire, they share the fire from home to home as well. When a family moves or when a young person marries, he or she takes the fire from the first hearth to start the first fire in the new hearth. Irish know that no fire lasts forever, that new fire comes from somewhere, that fire energizes our homes, and that the fire that has served us in the past is worthy of serving us in the present and in the days to come.[47]

17. LIVING THE QUESTIONS

It would not take much time to recognize that the way this last competency is formulated comes from the words of Rainer Maria Rilke, in *Letters to a Young Poet*:

> [H]ave patience with everything that remains unsolved in your heart. *Try to love the questions themselves,* like locked rooms and like books written in a foreign language. Do not now look

---

46. Rice, *The Pastor as Spiritual Guide,* 131.

47. Chittister, *The Fire in these Ashes,* 174.

for the answers. They cannot now be given to you because you could not live them. It is a question of experiencing everything. At present you *need to live the question.* Perhaps you will gradually, without even noticing it, find yourself experiencing the answer, some distant day.[48]

Questions, we will always have, and they are plenty and coming constantly. When we have thought that we have clarified and answered one, we are brought to the realization that something is getting more and more complex and, perhaps, muddled. In her work on *Leadership and the New Science,* Wheatley points to this hard reality: "This is a strange world, and it promises only to get stranger. Niels Bohr, who engaged with Heisenberg in those long, nighttime conversations that ended in despair, once said that great ideas, when they appear, seem muddled and strange. They are only half-understood by their discoverer and remain a mystery to everyone else."[49]

Mystery is all around us, and it should not be confused with mystification. Much as we try to probe the depth of mystery, it only continues to reveal its mysteriousness. Mystery is built into what is revealed. The more revelation we have, the more mystery we experience. Revelation is always a mystery. We can take the relationship of lovers as an example. I agree with Selmanovic: "What is hidden about the person is just as important as what is known, and only a relational experience can hold what is known and what is not known in harmony. Both knowing and not knowing become a part of revelation, a way love works."[50] As mystery is a part of life and deep questions will always be there, we must learn to live with mystery and learn to live the questions. We need to affirm with Harry Emerson Fosdick: "I would rather live in a world where my life is surrounded by mystery than live in a world so small that my mind could comprehend it."[51]

The desire for clarity and finality in us is strong. We want clear, unequivocal, and final answers. We get anxious in the presence of uncertainties. Without knowing it, we have much in common with religious fundamentalists. Slavok Žižek's statement on this matter is on target:

A fundamentalist does not believe, he *knows* directly. To put it in another way: liberal-skeptical cynicism and fundamentalism both *share* a basic underlying feature: the loss of the ability to believe in the proper sense of the term. For both of them,

48. Rilke, *Letters to a Young Poet,* 35; emphasis supplied.
49. Wheatley, *Leadership,* 193.
50. Selmanovic, *It's Really All About God,* 100–1.
51. Fosdick, *Neighbor,* 3.

religious statements are quasi-empirical statements of direct knowledge: fundamentalists accept them as such, while skeptical cynics mock them.[52]

Our desire for certainty has undermined faith. Faith has been confused with quasi-empirical propositions. Even if we follow the common people's language that makes faith identical with the word "belief," still there is a grave misunderstanding. Again, following Žižek, "belief is a reflexive attitude: it is never a case of simply believing—one has to believe in belief itself (one can also *not* believe one's belief)."[53]

We can embrace mystery and learn to live the questions if we embrace the posture of faith, from which springs forth hope. Faith is much more akin to trust (Greek—*pistis*). When what is around us or what is to come is not clear by sight, we have to live by faith (2 Cor 5:7). As Madeleine L'Engle puts it, "some things have to be believed in order to be seen."[54] Faith is a prelude to sight. Here is a line attributed to Saint Augustine: "Faith is to believe what you do not see; the reward of this faith is to see what you believe." We need the "eyes of faith" so we can see what is not immediately visible by ordinary sight, that life is full of mystery, complexities, and strange phenomena.

Much as we ache to know in advance, the future is not ours to see completely; we do not know completely about tomorrow, but by faith we trust who holds tomorrow and who holds our hands. Every beginning is an act of faith. In the beginning is faith. We may wish we had a searchlight to see clearly what is ahead of us, but what we have is a lantern, the lantern of faith. Like Indiana Jones in the movie, *Raiders of the Lost Ark*, we have to cross the chasm without a clear sight of the path, because the "path reveals itself one step at a time—and only *after* we've committed ourselves to moving ahead."[55]

So, we have to walk by faith, not only by sight, because the road is not given in advance. The poet Antonio Machado has these words for us: "*Caminante no hay camino. Se hace camino al andar*" ("Traveler, there is no road; the road is made by walking").[56] And, it is only in the walking that we will know the path (*solvitur ambulando*). Moreover, according to Buddhist teachings: "You cannot travel the path until you have become the path."[57] We must become the path. This dovetails well with an understanding of

52. Žižek and Gunjević, *God in Pain*, 191.

53. Ibid., 189.

54. L'Engle, *Many Waters*, 290.

55. Wheatley, *Walk Out Walk On*, 233.

56. Machado, "Proverbio 29," in *Campos de Castilla*, 138–39.

57. Kujawa-Holbrook, *Pilgrimage*, 70.

faith as a verb, in which once it finds a home in us, it "helps us carry our home within, which is where the true sense of home must begin." And, when this happens, our "life speaks"[58] or the "journey and destination get a little intertwined."[59]

Faith, not fundamentalist certainty, enables us to live with mystery and live the questions—unresolved questions. Along with many wise teachers, Wheatley calls us to "live with the strange and the bizarre, directed to the unseen lands by distant faint glimmers of hope. Every moment of this journey requires that we be comfortable with uncertainty. . . ." The religious leader of a multifaith world must have the competency to live with mystery with wonder and embrace the unresolved questions with grace and hospitality.

BIBLIOGRAPHY

Achcar, Gilbert. *The Clash of Barbarisms: The Making of the New World Disorder.* New York: Routledge, 2016.

Ali, Tariq. *The Clash of Fundamentalisms: Crusades, Jihads and Modernity.* London: Verso, 2002.

Appiah, Kwame Anthony. *Cosmopolitanism: Ethics in a World of Strangers.* New York: Norton, 2006.

Blake, William. "Auguries of Innocence." In *The Pickering Manuscript.* Originally published in *Songs of Innocence and Experience, with Other Poems,* edited by R. H. Shephard. London: n.p., 1866. https://www.poetryfoundation.org/poems-and-poets/poems/detail/43650.

Chittister, Joan. *Welcome to the Wisdom of the World and Its Meaning for You: Universal Spiritual Insights Distilled From Five Religious Traditions.* Grand Rapids: Eerdmans, 2007.

———. *The Fire in These Ashes: A Spirituality of Contemporary Religious Life.* Kansas City: Sheed & Ward, 1995.

Cobb, John. *Transforming Christianity and the World: A Way Beyond Absolutism and Relativism,* edited by Paul Knitter. Maryknoll, NY: Orbis, 1999.

Daniel, Ben. *Neighbor: Christian Encounters with "Illegal" Immigration.* Louisville: Westminster John Knox, 2010.

Fernandez, Eleazar S. *Burning Center, Porous Borders: The Church in a Globalized World.* Eugene, OR: Wipf & Stock, 2011.

———. *Reimagining the Human: Theological Anthropology in Response to Systemic Evil.* St. Louis: Chalice, 2004.

Fornet-Betancourt, Raúl. "Hermeneutics and Politics of Strangers: A Philosophical Contribution on the Challenge of *Convivencia* in Multicultural Societies." In *A Promised Land, a Perilous Journey: Theological Perspectives on Migration,* edited by Daniel Groody and Gioacchino Campese, 210–24. Notre Dame: University of Notre Dame Press, 2008.

58. Palmer, *Let Your Life Speak.*

59. Hering, *Writing to Wake the Soul,* 65.

Gopin, Marc. "The Heart of the Stranger." In *Explorations in Reconciliation: New Directions in Theology*, edited by David Tombs and Joseph Liechty 3–21. Aldershot, UK: Ashgate, 2006.

Halevi, Yossi Klein. "A Coming Together We Must Take on Faith." *Washington Post* B3 (December 23, 2001). Cited in David Smock, ed., *Interfaith Dialogue and Peace Building*. Washington, DC: United States Institute of Peace, 2002.

Heifetz, Ronald, and Marty Linsky. *Leadership on the Line: Staying Alive through the Danger of Leading*. Boston: Harvard Business School Press, 2002.

Hering, Karen. *Writing to Wake the Soul: Opening the Sacred Conversation Within*. New York: Atria, 2013.

Hunter, Victor. *Desert Hearts and Healing Fountains: Gaining Pastoral Vocational Clarity*. St. Louis: Chalice, 2003.

Huntington, Samuel. *The Clash of Civilizations and the Remaking World Order*. New York: Simon & Schuster, 1996.

Kim, Eunjoo Mary. *Preaching in an Age of Globalization*. Louisville: Westminster John Knox, 2010.

Kinnamon, Michael. *Can a Renewal Movement be Renewed? Questions for the Future of Ecumenism*. Grand Rapids: Eerdmans, 2014.

Knitter, Paul F. *Introducing Theologies of Religions*. Maryknoll, NY: Orbis, 2002.

———. *One Earth, Many Religions: Multifaith Dialogue and Global Responsibility*. Maryknoll, NY: Orbis, 1995.

Kujawa-Holbrook, Sheryl A. *God beyond Borders: Interreligious Learning among Faith Communities*. Horizons in Religious Education 1. Eugene, OR: Pickwick, 2014.

———. *Pilgrimage—The Sacred Art: Journey to the Center of the Heart*. Woodstock, VT: Skylight Paths, 2013.

L'Engle, Madeleine. *Many Waters*. New York: Farrar, Straus & Giroux, 1986.

Nouwen, Henri. *Reaching Out: Three Movements of the Spiritual Life*. New York: Image, 1975.

Palmer, Parker J. *Let Your Life Speak: Listening to the Voice of Vocation*. San Francisco: Jossey-Bass, 2000.

Panikkar, Raimon. *Cultural Disarmament: The Way to Peace*. Louisville: Westminster John Knox, 1998.

Rice, Howard. *The Pastor as Spiritual Guide*. Nashville: Upper Room, 1998.

Rilke, Maria Reiner. *Letter to a Young Poet*. Novato, CA: New World Library. 2000.

Sacks, Jonathan. *The Dignity of Difference: How to Avoid the Clash of Civilizations*. New York: Continuum, 2003.

Selmanovic, Samir. *It's Really All about God: Reflections of a Muslim Atheist Jewish Christian*. San Francisco: Jossey-Bass, 2009.

Smock, David., ed. *Interfaith Dialogue and Peace Building*. Washington, DC: United States Institute of Peace, 2002.

Thompson, Marjorie. *Soul Feast: An Invitation to the Christian Spiritual Life*. Louisville: Westminster John Knox, 2005.

Wheatley, Margaret. *Leadership and the New Science: Discovering Order in a Chaotic World*. San Francisco: Berrett-Koehler, 2006.

Wheatley, Margaret, and Deborah Frieze. *Walk Out Walk On: A Learning Journey into Communities Daring to Live the Future Now*. San Francisco: Berrett-Koehler, 2011.

Yoder, Carolyn. *The Little Book of Trauma Healing: When Violence Strikes and Community Security is Threatened*. Intercourse, PA: Good Books, 2005.

Žižek, Slavoj, and Boris Gunjević. *God in Pain: Inversions of Apocalypse.* New York: Seven Stories, 2012.

3

Designing Curricular Approaches for Interfaith Competency

or

Why Does Learning How to Live in a "Community of Communities" Matter?

—Mary E. Hess

What is a curriculum? How can you tell if it is working or not? What do you do when it does not work? If we are serious about designing curricular approaches for interfaith competency then along with defining what we mean by "interfaith competency" we need to answer these basic questions.[1]

Before moving into that discussion, I want to begin by noting that I am a Roman Catholic layperson who is on the faculty of a Lutheran seminary in the upper Midwest of the United States. What I offer in the following

1. Please note that other authors in this volume will address at more length the definitions of "interfaith" and "multifaith," but a quick distinction would be that "interfaith" refers more specifically to dialogue and encounter between specific faiths. Many organizations, for instance, put together "interfaith" worship services that are structured so that people of the faiths represented can be comfortable with the words being shared. "Multifaith," on the other hand, is more descriptive of the basic reality that we live in a world populated by multiple faith traditions, some of which find it very difficult to agree on any shared meaning. I would offer that "interfaith" is a smaller more specialized category within a larger "multifaith" reality.

chapter is deeply situated in these elements of my experience, and is intended to evoke thoughtful engagement rather than be a definitive prescription for specific actions. I speak from a Christian standpoint, knowing how problematic and charged this standpoint can be, but hoping that I can do so in ways that invite exploration and wonder.

As I write this chapter in the winter of 2016, the United States is in the early stages of a presidential political campaign that is already noteworthy for the level of hostile discourse and demagoguery being employed. This discursive terrain is particularly problematic for religious identity and understanding, as the charges being flung about include misconceptions about the relationships between Christianity and other religions, as well as specific allegations aimed at Islam. Whether it is Donald Trump's vociferous assertions about Syrian refugees,[2] or Wheaton College's concerns about the speech of one of its tenured faculty members,[3] the public sphere is awash in statements that invite religious intolerance. Our religious leaders appear ill-equipped to engage such pronouncements, while our congregations, let alone members of the general public, drift from specious claim to specious claim, caught up in the passions of the moment with little ability to confront and critically engage such rhetoric. In this atmosphere it is more urgent than ever that theological educators take up the challenges of interfaith learning. We need to be able to make the case for religious identity that is comfortable within a community of communities, rather than in one community over and against another. We need to ask with Michael Rosenak, "How *does* one really educate a young person, really *help* a young person to become loyal, disciplined by the regimen of revealed norms and, at the same time, curious, open, and endowed with an expansive spirituality?"[4]

DEFINING CURRICULUM

So what *is* a curriculum? In *Fashion Me a People*, Maria Harris draws on ancient elements of Christian community—particularly Acts 2:42—to describe five arenas of Christian learning: *kerygma*, or proclamation; *didache*, or teaching; *diakonia*, or service; *leiturgia*, or prayer; and *koinonia*, or community. She argues that each of these elements entails particular kinds of engagement, and together they form the curriculum—or "course

2. For instance, *The Economist* reports: http://www.economist.com/blogs/democracyinamerica/2015/12/trump-muslims.

3. For instance, *The Chronicle of Higher Ed*: http://chronicle.com/article/The-Week/234774.

4. Rosenak, *Commandments and Concerns*, 256–57.

to be run"—of Christian community.[5] Boyung Lee has taken this argument further by considering it through the lens of post-colonial theology rooted in the experiences of Korean immigrants.[6] She helps us to see that in the midst of discussions of curriculum, at least in the U.S. and similar contexts, we must also and always attend to the challenges of individualism vs. communalism. In many ways Lee's embrace and further critique of Harris echoes recent scholarship that begins with H. Richard Niebuhr's discussions of Christianity and culture, and then pushes it further to explore the consequences of understanding culture in more fluid, dynamic, and emerging ways.[7] Such scholarship prods us to understand both the power dynamics embedded in any assertion of what constitutes "reality," as well as invites us to respect the creativity and agency of persons in communities. It draws us towards an understanding that relishes knowing ourselves to be in a specific religious community and at the same time deeply respectful of other religious communities, that cherishes identity which is multiply grounded and shaped both personally and communally.

"Curriculum" has to be understood as all that is involved with learning, and particularly all that is entailed by seeking to shape specific kinds of learning towards specific learning goals. A curriculum requires a systemic view that takes account of interacting dynamics. Contrary to prevailing stereotypes, "curriculum" should never be heard as "printed materials to be used in Sunday school classrooms." Developing, implementing, and assessing a curriculum is truly "running a course," and it is never free from considerations of power. It is a marathon, not a sprint. We must be alert to the dangers of ignoring systemic issues when we consider curricula.

Another way to make this point is to note that while many people confronted with a need to develop a curriculum will focus on the *content* a curriculum should *cover*, education scholars assert that it is more effective to focus on the forms of knowing that a curriculum will *uncover* and *strengthen*.[8] We need to recognize that *how* we teach is often a far more powerful predictor of what is learned, than *what* we teach. Later in this essay I will point out why this assertion is even more pointed in an era in which massive amounts of content are easily accessible via digital devices, but for now let us note that the *ways* in which knowing is uncovered are shaped in distinctively different ways in various settings. In the Christian context,

5. Harris, *Fashion Me a People*, 55.

6. Lee, *Transforming Congregations*.

7. Niebuhr, *Christ and Culture*; and then see, for example, Tanner, *Theories of Culture*.

8. Wiggins and McTighe, *Understanding by Design*, 4.

the area with which I am most familiar, all five of the curricular intentions named by Harris and Lee are ubiquitous in theological education, but they are structured quite differently in different denominational settings.[9]

The distinctive characteristics of specific curricula can be teased out by considering which areas are emphasized, and in what ways. A particularly useful framework for perceiving such emphases comes to us through Elliott Eisner's work in describing the functions of explicit, implicit, and null curricula.[10] An "explicit" curriculum might best be described as that which an institution strives deliberately and intentionally to teach. This is the curriculum embodied in the written documents, described in an institution's catalog, and assessed by accreditors. An "implicit" curriculum, in contrast, is what is generally learned incidentally by students. Dining room conversations, late night group study sessions, peer "buzz" about courses; even the basic forms of tacit knowing that define styles of clothing, forms of personal address, and so on, constitute an implicit curriculum. The "null curriculum," by way of contrast, are the things that are learned through the silences, the taboos, the deliberate evasions of engagement that take place in a learning environment. The example I most often use because I teach in a predominately white environment has to do with race. In majority white communities, race is often the unspoken, unacknowledged, null curriculum. White privilege, for instance, is rarely even named in such settings, let alone interrogated.[11]

One of the most challenging consequences of the interaction between explicit, implicit, and null curricula is that when they contradict each other the implicit and null curricula overwhelm any explicit intentionality. A common complaint that Pew and other research survey organizations describe is that of people who condemn religious institutions for being hypocritical.[12] There is no person or organization that does not at some point express hypocrisy, but the frequent criticism of religious institutions as "hypocritical" often occurs because of a mismatch between the explicit assertions of a given community—love of neighbor, for instance—and the inferences drawn by participants through tacit forms of knowing that emerge from participation in other communities at the same time. Young people, for instance, might

---

9. See, in particular, Seymour, *Theological Approaches to Christian Education.*

10. Eisner, *The Educational Imagination.*

11. For more on this specific challenge, see Hess and Brookfield, "'How Can White Teachers,'" 162–89.

12. See, for instance, the Pew Research Center on Religion and Public Life (http://www.pewforum.org), or other major surveys run by Gallup, Barna and others. Voluminous data is available at the Association of Religion Data Archives (http://www.thearda.com).

find themselves being forced to choose between their sense of themselves as humans who respect GLBTQ issues and humans who go to church. In other words, we all find ourselves embedded in multiple communities even while being one person, so how are the various communities of which we are a part respected in a specific community?

Does the implicit curriculum respect a community of communities? Or does it require identity to be constructed through only one community? In settings in which the explicit and implicit contradict each other, the implicit most often holds primacy. Answering the question "How can you tell if a curriculum is *working* or not?" requires consideration of all three of these curricula: explicit, implicit, null.

No matter how strongly a church community proclaims its commitment to inclusivity or to "Bible-based authority" (two claims which might be found at opposite ends of theological spectra), if that church does not embody hospitality, its claims are perceived as hypocritical. On the other hand, a church that begins with the assertion that "you will be disappointed by us" (an assertion proffered by The House for All Sinners and Saints in Denver, CO, for instance)[13] matches its explicit assertions with its implicit forms of knowing and finds its identity growing deeper and stronger.

In the context of theological education, a school that explicitly affirms its openness to engaging "the neighbor" but offers no way for students to learn about and develop relationships with their neighbors, is posing a conundrum. In the specific area that is the focus of this book, the absence of broad-based engagement with issues of religious pluralism sends a very problematic message to students.

Engagement alone is not enough, because a curriculum that explicitly names religious pluralism as a contemporary issue, but then marginalizes it to study in only a few courses, or only in electives, implicitly teaches that religious pluralism is actually not all that relevant or important to practices of faith. Indeed, it can even teach students that formation in one community requires ignorance of other communities.

A school, on the other hand, which in its student, staff, and faculty bodies is already religiously diverse, which regularly offers its students opportunities to explore varieties of ways in which to engage theologies of religion, which invites students to do comparative theology, which offers multiple occasions for exploring multifaith conversation, and so on, teaches both explicitly and implicitly that living in the 21st century means living in a multifaith world.

---

13. Bolz-Webber, "Seeing the Underside."

It is fairly clear, even from a cursory sweep of current national discourse in the United States, that our curricula of engagement with multifaith realities have not been very effective.[14] Nearly every major "world religion"[15] makes claims that fall under the rubric of "the golden rule" or what some scholars term an "ethics of reciprocity,"[16] yet national surveys report, over and over again, that the vast majority of those surveyed in the U.S. either are ignorant of such commitments, or actively disbelieve them, preferring to label whole swaths of a religious tradition as "terrorist" or "fundamentalist."

From the vantage point of having a learning goal of robust and shared public engagement across religious communities, our curricula for interfaith relationship in a multifaith society are clearly not effective. But how we diagnose that lack of learning is crucial, for it will define the responses we develop for future learning.

Some scholars diagnose the problem as a lack of literacy in the "home" religion of the community. How can one engage in interfaith discussion, these scholars argue, if one doesn't even understand one's own tradition? Christian Smith's research, for instance, suggests that young people in the United States hold a theology of "moralistic therapeutic deism," which is to say, a majority of young people believe there is a God (deism), but perceive that God as mostly an abstract or removed transcendence that is primarily concerned with rewarding good behavior and punishing bad behavior (moralistic therapy).[17] This is a belief substantially at odds with most Christian theological convictions.

If you diagnose the "problem" as being lack of theological depth, then the prescription for solving that problem requires finding ways to develop deeper theological content for young people in their home tradition. Such a prescription begs engagement with theologies of religious pluralism— how does one's home tradition make sense of the vibrant presence of other faiths?—but discussions of multifaith learning, let alone theologies of religious pluralism, are for the most part routinely absent from youth and young adult programs in the Christian context.

A different group of scholars diagnoses the problem of lack of multifaith awareness, and even more so the lack of substantial interfaith dialogue, as stemming not from a lack of theological knowledge, but rather from too

14. For an extensive exploration of this lack of literacy, see Prothero, *Religious Literacy*.

15. This is a label which is highly problematic for a variety of reasons, but I'm not sure what a good alternative in this space would be, so I use it—but with caution.

16. For more on an "ethics of reciprocity," see http://www.religioustolerance.org/reciproc.htm.

17. Smith, *Soul Searching*, 163.

strong an insistence on a narrow strain of Christian theology that confesses what Paul Knitter labels a "replacement model" stance.[18] That is, these scholars believe that too much formation has focused on a conception of the Christian God as the one and only route to salvation, which, when combined with an impositional form of proselytism, forms Christians as people who can "see" people of other faiths only as targets for missionary conversion.

Consider: the former diagnosis requires deeper learning in one's own tradition internally, and the latter prescribes taking one's own learning and imposing it on others externally. It is important to recognize that both of these stances assume the strength and orthodoxy of the observer's community. There is little room in these formulations for a stance that begins in humility and proceeds to understand that in learning one is always risking one's understanding.[19] Or that learning in community can and should deepen one's sense of being part of multiple communities, and learning that a community of communities can be the embodiment of authentic education.

This is a clear example of how the implicit and null curricula overwhelm the explicit curricula. By refusing to see the power dynamics embedded—implicitly and through null curricula—in a specific religious community's stance, any curricula developed blindly reinforce these power dynamics. You can read Matthew 28:19–20—"Go, therefore, and make disciples of all nations, baptizing them in the name of the Father, and of the Son, and of the holy Spirit, teaching them to observe all that I have commanded you"—from a standpoint in which "make disciples" is heard as "impose this belief system on people" or you can hear this same text as "make disciples" being a claim to spread learning, and recognize in doing so that any time you seek learning you begin by risking your current understanding. The former stance refuses to see that "make disciples" is a dynamic, changing set of relationships, while the latter attempts to make clear that God is the primary Maker, and that ongoing learning is deeply relational and must begin in humility.

Note that in all cases the diagnosis one makes as to the need for learning and the prescriptions offered are themselves profoundly theological

---

18. Knitter, *Introducing Theologies of Religions*, 19–60.

19. It is beyond the scope of this essay to explore the assertion more fully, but I would note here that I am deeply convicted by the argument Willie James Jennings puts forth in his recent book *The Christian Imagination*. His argument in that book pushes back against the centuries-long search for orthodoxy in Christianity, and makes clear that there are alternative pathways which have much more resonance with the earlier communities following Jesus and which do not prize orthodoxy above all else.

assertions. Consider how Parker Palmer's "grace of great things" poses a keenly different theological stance:

> We invite *diversity* into our community not because it is politically correct but because diverse viewpoints are demanded by the manifold mysteries of great things.
>
> We embrace *ambiguity* not because we are confused or indecisive but because we understand the inadequacy of our concepts to embrace the vastness of great things.
>
> We welcome *creative conflict* not because we are angry or hostile but because conflict is required to correct our biases and prejudices about the nature of great things.
>
> We practice *honesty* not only because we owe it to one another but because to lie about what we have seen would be to betray the truth of great things.
>
> We experience *humility* not because we have fought and lost but because humility is the only lens through which great things can be seen—and once we have seen them, humility is the only posture possible.
>
> We become *free men and women* through education not because we have privileged information but because tyranny in any form can only be overcome by invoking the grace of great things.[20]

As a Christian I frequently invite my students to read Palmer's statements replacing "great things" with the name "Jesus Christ"—and my students discover a very different starting point for theological assertion. I believe that other religious traditions can and have made similar assertions that require recognizing one's own standpoint as profoundly human and fallible, thus in need of continual engagement in learning.

The implicit curricular issue at stake is: are we perceiving learning as something that opens people up and enlarges their understanding, or are we seeing teaching as transferring information that is stable and unchanging? Are we teaching that religious community is made up of many distinctive communities, all of whom share a central commitment to learning? Or are we teaching that religious identity must have rigid and even impermeable boundaries, must be "over and against" other communities?

The conclusion I draw here is that a theological curriculum focused on interfaith engagement in a multifaith world needs to be both explicitly and implicitly committed to learning that begins in humble acknowledgement of human fallibility, and recognizes the dynamic and changing nature of all

20. Palmer, *Courage to Teach*, 107–8.

knowledge bases. Such a foundation needs to be expressed in the theological language of the community of origin, but remain ever mindful of the implicit and null curricula that can attach to such language—and it must always be aware that communities of knowing are large and various, that we are teaching towards a "community of communities." We must, per Boyung Lee, refuse the individualism vs. communalism dichotomy for a stance that deeply respects the formative power of both.

EXPLORING TRANSFORMATIVE LEARNING

What is the next step? To answer that question I want to bring into this discussion Robert Kegan's description of transformative adult learning.[21] We are in a time, an era, when religious fluency is more important than ever before. Not "literacy" but fluency, because we need not only to be comfortable with our neighbors, we also need to be able to communicate across deep divides and in the face of multiple global challenges.

This is an era that requires *transformative* learning, learning that is not simply about acquiring the ability to read and write in a language, to "speak Christian" for example, but the ability to speak one's personal and communal truths with integrity, to discern authentic and authoritative speaking from inauthentic and specious claims, to create in new ways, to share and to learn, and to collaborate from a specific religious identity that is open to engagement beyond its borders.[22] We need to be about nurturing identities that, while rooted in one specific community, understand the ways in which a "community of communities" must exist for respect to exist for all.

Kegan has identified a spiral for this kind of transformative learning that is based in developmental awareness and is traced through three movements—confirmation, contradiction, and continuity.

"Confirmation" begins in understanding the space, persons, and goals of learning at the moment. Where are learners right now? How do they understand their own identities and those of people around them? What is it they want to learn? Are they aware of their own biases towards individualism or communalism? If, for instance, pervasive anxiety and fear of terrorism invites an understanding of Christianity that is at once both exclusively the arbiter of salvation and at the same time institutionally embattled, then the context in which people come to learn about other faiths has already drawn certain conclusions for them. You cannot simply "tell" people that Christianity is a faith of openness and love, even love of enemies, if their

21. Kegan, *The Evolving Self*, and *In Over Our Heads*.
22. Tran's work is particularly pertinent here: "Narrating Lives," 188–203.

experience of Christianity is the opposite. That message will have no authentic integrity. But you can begin by acknowledging the fears and the environments in which people live and then—in Kegan's second movement—seek to contradict the misperceptions that lead to such fears.

"Contradiction" can occur in many ways. A teacher might offer an alternative interpretation, or invite people into the classroom who can testify to the reality of open-handed love of neighbor. But contradictions also arise without intention, from the sheer proximity of different experiences. Many Christians in the state of Minnesota where I live encounter Muslim families through their children's public school classrooms. These Christians begin to experience contradictions to their taken-for-granted negative assumptions when they experience resonance and see similarities amongst Muslim parents who are also concerned for their children's education.

It is Kegan's third movement however, "continuity," which is key to transformative learning. Without continuity people caught in the grip of contradictions to their default understandings may simply retreat into one of two ends of a spectrum—fundamentalism or relativism. They may retreat into a tightly defended position which brooks no awareness of the contradiction, a kind of fundamentalism, or they may give up on making sense of the contradiction and simply assert that their perception is profoundly personal and there is no way to arbitrate amongst differences let alone accept shared truths amongst people. "You have your belief and I have mine, and that's the way the world is." I noted Smith's research earlier, and his claim that the majority of young people in the U.S. see the world through a lens of "moralistic therapeutic deism." It might well be that this stance has more to do with a vague acceptance of relativism, which is founded in the contradictions they perceive, than it does with any religious conceptualizations.

"Continuity" involves providing a clear narrative of how certain underlying beliefs can be maintained even as they are critiqued, deepened, and perhaps shifted. One clear example that many seminary faculty recognize comes from watching students enter biblical studies classes at the graduate level. Many of these students come to theological education with a wholehearted affection for the Bible, and with an intense loyalty to the community of interpretation within which they formed that affection. When their interpretation is contradicted by various kinds of biblical scholarship, students can react with anxiety and sometimes even outright refusal to take seriously such scholarship. I still remember the anguish on the face of the student in one of my classes who could not grasp that her conviction that Moses had written the Pentateuch did not square with recent scholarship. Or, similarly, there are students (many of whom live in white majority settings) who are quite comfortable with some forms of scholarly biblical criticism but who cannot fathom how post-colonial interpretations might have relevance or interest to them personally. The key for transformative learning is finding the underlying commitments that can endure and even be deepened by taking seriously the existing contradictions.

In biblical studies I have witnessed faculty who manage these contradictions with grace and ease as they help students to discover that taking critical work seriously, far from lessening a sense of the Bible's authority, can actually deepen a sense of its relevance and authority over time. These faculty are adept at inviting students into a "community of communities." In this instance the underlying faculty commitment has to do with finding ways for the Bible's authority to remain strong even as the interpretive field in which the student understands that authority is broadened and made more complex. The commitment is to expressions of biblical authority that are not frightened of or made defensive by more complex engagement, but rather invite it. Such a commitment is, incidentally, strengthened by a starting point of humility and openness.

Finding continuity requires taking seriously the starting place of a learner, tracing the trajectory of the learner's engagement with contradictions, and finding ways for the contradictions to be encompassed in a new-found resolution of meaning which can draw on underlying commitments that continue in spite of contradictions.

So where is theological education right now when it comes to questions of living faithfully in a world of many faiths? Where are seminarians and other students finding themselves? In my context, far too many U.S. Christian graduate theological programs are caught up in a fever of anxiety about our survival, clutching past understandings to ourselves in fear, seeking to shore up what we know, and fearful of what we might be becoming. Faculty read survey data avidly, wondering aloud how students who are "spiritual but not religious" might find their way into our programs, and seeking to discern what we can do with them once they are here. Questions of other faiths can feel like distractions to some colleagues, or like luxuries for which we do not have time in the midst of trying to share classical understandings of Christianity with students who do not have even basic literacy in Christianity. To return to the diagnoses I explored earlier in this chapter, these faculty are focused on strengthening what they believe to have been a faulty "transfer" of deep theological content to students.

Yet many of our students find themselves on the opposite end of these discussions, coming to seminary with a deep desire to see how Christianity can be made to "make sense" in the midst of a world of many faiths.

Living in a world of networked religion,[23] these students find themselves in the midst of convergent practices with little respect for the time and attention it requires to trace the origins and traditions of specific ideas. From their perspective, the key issue is not transfer of ideas, but rather support for their own creative and experiential embodiment of religious ideas that excite them.

Where theological curricula used to be structured to transfer stable accounts of religious knowing, and thus were primarily concerned with clarifying specific kinds of content, now curricula, to be effective, have to be much more focused on igniting basic interest in religious knowing, and developing critical engagement skills for students who must learn tacitly in the midst of fluid and rapidly changing accounts of religious experience. We have to offer both the contradictions that expand students' view of the world and the continuity that can draw them more deeply into faithful engagement.

It is at the juncture of these intersecting streams—the desire of faculty to transfer stable content coming into conflict with the desire of students to learn experientially amidst the flux of change—that the framework of the "explicit, implicit, and null" curriculum, in conjunction with the "confirmation, contradiction, and continuity" of Kegan's framing, becomes so useful. It can help us see that our current environment both requires and embodies the possibility of living in a community of communities. Where in previous centuries a certain kind of "stable" content knowledge could be asserted, in the midst of the firehose of data that is the internet we can no longer deny the many and varied forms of religious experience and religious knowing that surround us. But we also do not need to be limited to a "content transfer" mode of learning. Instead these frames for discerning what is happening in our curricula point to new opportunities for interfaith and multifaith engagement in the worlds we inhabit.

A NEW CULTURE OF LEARNING
FOR A MULTIFAITH SOCIETY

Scholars who write about this "new culture of learning" emerging in the midst of digital spaces have noted that people growing up in the midst of

---

23. Campbell, "Understanding the Relationship." Campbell has argued that the concept of "networked religion" names well how religion functions online and she further suggests that online religion exemplifies five key social and cultural changes at work in religion in general in society: networked community, storied identities, shifting authority, convergent practice, and a multisite reality.

widespread digital gaming (with 97 perent of young people playing video games) as well as deep immersion in social media, have developed skills for active learning that are catalyzed by project-based assignments.[24] When you spend large amounts of time playing games that require you to explore environments, seeking treasures in hidden ways, you hone inquiry skills that are quite useful for ferreting out information. At the same time, these games also privilege collaborative forms of engagement that build team learning skills, and which require repetitive engagement with failure prior to eventual success. Indeed, one scholar of game design has pointed out that the most successful games have an 80 percent failure rate.[25] Players of such games find the challenges exciting, rather than an obstacle, and work together to overcome them.

This kind of learning is increasingly familiar to people, and carries an implicit curriculum of openness to change, human fallibility, and support for participation. Can you hear the resonances to my earlier assertions? Indeed, millennial students are often more interested in other faiths than in the one they nominally grew up within, because these other faiths hold esoteric intrigue for them—something they have learned to value in the games they play.[26]

In my context I need to ask about the ways in which I might ignite student interest in Christianity by drawing students into respectful comparisons with other faiths. How might an inquiry into the practices of meditation in Sufi Islam, for instance, invite recognition of the power of centering prayer in the Christian tradition? Or how might an exploration of the notion of *logos* in John's Gospel and in Advaita Vedanta elicit new and fruitful questions?[27] I ask these questions because they point to ways to engage traditional, even classical, content from an entry point that *values* other faith traditions. It is a path forward, which unites the explicit curriculum (specific content about a specific tradition) with the implicit curriculum (the surround of a multifaith environment heavy on experiential learning). As Kristen Largen has written, this is an attempt to consider interreligious engagement as "part of the *foundation* of Christian theology, rather than its decoration."[28]

24. See, in particular, Thomas and Seely Brown, *A New Culture of Learning*; and Ito, et al., *Hanging Out.*

25. McGonigal, *Reality is Broken,* 64.

26. Hess, "Teaching and Learning," 55.

27. This particular example comes to mind due to a discussion I once heard Anant Rambachan and Gregory Walter have concerning a paper they were working on together at St. Olaf College (http://wp.stolaf.edu/religion/people/gregory-a-walter/).

28. Largen, *Finding God,* 1, emphasis in original.

By paying careful attention to where students begin from—particularly their experiences of less than deep immersion in a worshiping community, as well as widespread shallow awareness of other faith traditions—theological educators can draw them through the kinds of contradictions that exist in our environment, towards a deeper grasp of their specific religious identity as well as basic information about other religious traditions in ways that are open-hearted and thoughtful.

Scholars of this "new culture of learning" point to three distinctive shifts to which we must attend.[29] The first has to do with a clear shift from teaching-based to learning-based approaches. This is not a simplistic "cater to students" paradigm, but rather an evidence-based recognition that when you put learning at the heart of an educational enterprise your pedagogy shifts. Many theological faculty are coming to this awareness firsthand as they begin to teach in fully distributed or online formats. The kinds of pedagogical strategies often used in "in person" classrooms have significant negative aspects when ported without adaptation to an online format.[30] Body language, for instance, which is often used as a clue to student attention and understanding in an "in person" classroom, is much harder to read in a video-streaming format and completely inaccessible in a text-based learning management system. Without such indicators, educators have had to move to other pedagogical tools: carefully curated small group discussions, structured debates, webquests, and many other forms of learning-centered processes that become tangibly useful in distributed formats.

These processes offer educators much more robust insight into levels of student comprehension, in turn providing opportunities for more significant learning. Once a teacher has experienced student understanding in a learning-centered mode, it is difficult to return to more instructional or teacher-centered modes. Faculty member after faculty member has testified to the ways in which their pedagogies have shifted in their "in person" classrooms after a stint teaching online.[31]

A second shift scholars are naming has to do with larger cultural patterns that are making the distinctions between "public" and "private" less relevant, given our social media spaces, than the distinctions between "personal" and "collective." Most educators who work in seminary settings will be familiar with the level of anxiety that exists around student discussions of what "could" versus what "should" be shared in social media. But fewer are aware of why there are such sharp disagreements about such issues.

29. Hess, "A New Culture of Learning," 227–32.
30. Hess, "What Difference Does it Make?" 77–91.
31. Nysse, "Online Education."

Most social media sites promise a certain degree of functionality that increases based on how much you share about yourself, and how willing your friends are to share. That is, the more you share personally, the more collectively useful a site can be. Yelp, for instance, collates reviews of specific restaurants and so on, based on the experiences of its members. The more willing you are to post your experiences—including your location and time of visit—the more effective such reviews can be when peer sharing is more trusted than commercial marketing. On the other hand, users have to be careful about how and what they're sharing, and how it will be used. Many people love to play with the ubiquitous quizzes in Facebook—"Which Harry Potter character are you?" "What denomination is really yours?" etc. etc.—but these quizzes primarily exist to extract information from people so as to create more efficient commercial marketing. In these cases sharing personal information does not benefit collective agency, but rather consumer commodification.

Thus the shift in focus from "public and private" to "personal and collective" is not without its challenges, but it does have one very pertinent opportunity to offer: renewed attention to collectivity. Here I want to return to Boyung Lee's description of the crucial role asking questions of individualism and communalism must play in developing, implementing, and assessing faith curricula.

Religious communities, and particularly the institutions that sustain them, depend nearly universally on commitments to collective action in response to God's agency. Christian liturgical action, for instance, is generally collective worship of a God whose divine agency creates, redeems, and saves human beings. God is the primary Agent, and human response to such agency is shared—through time, through participation in shared ritual, and so on. Such experiential awareness of collective action has been waning for the last several decades, with the modernist emphases on individualism and neo-liberal economic processes overwhelming historical patterns of commitment to common goods. Yet this emerging shift in digital spaces to awareness of and participation in "personal and collective" processes offers new hope for retrieving ancient understandings and renewing such shared action even in the hegemonic contexts that have been most resistant to communalism.

Finally, the third shift that scholars of a new culture of learning are exploring is the shift observed when knowledge increasingly is perceived as fluid, dynamic, and rapidly changing rather than stable, constant, and unchanging. These scholars argue that stable, constant knowledge can navigate simple pedagogical tools of information transfer, whereas fluid, changing forms of knowledge require the ability to learn through tacit forms of knowing, to discern amidst a diverse array of pedagogical tools, and to be particularly attentive to context. Post-modern and post-colonial insights, for instance, demand different kinds of pedagogical tools to be employed if students are to comprehend well the subjects they are engaging. The forms of theological argument I noted earlier when citing Parker Palmer's "grace of great things" are highly congruent with these kind of tools, offering very specific forms of continuity.[32]

It should be no surprise to us that students entering into theological education have a high level of individualist interest in their studies, and very little experience with, let alone desire for, engagement in modes of learning that require them to submit their individual desires to a larger good. How does one respond to such fear and ignorance? For many of us the implicit curriculum suggests turning in upon ourselves, clutching our identities tightly. Yet the experience of people of faith over time actually points to the need to take the opposite stance. As Sr. Simone Campbell has noted:

> 'How do you handle the things that scare you?' Walk towards them. That's the only way. Because fear is just my insecurity or my apprehension about the unknown or something that I don't want to acknowledge. My experience is that if you walk towards fear then it dissipates. It's when we get curled up and keep obsessing about the fear that it's crippling.[33]

So how might we draw on our individual interests, contradict our perceived sense that individualism is the "sine qua non," and face the fears that might come from truly engaging the multifaith realities in which we

32. There has been abundant writing in this area, but I would note a few books which have proven particularly useful in my context: Sacks, *Not in God's Name*; Foley, *Theological Reflection Across Religious Traditions*; Largen, *Interreligious Learning and Teaching*; Kujawa, *God Beyond Borders*; King and Tan, eds. *(un)Common Sounds*; and Davis, ed., *Hearing the Call across Traditions*.

33. Campbell, "Interview." Simone Campbell is the executive director of *Network*, which is a Catholic lobbying group focused on education for social justice. As the chief spokesperson for the "Nuns on the Bus" tour of 2014, she has become nationally recognized for her ability to inspire diverse groups of people to work for social change.

find ourselves? How might we draw each other into a deeper engagement in a community of communities through the development and implementation of curricula that acknowledge deep and incommensurable differences amongst specific religious communities *and* a shared conviction that religious commitments should be respected?

PRAGMATIC QUESTIONS AND STEPS FORWARD

In an essay entitled "Designing Curricular Approaches for Interfaith Competency" it is likely that readers expected me to take a stance on whether it was better to require specific courses on interfaith content, or to integrate such content throughout the entire curriculum. My argument, instead, is that rather than focusing on how content is packaged and how to transfer that content effectively, we need instead to recognize that *pedagogical mode in which* we teach is often a far more powerful predictor of what is learned than *what* we teach.

If you are in a school in which the implicit curriculum thoroughly supports and enriches an understanding that interfaith competencies are crucial for pastoral leaders, then the question of how to arrange the content in the curriculum will naturally flow from what must already be collaborative processes on the part of the faculty.

In settings in which interfaith competency is explicitly named as important, but which in practice the implicit curriculum teaches is ephemeral, irrelevant, or not useful to pastoral identity, then a first step would be to include courses that explicitly unite the explicit and implicit curricula around interfaith competency.

Years ago I shared a "reflectivity matrix" as a way for seminary faculties to identify the extent to which reflective practice currently shaped their curriculum, and then to choose ways to deepen such practice.[34] That chart asserted that it was nearly impossible to move from the left side, which was highly unreflective, to the far end of the right side, which was highly reflective, in one move. Rather, schools needed to move through various positions more organically, developing their pedagogical strategies over time. That same chart is useful in this context if you keep in mind interfaith competencies as one element of cultural awareness and theological skill.[35]

Thus schools whose stances on reflective practice live on the far left side of the chart will more likely need to build specific courses with titles

34. This matrix is reprinted with permission in the appendix to this book.

35. For the original context of the chart and an explanation of how to use it for faculty development see Warford, *Revitalizing Practice*.

such as "interfaith leadership" into their curriculum, whereas schools on the far right side of the chart will already be organically addressing such questions throughout their entire curriculum in both explicit and implicit ways. In all cases, however, the goal is continually to grow and learn, expanding the capacity of a community to engage in interfaith learning. The underlying commitment which resources moving through the inevitable contradictions that arise is a commitment to development and learning in the midst of fluid and changing environments. What follows here is a series of questions that I hope can spark the curricular discussions necessary for moving into interfaith learning in a multifaith society in ways that are constructive and sensitive to the context of a particular school.

Begin with the basic questions of curricular design—Who is in the learning space? Where is the learning occurring? And why have they gathered? (person, place, purpose). These questions can be stated more specifically:

- What percentage of your student body, staff cohort, and faculty come from differing faith traditions?[36]

- What are the varieties of religious community in your immediate geographic environment?[37]

- In what ways does your school or program's mission statement name or ignore the reality of a multifaith context?

- What are the primary pedagogical modes in place in your school or program?

- How aware are your faculty of the diverse resources within their own scholarly disciplines for developing and resourcing interfaith competencies?

- What kinds of anxieties currently flow through the learning systems in your setting?

- In what ways do energy and even joy find expression in your setting?

- What degree of relational trust currently exists across the ecology of your school and its immediate contexts?

These last three questions may seem too ephemeral or emotional for a discussion of curriculum, but there is significant educational literature

36. Some of this information is available in ATS schools through the various student surveys. Other will need to be gathered locally.

37. Here the Pluralism Project will often prove a helpful source of information (http://pluralism.org).

which points to "degree of relational trust" as a key factor in ensuring successful education reform.[38] Once you have a shared sense of this information, you can bring it to the matrix chart and begin to discern next steps for your specific context.

Finally, there is always the challenge of sustaining your energy for getting to where you are headed. There are many useful essays in this book that address specific elements of that challenge. I would like to conclude this chapter by drawing on the wisdom of Bryan Stevenson, a lawyer, social justice advocate, clinical law professor, and founder of the *Equal Justice Initiative*. Stevenson has outlined four necessary actions in pursuit of reform in criminal justice, but his actions are equally relevant and useful in our work here as well. He suggests that we need to:

- Get proximate
- Change the narratives
- Find your hope
- Risk being uncomfortable.[39]

This formulation nicely summarizes the pragmatic ideas of this chapter. To shape curricula for interfaith engagement in a multifaith world we need to "get proximate" to the challenges. We need to develop relationships across religious community boundaries, finding ways to learn from each other.

"Change the narratives"—in particular, we need to recognize how strongly the implicit and null curricula of a school can shape the learning that emerges. We need to concentrate on forming a "community of communities" so that our students can be invited into respect for the distinctiveness of their specific religious communities while yet affirming shared respect across our differences.

"Find your hope"—in a context of fear, in a world in which our current efforts are bearing so little fruit, it can be hard to find grounds for hope. Here is a space in which specific theological convictions can be life-giving. Those convictions will be expressed in different ways in different communities, but nearly all religious traditions ground their witness in expressions of hope, and that hope sustains the resilience necessary for real change and growth.

---

38. Bryk and Schneider, *Trust in Schools*.

39. Stevenson, "Four Steps." These four elements are concisely stated in the interview Stevenson did for *Christian Today* in 2015, but I would also recommend his book, *Just Mercy: A Story of Justice and Redemption*.

"Risk being uncomfortable"—an excellent reminder that the contradictions many of us as faculty need to engage and move beyond have to do with our taken-for-granted assumptions about the stable, unchanging nature of religious knowing and our professions as teachers. We may well be uncomfortable as we venture into this terrain, but Stevenson and others remind us that discomfort can be a sign of transformative learning.

I began this chapter with Maria Harris' evocation of Acts 2:42—"They devoted themselves to the teaching of the apostles and to the communal life, to the breaking of the bread and to the prayers." If we can hear that phrase as rooted in a desire to learn in community, and with a broader openness to the diversity of the communities in which we learn, then I hope that we may all find ways to devote ourselves to these simple, but profound commitments. Whether we are Christian, Muslim, Jewish, Jain, Hindu, Buddhist, and on and on, we share a society. Learning how to share a communal life, to learn from each others' teachers, to find ways to eat together, and to share our differing experiences of prayer can only contribute to our common good, to a "community of communities."

BIBLIOGRAPHY

Bolz-Webber, Nadia. "Seeing the Underside and Seeing God: Tattoos, Tradition, and Grace." Interview with Krista Tippett on *On Being* (Sept 2013). http://www.onbeing.org/program/transcript/nadia-bolz-weber-seeing-the-underside-and-seeing-god-tattoos-tradition-and-grace.

Bryk, Anthony, and Barbara Schneider. *Trust in Schools: A Core Resource for Improvement.* New York: Sage Foundation, 2002.

Campbell, Heidi. "Understanding the Relationship between Religion Online and Offline in a Networked Society." *Journal of the American Academy of Religion* 80 (2012) 64–93.

Campbell, Sr. Simone. "Interview: Sister Simone Campbell." Interview with Caitie Whelan on *The Lightning Notes* (Jan 2016). http://thelightningnotes.com/2016/01/15/interview-sister-simone-campbell/.

Davis, Adam, ed. *Hearing the Call across Traditions: Readings on Faith and Service.* New York: Skylight Paths, 2009.

Eisner, Elliott. *The Educational Imagination: On the Design and Evaluation of School Programs.* Upper Saddle River, NJ: Merrill Prentice Hall, 2002.

Foley, Edward. *Theological Reflection across Religious Traditions: The Turn to Reflective Believing.* New York: Rowman & Littlefield, 2015.

Harris, Maria. *Fashion Me a People: Curriculum in the Church.* Louisville: Westminster John Knox, 1989.

Hess, Mary. "Teaching and Learning Comparative Theology with Millennial Students." In *Comparative Theology in the Millennial Classroom*, edited by Mara Brecht and Reid Locklin, 50–60. New York: Routledge, 2016.

―――. "A New Culture of Learning: What Are the Implications for Theological Educators?" *Teaching Theology and Religion* 17 (July 2014) 227–32.

―――. "The Pastoral Practice of Christian Hospitality as Presence in Muslim-Christian Engagement: Contextualizing the Classroom." *Theological Education* 47 (2013) 7–12.

―――. "What Difference Does it Make? Digital Technology in the Theological Classroom." *Theological Education* 41 (2006) 77–91.

Hess, Mary, and Stephen Brookfield. "'How Can White Teachers Recognize and Challenge Racism?' Acknowledging Collusion and Learning an Aggressive Humility." In *Teaching Reflectively in Theological Contexts: Promises and Contradictions*, Mary Hess and Stephen Brookfield, eds., 162–189. Malabar, FL: Krieger, 2008.

Ito, Mizuko, et al. *Hanging Out, Messing Around and Geeking Out: Kids Learning and Living with New Media*. Cambridge: MIT University Press, 2010.

Jennings, Willie James. *The Christian Imagination: Theology and the Origins of Race*. New Haven: Yale University Press, 2010.

Kegan, Robert. *The Evolving Self: Problem and Process in Human Development*. Cambridge: Harvard University Press, 1982.

―――. *In Over Our Heads: The Mental Demands of Modern Life*. Cambridge: Harvard University Press, 1994.

King, Roberta, and Sooi Ling Tan, eds. *(un)Common Sounds: Songs of Peace and Reconciliation Among Muslims and Christians*. Eugene, OR: Cascade Books, 2014.

Knitter, Paul F. *Introducing Theologies of Religions*. Maryknoll, NY: Orbis, 2002.

Kujawa-Holbrook, Sheryl. *God beyond Borders: Interreligious Learning among Faith Communities*. Horizons in Religious Education 1. Eugene, OR: Pickwick, 2014.

Largen, Kristen. *Interreligious Learning and Teaching: A Christian Rationale for a Transformative Praxis*. Minneapolis: Fortress, 2014.

―――. *Finding God among Our Neighbors: An Interfaith Systematic Theology*. Minneapolis: Fortress, 2013.

Lee, Boyung. *Transforming Congregations through Community: Faith Formation from the Seminary to the Church*. Louisville: Westminster John Knox, 2013.

McGonigal, Jane. *Reality is Broken: Why Games Make Us Better and How They Can Change the World*. New York: Penguin, 2011.

Niebuhr, H. Richard. *Christ and Culture*. New York: Harper, 1951.

Nysse, Richard. "Online Education: An Asset in a Period of Change." In *Practical Wisdom: On Theological Teaching and Learning*, edited by Malcolm Warford, 197–214. New York: Lang, 2004.

Palmer, Parker. *The Courage to Teach: Exploring the Inner Landscape of a Teacher's Life*. San Francisco: Jossey-Bass, 1998.

Prothero, Stephen. *Religious Literacy: What Every American Needs to Know—And Doesn't*. San Francisco: HarperSanFrancisco, 2007.

Rosenak, Michael. *Commandments and Concerns: Jewish Religious Education in a Secular Society*. Philadelphia: Jewish Publication Society, 1987.

Sacks, Jonathan. *Not in God's Name: Confronting Religious Violence*. New York: Schocken, 2015.

Seymour, Jack. *Theological Approaches to Christian Education*. Nashville: Abingdon, 1990.

Smith, Christian. *Soul Searching: The Religious and Spiritual Lives of American Teenagers.* New York: Oxford University Press, 2005.

Stevenson, Bryan. "Four Steps to Really Change the World." Interview by Martin Saunders in *Christian Today* (July 16, 2015). http://www.christiantoday.com/article/bryan.stevenson.four.steps.to.really.change.the.world/59211.htm.

———. *Just Mercy: A Story of Justice and Redemption.* New York: Spiegel & Grau, 2014.

Tanner, Kathryn. *Theories of Culture: A New Agenda for Theology.* Minneapolis: Fortress, 1997.

Thomas, Douglas, and John Seely Brown. *A New Culture of Learning: Cultivating the Imagination for a World of Constant Change.* Scott's Valley, CA: CreateSpace, 2011.

Tran, Mai-Anh Le. "Narrating Lives, Narrating Faith: 'Organic Hybridity' for Contemporary Christian Religious Education." *Religious Education* 105 (2010) 188–203.

Warford, Malcolm. *Revitalizing Practice: Collaborative Models for Theological Faculties.* New York: Lang, 2008.

Wiggins, Grant, and Jay McTighe. *Understanding by Design.* Alexandria, VA: Association for Supervision and Curriculum Development, 2005.

4

Religious Self, Religious Other

Coformation as a Model
for Interreligious Education

—Jennifer Peace

INTRODUCTION

One of the enduring insights of my own intellectual formation in the historical and cultural study of religions is that "we know by way of contrast." This building block of knowledge applies not only to concepts and ideas but to our sense of identity. In other words, "I" can be defined in many ways, but one primary way to define myself is to notice that "I" am not "you." While this simple binary is an essential part of the earliest differentiation each infant makes as he or she begins to make sense of the world, when taken to an extreme it can create problems. Distinguishing between the healthy process of differentiation and meaning making, versus a pathological commitment to two inviolable categories of *us=good* and *them=evil* is essential. Understanding and dismantling what Jonathan Sacks refers to as "pathological dualism" is at the heart of my approach to interfaith education in the context of seminary formation.[1] The story of how this central concern

1 Sacks, *Not in God's Name,* 51. "Dualism comes in many forms, not all of them dangerous. There is the Platonic dualism that differentiates sharply between mind and body, the spiritual and the physical. There is the theological dualism that sees two

might translate into a model for interreligious education is the focus of this chapter.

Since 2008 I have had the privilege of being at the heart of a remarkable initiative to re-imagine seminary education for a multireligious world in my position as founding co-director of the Center for Interreligious and Communal Leadership Education (CIRCLE), a shared initiative between Andover Newton Theological School (ANTS) and Hebrew College (HC). This work began with the providence of proximity thanks to the co-location of Hebrew College in 2002 and the launching of its rabbinical school in 2003. But proximity alone does not ensure creative partnership. The interreligious work between the two schools developed over many years of deliberate relationship building, ongoing financial commitments, and the combined intellectual and spiritual resources of our two communities.[2]

Our quest began with a question: What does adequate preparation for the next generation of religious leaders and educators look like given the complex multireligious contexts where our graduates will serve? Significantly, the first constituents to pose this question in a serious way were students. Betty Ann Miller, a rabbinical student, began to wonder what, if anything, the formation for ministry process taking place a few hundred yards across the hill at Andover Newton had to do with her own rabbinic training. So she looked for a conversation partner and soon her personal quest became a collective journey. This group of pioneering students, Jewish, Christian, and Unitarian Universalists (UUs), called themselves Journeys on the Hill or JOTH. Their peer-led conversations about both the practical and theological concerns associated with formation for religious leadership created the template for what became the CIRCLE fellowship program, a cornerstone of the Center's work. Under the auspices of this joint program, up to twelve CIRCLE fellows are selected through a competitive application process to participate in a yearlong process of interfaith learning and leadership. The

different supernatural forces at work in the universe. There is the moral dualism that sees good and evil as instincts within us between which we must choose. But there is also what I will call *pathological dualism* that sees humanity itself as radically, ontologically divided into the unimpeachably good and the irredeemably bad. You are either one or the other: either one of the saved, the redeemed, the chosen, or a child of Satan, the devil's disciple."

2. In particular, the leadership of founding co-directors Or Rose from Hebrew College and Gregory Mobley from Andover Newton has been essential to the evolution and success of this work. More recently the addition in 2014 of Islamic-scholar-in residence Celene Ibrahim and CIRCLE administrator Soren Hessler has allowed the work to expand in new ways. In addition, this work has been supported by the efforts and leadership of key administrators, faculty, board members, and dedicated students at both schools.

fellowship involves both professional development sessions for the whole cohort as well as individual initiatives led by pairs of fellows, designed to increase positive relations across religious lines. While the particular story of how interreligious education became integral to ANTS and HC is perhaps idiosyncratic, the underlying assumptions, attitudes, strategies, and vision that undergird our approach may be instructive to other educators looking to effect institutional change in their own settings.

PART I: FROM EDUCATION TO COFORMATION

In the Fall of 2011, as I was beginning my third year with CIRCLE, I was invited to contribute an article to *Colloquy* magazine, a publication of the Association of Theological Schools, the largest accreditor of seminaries in North America. The focus of the issue was on "multifaith education initiatives." As I crafted a piece to describe the details of our curricular design and articulate what makes it distinctive or new, I realized that ultimately we were not just interested in adding new classes or opportunities for interfaith engagement to an already full schedule of courses and requirements. Rather, more radically, we were hoping to influence the conversation and ultimately shift the paradigm about what constitutes adequate seminary education.

Thinking back to my own experiences in both seminary and doctoral studies, I understood that training for ministry and related religious leadership roles was, at its best, a profound formation process. Beyond learning the essentials of history, theology, ethics, Bible, pastoral care, etc., seminary education is about forming a person. What was new about the model we were developing at CIRCLE was a fundamental assertion that we cannot form our religious leaders and educators in mono-religious isolation. The religious blinders of my own seminary training, revealed through what was explicitly or implicitly left out of the curriculum, gave me the impression that everything I needed to know or be able to do was fully contained in the teachings and traditions of fellow Christians (and more often than not, white, male, Protestant Christians). In a world where religiously-motivated violence and polarizing rhetoric rooted in religious stereotypes dominate the daily news, I am convinced that this model is inadequate for the current realities and demands that our graduates face (if indeed it was ever adequate).

The theory driving CIRCLE's work posits the essential role of learning *with* the "religious other" as we construct a clearer sense of our "religious self." This contrasts with the dominant world religion paradigms where learning *about* the religious other is the norm. While the emphasis on religious literacy at the heart of this model is essential, it is not sufficient. In the opening lines of my article for *Colloquy* I coined the term "coformation" to signal the new paradigm of the model we were promoting:

> To add the prefix 'co' to 'formation' and apply it to seminary education is to assert that students are not formed in isolation but in connection to a dynamic web of relationships. Making formation an intentionally interfaith process reflects the reality that our particular beliefs exist in a larger and complex multi-religious (and nonreligious) human community, a community we want to prepare our students to both encounter and engage on multiple levels—theological, ethical, and pastoral—as community organizers, educators, preachers, and citizens.[3]

Beyond the relational skills and civic priorities inherent in this model, the term "coformation" signals another fundamental aspect of this work for me—the inner work that is part of forming the whole person. A key theological insight that underpins my commitment to interfaith education as part of seminary formation is the assertion that interreligious engagement is a *way* of being Christian. Rather than tangential to faithful Christian life, how we understand and treat our religious neighbors is central to it.

In my doctoral training in the Historical and Cultural Study of Religions program at the Graduate Theological Union, my work was anchored by a focus on Christian spirituality even as I explored similarities and differences across religious traditions. Attention to my own religious life and the spiritual practices that animate it is fundamental to the process of forming my sense of self as a Christian. Coformation is a process of learning alongside religious others, attending to both the external and internal demands of coming to know the religious *other* in relation to the religious *self*. While prioritizing interreligious relationships in the process of training future religious leaders, attending to the inner dimensions of one's own spiritual formation is an essential part of the equation.

One oft-repeated sentiment in CIRCLE's work is that we are interested in helping Jews be better Jews, Christians be better Christians, UUs be better UUs, Muslims be better Muslims, and so on. This is not a model of interreligious education that skirts particularity for the sake of commonality. In fact we would argue that to the contrary, when the work is done well, students come away with a deeper understanding and appreciation of their own identity even as they may experience some "holy envy" in the face of the practices and commitments of their fellow students from different religions.

---

3. Peace, "Coformation," 24.

Two anecdotes from the early years of our program are illustrative of this point. The first occurred in the context of our CIRCLE fellowship program. We were still in the early weeks of the program and the cohort was getting to know each other. As we shared stories, Dan, an articulate rabbinical student, talked about his deep relationship to Judaism and what he appreciates about it. Following his comments one of the Christian students, Tim, said, "Hearing you describe what you love about Judaism makes me want to take the irony out of my voice when I talk about Christianity." Rather than only focusing on critiques of his tradition, Tim was moved to talk about what he finds beautiful in Christianity or as Tim put it, a "theo-aesthetics" of his faith.

The second illustration of the relationship between personal formation in this process of coformation comes from the classroom. I was co-teaching a yearlong class on Jewish-Christian relations with my colleague from Hebrew College and CIRCLE co-director Or Rose. One student, Greg, came into the class with a lot of confidence about his knowledge of the topic. He described himself as an interfaith minister and shared with the class the fact that he had been married for many years to a woman who was Jewish. But after a year of conversation, reflection, and reading, Greg arrived at an unexpected revelation. He came into the class with a deep appreciation for the similarities across religious traditions but as he wrote in his final reflection paper:

> What I had yet to realize was that there is even more need to understand and appreciate each other's differences, and in the process, move beyond tolerance, and beyond simply seeking the familiar. Not everything is a commonality, and that is perfectly okay. In fact, it is necessary. In our difference lies our dimensionality, our depth, our richness.

As a result, Greg was inspired to explore his Baptist roots again, with a view to the distinct contours and evolution of his own religious identity. I like to use the analogy of a potluck supper when I talk about interfaith engagement; understanding and owning your particular religious identity is akin to bringing your own dish to the interfaith table.

I often encounter students, like Greg, who come to interfaith work with a default emphasis on sameness. If "sameness" is the entry fee for interreligious relationships, religious commitment and particularity can be seen as antithetical to that goal. While there is typically an altruistic impulse behind this emphasis on sameness, it reveals an implicit assumption that difference is threatening. While underscoring our shared humanity and the dignity that affords each of us, an important counterbalance in my approach to interfaith education is to dive deep into the irreducible differences that distinguish communities and individuals. An interfaith leader is someone who understands that these differences are to be safeguarded and celebrated rather than erased or flattened.

PART II: INTERFAITH EDUCATION AND TRANSFORMATIVE LEARNING

Implicit in the idea of coformation is an expectation of change. Genuine learning is a transformative process. Max Stackhouse, a former professor of ethics at Andover Newton, once remarked that to truly be a Christian one must be continually open to conversion. When I did field work for part of my doctoral research at a Benedictine Abby, I saw this sentiment reflected in the community's vow to "*conversatio morum*," a vow they interpret as a daily openness to change.[4] This posture of openness coupled with a sense of epistemological humility is essential for learning and essential for the model of interreligious coformation we are committed to at CIRCLE.

As a professor, I've had the privilege over the years of watching students experience those moments of awe when a genuinely new insight takes hold and they sense that who they were when they came into the class has been altered or impacted in some significant way. The classroom is a protected space on a certain level where students are free to explore new ideas and follow lines of thought. They can trace the implications of their theories and theologies while being spared from the consequences of these thought experiments. Imagining themselves tackling complex interreligious dilemmas from the relative safety of the classroom allows students to create mental muscle memory, preparing them for analogous scenarios they may encounter beyond the classroom. To train religious leaders with the confidence, curiosity, and capacity to work across religious lines on complex questions, we need to attend to the explicit, implicit, and null curricula in our seminaries.

"Our experiences change us." I was teaching a class with Or Rose and Celene Ibrahim on interfaith leadership in the Boston area when Basma, a

---

4. "The three vows taken by a Benedictine, presented by St. Benedict in Chapter 58 of the *Rule* are: Stability, *Conversatio Morum,* and *Obedience.* The vows of *Stability* and *Conversatio Morum* are unique to Benedictines. Stability implies not only binding oneself to the physical "place" and land that is Regina Laudis, but also the personal identification with the spirit and aspirations of the community. *Conversatio Morum,* rooted in the Latin "conversation" complements Stability, and asks that the nun be willing 'to change' every day of her life." http://abbeyofreginalaudis.org/ceremonies-MotherAlma.html

Muslim student from Egypt who sat in the back row, offered this simple but profound observation. She was talking about her own experiences growing up in a Muslim majority country where all her significant interactions were with fellow Muslims. Coming to the U.S. with her husband for school, she had myriad new experiences with people from various religious backgrounds. In fact, Basma had become a CIRCLE fellow and had spent the year co-leading a peer group with a Christian (Brethren) student from Andover Newton. The topic was on portrayals of the religious other in scripture and the peer group looked at Jewish, Christian, and Islamic texts in Hebrew, Arabic, and English because of the expertise in the group. Basma's comment reminded me of the importance of thinking carefully about the kinds of experiences we create for our students.

Interreligious education is understood in many different ways. In some seminaries in particular it is located squarely under the auspices of comparative theology.[5] In many secular college and university settings, religious literacy is the dominant paradigm.[6] CIRCLE's approach focuses on the broader process of formation for ministry with an emphasis on the power of "interreligious learning through relationship building." When students are in relationship over time (students spend anywhere from two to six years in degree programs at ANTS or HC) the kinds of questions they ask and the kinds of answers they offer shift and deepen. Knowing that your conversation partner both understands and appreciates you as a person creates the possibility for the kind of trust and vulnerability that can lead to transformative learning.

My own training as an historian of religions influences my approach to interreligious education. History of religions is an interdisciplinary comparative approach to a diverse range of concerns related to how traditions have developed, interacted, and impacted both individuals and communities over time. For me, understanding stories from the past offers paradigms and patterns of thought that can provide insights and tools for analyzing current interreligious relations.

Beyond intellectual curiosity, my interest is fueled by an ethical concern that began to form when I was a young college student majoring in South Asian studies. As I read accounts of the partition of India in August 1947 and the massive violence that erupted along the border, my questions centered on how community is created and destroyed. How did those living side-by-side before the partition, shift from being defined primarily as

---

5. See Cornille, *The Im-Possibility of Interreligious Dialogue*; or Clooney, *The New Comparative Theology*.

6. See Prothero, *Religious Literacy*; or Moore, *Overcoming Religious Illiteracy*.

neighbors to being defined narrowly through the lens of religious identity? What turns one's neighbor into one's enemy seemingly overnight? How are these breaches repaired? Of course these are not questions confined to history books. They comes up again and again when we try to piece together what happened in April 1994 in Rwanda or July of 1995 in Srebrenica, to name just two stark and relatively recent examples.

Given both past and contemporary examples of communal violence, particularly where the lines of division are drawn in religious terms, I would argue that cultivating interreligious understanding among our future religious leaders is an ethical imperative. Those of us who identify as members of a religious community have a responsibility to both acknowledge and decry the violence done in the name of the traditions we claim. It is inadequate and perhaps immoral to educate future religious leaders without skills, attitudes, and experiences that will prepare them both to work for peace in the midst of religiously-motivated violence and to be "repairers of the breach" in the wake of communal violence.[7] I would argue that one of the central commitments of an interreligious leader is to safeguard the wellbeing and religious identity of the "other," particularly those from vulnerable religious minorities.[8]

Of course the lines that divide us can be drawn in many different ways and our identities are always more complex than our religious affiliations. This is where interfaith educators can draw on and contribute to scholarship related to the intersectionality of identity as well as scholarship focused on defining and dismantling systems of oppression such as racism, sexism, homophobia, anti-Semitism, ableism, ageism, and other forms of hatred based on particular identity categories. My own background in feminist studies, coupled with my experiences as a woman working in the male-dominated spheres of academia and religious leadership, have led me to see the parallels between the work of developing a feminist consciousness and the underlying tasks of interfaith education—both are forms of consciousness-raising. Ultimately, raising one's consciousness cannot be mandated, only invited. As an educator, my task is to set up the conditions where students feel safe enough and curious enough to accept the invitation to remove their blinders and be changed.

7. The phrase comes from Isa 58:12. "And your ancient ruins shall be rebuilt; you shall raise up the foundations of many generations; you shall be called the repairer of the breach, the restorer of streets to dwell in." English Standard Version.

8. For an exploration of the role of interreligious dialogue in civil society see Lervick, *Interreligious Studies*.

PART III: CURRICULUM DESIGN AND
INSTITUTIONAL TRANSFORMATION

Having articulated CIRCLE's vision and some key insights that shape our approach to interfaith education, this section outlines the curricular and co-curricular model that embodies these ideals. While the student led peer group, JOTH, and an ad hoc offering of joint courses and campus events were already underway when I came to Andover Newton in 2008, with the establishment of CIRCLE we began to develop a more strategic long-term vision for how this work could affect wider institutional change. The initial grant proposal to the Henry Luce Foundation framed the goal of our work in broad terms. Beyond adding new resources to develop our interfaith programming, we focused on how the Center might be a catalyst for institutional change—nurturing an ethos of interreligious understanding on both campuses.

Students from ANTS and HC laid the groundwork for the institutional change through their curiosity and entrepreneurial energy, which caused them to reach out across the two campuses and form a new interreligious student group, Journeys on the Hill. The students quickly found allies among the faculty who began to offer a handful of joint courses. The work continued to develop, gathered momentum, and eventually led to grant applications. With the infusion of significant financial resources in 2008, thanks to the Henry Luce Foundation, CIRCLE was established, creating the essential inter-institutional infrastructure on which the work could build.

Campus programs, a joint fellowship program, and joint courses were the three primary foci of CIRCLE's work that most impacted and shaped the curricular changes. It is worth noting the key features of each of these initiatives before noting some of the resulting curricular and institutional changes:

1. **Cross-campus programing**: CIRCLE often describes our two campuses as a "living laboratory" where we can explore various models of interreligious engagement. Campus programming is the crucible where new ideas are born, some of which find their way into the life of the schools. Broadly speaking, our campus programming typically serves one or more of these three goals: jointly acknowledging or celebrating key moments in the liturgical life of our respective traditions; lectures, panels, or conferences that increase religious literacy or interreligious understanding; and activities, events, or programs focused on strengthening or building relations across religious lines. These goals provide a kind of plumb line when we are considering sponsoring new programs.

Beyond the optional programs CIRCLE sponsors, co-sponsors, or supports each year, the annual event with the broadest institutional impact is our Joint Spring Community Day. This event evolved out of an existing practice at ANTS of holding two "community days" each year, once in the fall and once in the spring. After ANTS invited HC to participate in its joint day of service learning, the event evolved into an important shared tradition planned by CIRCLE fellows with guidance and input from the co-directors. It reflects a significant joint institutional commitment, as both schools close down operations for the day and "require," or at least strongly urge, students, staff, and faculty all to participate in a full day of relationship-building, shared meals, and shared learning. For some on our campuses, this is their first introduction to students from the neighboring school and it often leads to new connections and new commitments that sow the seeds for new initiatives, programs, and fellowship pairs in subsequent years.

Another example of how a singular event can become a shared tradition is the annual CIRCLE-sponsored celebration of *Sukkot*. This fall Jewish holiday has a built-in expectation of welcoming the stranger. This creates an authentic opportunity for Andover Newton students to visit Hebrew College early in the semester and get a peek into a particular Jewish practice while sitting in a *Sukkah* and experiencing the hospitality at the heart of this holiday. It has also become a great time to introduce our new CIRCLE fellows and invite students to participate in the range of peer-group opportunities that the fellows lead each year. After doing this together for many years, the annual celebration of *Sukkot* has become an anticipated shared tradition.

A final example is illustrative of how co-curricular programs can ultimately impact curricular design. This example underscores the importance of cultivating a culture of innovation and entrepreneurial energy to generate a vibrant model of interreligious education. We had a student one year, Kurt, who was interested in the criminal justice system. He initiated a relationship with a Boston-based organization, *Partakers*, that organizes volunteers into teams of mentors for individuals pursuing their GEDs or college degrees while incarcerated.[9] To ensure the continuity of this collaboration, before graduating Kurt worked with CIRCLE's co-directors to fold this work into the CIRCLE fellowship program. For many years, the program continued with a rotating set of two students (one from HC and one from ANTS) providing leadership for a "prison justice and ministry peer group." One year, ANTS faculty member Brita Gill-Austern, professor of psychology and

9. For an overview of Partakers' "College behind Bars" mentoring program go to: http://partakers.org/site/college-behind-bars/.

pastoral theology, participated in the group. This led Prof. Gill-Austern to offer a credit-bearing class on prison justice, taking a student-driven initiative and moving it into the curricular heart of the school. While not every program or event becomes a shared tradition or a part of the curriculum, the creative range of programs each year, influenced by the inclinations of students, in conversation with the experience of CIRCLE's co-directors, allows for a dynamic interaction of new ideas that influences the ethos on each campus.

2. **CIRCLE Fellowship program:** This model of "learning *with* rather than *about*" each other guides our work both inside and beyond the classroom and has become a key principle in our fellowship program. Over the years the fellowship program has been modified, refined, and altered to suit shifting resources and changes in our model of interreligious work, but it has remained a central and distinct feature of our program from the start. One of the goals of CIRCLE programming in general is to provide multiple entry points and levels of commitment to honor the range of goals and experiences of our seminary students. In the spectrum of participation students can attend a single event, take a joint class, join a yearlong interfaith peer group, or, at the most time intensive end of the spectrum, they can apply to become a CIRCLE fellow.

Two or three students (each from a different religious background) apply to the program in teams. This requires that students have begun a process of building relationships that is at the heart of our model.[10] It also ensures a certain amount of parity, a core value of the work, even in the initial planning stage. We ask students to conceive of a topic of shared concern where their respective traditions inspire, motivate, or equip them in some way to tackle the issue at hand. We have had fellowship projects over the years focused on environmental concerns, shared text study, artistic expression (from singing to poetry to multi-media art as a mode of spirituality), prison justice, issues of women's leadership, and LGBTQ issues to name a few. We have found that this model allows for powerful coformation experiences that radically broaden how students understand their roles and obligations as future religious leaders.

In addition to their leadership around a topic of shared concern, fellows engage as a cohort in a yearlong leadership development program

10. While it is beyond the scope of this chapter to go into details here, when designing programs that rely on relationship building it is important to consider the power dynamics among students and how racism and other forms of discrimination might disadvantage or even preclude certain students from participation. In our own program I have become increasingly aware of how biases can get in the way of forming the initial partnerships required to apply to become a CIRCLE fellow.

designed by CIRCLE's co-directors. One goal of the regular cohort meetings is to create a sense of community that can extend beyond graduation so that former CIRCLE fellows might become resources and colleagues out in the field. In addition to sharing personal stories and exploring theological questions, these sessions include everything from the nuts and bolts of running a successful interfaith event, to strategies and tools for facilitating difficult conversations, to an overview of grant writing.

To expand the model beyond Jewish, Christian, and Unitarian Universalist contexts, we actively built relationships with Muslims in the greater Boston area. To this end, in 2012, I formed an intra-Muslim women's group with the support and partnership of Islamic scholar Celene Ibrahim. Calling our group "Third Thursdays," we met together monthly for a year of conversation and relationship-building focusing on both the needs and resources of the wider Muslim community. Out of these conversations we decided to invite "Muslim community fellows" to apply for our CIRCLE fellowship program. Interest and participation grew each year and eventually laid the groundwork for a historic institutional decision to jointly appoint Celene Ibrahim as our third CIRCLE co-director and Islamic-Scholar-in Residence at HC and ANTS.

In the first years of the fellowship program we provided students with a large annual stipend and met weekly as a cohort. Over the years we've reduced the stipend to a sustainable amount and created endowments to support them, while also cutting back from weekly cohort meetings to monthly sessions. While the importance and impact of the innovation and leadership of these fellows cannot be overstated in terms of the impact on the ethos on our campuses over the years, we are currently in the process of conducting a qualitative study to evaluate the impact of the fellowship program on alums, conducting interviews and sending surveys to what is now more than 100 former fellows from both HC and ANTS. Initial feedback from fellows speaks to the power of the program and its relevance in their own work as religious leaders. Reflecting on her own changing paradigm for interfaith work influenced by CIRCLE's program, one Muslim fellow commented:

> I think most of my interfaith work was one-directional; people would come to the mosque looking for information on Islam and we would deliver that information. The models of interfaith partnership modeled at CIRCLE are different: often a single issue is engaged from multiple faith perspectives, with each partner learning equally about their own tradition in the process.

I've really appreciated this approach as more collaborative and more enriching than the models I've been using.[11]

3. **Joint Courses**: As early as the founding of JOTH, students began agitating for shared learning opportunities, not just as co-curricular options but as credit-bearing courses. They found willing partners on both campuses particularly in the persons of Rabbi Or Rose from Hebrew College and Rev. Dr. Gregory Mobley from Andover Newton, who provided critical early leadership and taught many joint courses over the years.

As more and more faculty became engaged and inspired by co-teaching, we began to systematize the offerings and create a coherent scope and sequence for students who wanted to leave seminary or rabbinical school with a solid grounding in interreligious leadership. As we considered the courses that had been particularly successful over the years, we noticed they seemed to fall into one of three areas: shared text study, practical or pastoral concerns, and social justice topics. These were areas where joint classes clearly enhanced mutual learning and where there appeared to be a strong sense of mutual motivation. These were also areas where we had complementary faculty expertise on each campus that allowed for joint course design and co-teaching. A final essential ingredient was that these areas appealed to a large number of students from each campus and contributed to their respective degree programs. In addition to these three areas, we began to offer a set of courses focused specifically on understanding the many dimensions of interfaith leadership. Identifying core areas for co-teaching has allowed us to offer a dynamic range of specific courses that speak to student and faculty interests while providing some consistency and predictability to the kinds of courses we offer.

PART IV: INSTITUTIONALIZING INTERFAITH WORK AT ANDOVER NEWTON

Institutionalization necessarily takes time and involves many stakeholders, including board members, administrators, faculty, staff, and students. While we consciously attend to parity in all our work, progress towards institutional change has necessarily followed distinct if parallel trajectories at Hebrew College and Andover Newton. Because of my own location at ANTS I will focus primarily on the shape of this path at Andover Newton.

One of the great success stories of CIRCLE's work towards institutionalization at Andover Newton was the creation of a tenure-track faculty

---

11. Peace, "Grant Report," 4.

position in Interfaith Studies. It is the first position of its kind in Andover Newton's history and one of a small handful of similar positions across the country. The new position was created with the unanimous approval of both the faculty and the ANTS Board of Trustees in June 2012. After going through the search process as the incumbent candidate, I was hired to be the first person to fill this position. In 2015, I received tenure and promotion to my current title of Associate Professor of Interfaith Studies. Anchoring the work under the auspices of a tenured faculty member was an important step in establishing its centrality in the academic heart of the school.

With leadership from dean of faculty, Sarah Drummond, interfaith education moved from a series of ad hoc courses to the center of our academic programs. Initially interfaith courses were electives. During a scheduled curriculum revision process, we added an expectation that all MDiv students would take at least one class with an interfaith focus. The next step was the creating of a five-course "Certificate in Interfaith Leadership." CIRCLE's co-directors designed the interfaith certificate jointly with the needs and curricular models of both institutions in mind. However, it was an easier adaptation for ANTS because previously we had established a number of certificates in other areas. At HC adding a certificate would require creating a new academic category, which ultimately meant it was never fully implemented as a joint certificate program. We learned important lessons about the challenges of coordinating curricular changes across schools with very distinct educational designs. We applied these lessons when CIRCLE turned its attention to the task of creating parallel interreligious MA programs, a degree with greater "currency" both on our two campuses and in the wider world.

In a major milestone for institutionalization, ANTS and HC both launched their own versions of new Masters degree programs in 2015. Andover Newton's Master in Global Interreligious Leadership (MGIL), approved by the ATS, is a pioneering program that attracted a diverse group of students to its inaugural class in the Fall of 2015. We have a cohort of Muslim, Christian, and UU students in Andover Newton's version of the degree and a second cohort of Jewish students in Hebrew College's program. As we described the MA in our report to the Luce Foundation:

> The goal of this program is to help current and future communal leaders develop the knowledge and skills to serve effectively in an age of unprecedented interaction among people from different religious and cultural traditions. MGIL addresses an urgent need in the educational formation of emerging and veteran clergy and others serving as religious educators, community

organizers, and non-profit and civic leaders. The program is designed in such a way that students from each school will earn a Masters Degree from Andover Newton or Hebrew College, and a certificate from the other institution. The program can be completed in 18 months at either school, with various components available online.[12]

The MA programs were built on the foundation of strong relationships fostered through cross-campus events, jointly taught courses, shared faculty development, and inter-institutional structures that allowed for ongoing communication and shared decision-making.

If faculty buy-in, administrative leadership, and curricular and co-curricular programs are all essential ingredients of institutionalizing interreligious understanding, one added and often overlooked ingredient for this work is physical space. While our work evolved over time through sharing our respective spaces, a long-standing vision for creating a space specifically dedicated to this work goes back as early as the first grant to the Luce Foundation in 2008. When Nick Carter finished a ten year term as president of Andover Newton and incoming president Martin Copenhaver chose to live off campus, the historic President's House no longer had an obvious use. The idea of designating the house as a dedicated space to create a vibrant center for interreligious living, learning, and research for Jewish, Christian, UU, and Muslim community members on our hilltop campus inspired many, including the Andover Newton board of trustees who voted unanimously to do just that in the summer of 2015.

"CIRCLE House" has created a much-needed community-building space for Hebrew College, ANTS, and our Muslim partners. It has extended the possibility for new partnerships as community-based organizations doing innovative interfaith and/or Islamic educational work affiliate with us. It creates a natural space to host interreligious events and group meetings. The decision to convert the President's House into a center for interreligious learning also signals an ever-deepening institutional commitment to interreligious work. Perhaps, most importantly, it has created a new shared space on our campuses where students can bump into each other and get to know each other in the kind of relaxed, informal setting that is essential to building genuine friendships across lines of religious difference. The world is in desperate need of more such spaces.

What is at stake in interfaith education is related for me as a Christian educator to what is at stake for seminary education in general. I see this work as a paradigm shift in our understanding of and relationship to the

---

12. Ibrahim and Rose, "Annual Grant Report," 8.

"religious other." In earlier days (and still in some seminaries today) exposure to the religious other comes primarily through the lens of missionary accounts or classes outlining the tenants of other faiths only as a tool for proselytizing.[13] The approach that CIRCLE has charted goes beyond a more neutral religious literacy approach found in many programs to a model of transformative learning that results in both better religious leaders and better interreligious leaders.[14] Deep knowledge of one's self in relation to the religious other is not an option but an obligation if our students are going to responsibly and effectively engage in the pressing needs and current issue of our religiously diverse 21st century context.

This is why, after close to a decade co-directing CIRCLE, I am more convinced than ever that interfaith education is an essential part of seminary formation. While the trajectory of CIRCLE's work from ad hoc student-led programs to a new tenure track faculty position and an accredited MA in Global Interreligious leadership is particular to our context, the need for similar innovations and the adoption of interreligious coformation as a key paradigm for seminary education is widely applicable.

My greatest hope is that the work we have done through CIRCLE might be a model or source of inspiration for others even as we learn from other models how to deepen and develop our own work. This interest in being part of a dynamic conversation has led to my work in establishing new platforms where these conversations can take place on the national level. In 2013, I cofounded (with Homayra Ziad) the "Interreligious and Interfaith Studies" group as part of the American Academy of Religions. Because of the overwhelming response and interest in this group at the AAR, I'm leading a process to establish a new Association for Interreligious Studies as a scholarly society dedicated to developing and exploring the potential of this emerging paradigm in the study of religions and its implications for both our educational institutions and our civic life.

Many of the details of how this work happens falls under the radar of the major news outlets or the lines of academic journals. But ripple effects of one program, one class, one changed heart, one institutional transformation play out every day in countless ways. I tried to capture a glimpse of these

13. Auburn Seminary released a study in 2009 on the state of multifaith education in American theological schools. Summarizing the results, the report found that "multifaith education enhances proselytizing" was one of the top three rationales for American seminaries to include classes in this area.

14. Ibid. It is interesting to note that the other two rationales Auburn found for "multifaith education" were that it "makes better religious leaders," and that it "strengthens faith."

ripples in one of the annual grant reports on our activities to the Henry Luce Foundation:

> I am keenly aware of both the slow pace of making institutional change and the urgent need for transformed leaders working across religious divides. In the two years covered by this report alone, we have seen countless news stories of religious bigotry eclipsing our higher civic values: From the national controversy that erupted in 2010 over the Park 51 Community Center in NYC, to Peter King's anti-Muslim congressional hearings, to the shootings this August in Oak Creek, Wisconsin at a Sikh Gurdwara that left six people dead.
>
> But in each of these moments when fault lines in our country's civic life have been exposed, we have also seen people called to acts of courage and vision—people who step into the breeches and act as agents for healing. When the Park 51 controversy erupted, a Jew, a born-again Christian, and an atheist teamed up and committed hundreds of hours of time to help counter the false propaganda about the Park 51 (one of whom, Josh Stanton, cofounded CIRCLE's online publications, the *Journal of Interreligious Studies* and the *State of Formation* blog site). When Congressman Peter King convened hearings on the 'extent of the radicalization of American Muslims,' Muslim, Jewish, and Christian leaders from the ICPL (Interreligious Center for Public Life, founded by ANTS and HC) joined their voices with others to send a joint letter of concern to elected officials, posted articles condemning the hearings, and convened conversations in their respective communities. In the wake of the killings at the Gurdwara in Oak Creek, WI, students from the summer seminar 'Building Interfaith Community and Leadership,' that I co-taught with Diana Eck, responded with letters of condolence, public letters of support, sermons, and solidarity at gatherings in local Gurdwaras the week following the attack.
>
> All of these responses confirm my conviction that CIRCLE's work can and does have ripple effects beyond our hilltop. We are creating programing and structures but most importantly an ethos of understanding that contributes to our collective ability to respond—with skill and courage—to acts of religious violence. The commitment of CIRCLE and countless others to interreligious bridge-building is bolstered every time a connection is built, every time ignorance is countered with understanding, every time love and solidarity trump hatred and isolation. While we can't predict when the breeches will occur,

we can continue to prepare leaders who are equipped for the slow, patient work of repair.[15]

CONCLUSION

At the outset of this chapter I noted that the interfaith work at Andover Newton and Hebrew College began with a key question: What does adequate preparation for the next generation of religious leaders and educators look like given the complex multireligious contexts where our graduates will serve? Over the years of experimentation, reflection, and strategic development, our questions have shifted and multiplied. We are no longer asking whether or not the competencies of interreligious leadership are necessary for adequate preparation. Instead our questions focus more on the details of "how" and "what." How can we design a curriculum to move from a model of religious formation to a model of interreligious coformation? How can we integrate interfaith concerns in a curriculum so that they do not remain peripheral or optional? What curriculum designs, educational programs, and pedagogical strategies best serve this work? What does a competent religious leader need to know or do to effectively work with colleagues and community stake-holders across religious lines? These are not questions we can answer alone. The many contributions in the chapters that precede and follow my own each help to frame and fill in the details as we collectively confront these pressing questions.

BIBLIOGRAPHY

Auburn Seminary, Center for Multifaith Education. "*Beyond World Religions: The State of Multifaith Education in American Theological Schools.*" 2009. http://www.auburnseminary.org/seminarystudy.

Clooney, Francis X., S.J. *The New Comparative Theology: Interreligious Insights from the Next Generation.* New York: Continuum, 2010.

Cornille, Catherine. *The Im-Possibility of Interreligious Dialogue.* New York: Crossroad, 2008.

Ibrahim, Celene, and Or Rose. "Annual Grant Report." Unpublished grant report to the Henry Luce Foundation. Submitted May 2015.

Leirvik, Oddbørn. *Interreligious Studies: A Relational Approach to Religious Activism and the Study of Religion.* New York: Bloomsbury, 2014.

Moore, Diane. *Overcoming Religious Illiteracy: A Cultural Studies Approach to the Study of Religion in Secondary Education.* New York: Palgrave Macmillan, 2007.

15. Peace, "Final Report," 17–18.

Peace, Jennifer. "Coformation Through Interreligious Learning." *Colloquy* 20:1 (2011) 24–27. http://www.ats.edu/uploads/resources/publications-presentations/colloquy/colloquy-2011-fall.pdf.

———. "Final Report on Luce Grant funding from July 2010–June 2012." Unpublished grant report to the Henry Luce Foundation. Submitted September 2012.

———. "Grant Report: July 1, 2013–June 30, 2014" Unpublished grant report to the Henry Luce Foundation. Submitted May 15, 2014.

Prothero, Stephen. *Religious Literacy: What Every American Needs to Know—And Doesn't*. New York: HarperOne, 2008.

Sacks, Jonathan. *Not in God's Name: Confronting Religious Violence*. New York: Schocken, 2015.

5

Beyond World Religions

Pedagogical Principles and Practices for the Encouragement of Interfaith Hospitality and Collaboration

—Lucinda Mosher

In 2012, the Association of Theological Schools mandated that study for a Master of Divinity degree shall include engagement with "ministry in the multifaith and multicultural context of contemporary society" and "attention to the wide diversity of religious traditions present in potential ministry settings."[1] I was glad to see the institution of this standard. However, by 2012, it had already been my good fortune to teach at several institutions that saw multifaith engagement and multireligious literacy as serious concerns in the formation of religious leaders. Additionally, I had long been involved as a researcher into multifaith education pedagogy and as a facilitator of projects meant to encourage interfaith hospitality and col-

---

1. Association of Theological Schools Commission on Accrediting, Degree Program Standard A.2.3.2. http://www.ats.edu/uploads/accrediting/documents/degree-program-standards.pdf. See also http://www.auburnseminary.org/mfats. For further background on the development of this standard, see Stephen Graham, "Christian Hospitality and Pastoral Practices in a Multifaith Society: An ATS Project, 2010–2012" in *Theological Education* 47:1 (2012): 1–10, available at http://www.auburnseminary.org/sites/default/files/graham-ats-mf.pdf.

laboration.[2] In what follows, I describe some of that work, share my preferred models and methods for the formation of religious leaders with heart and skills for interfaith hospitality and collaboration, and reflect briefly on the assessment of students' progress toward the competencies that will allow them not only to offer interfaith hospitality and collaboration effectively, but to encourage it in others.

BEYOND "WORLD RELIGIONS"

Early in this century, Auburn Theological Seminary's Center for Multifaith Education (CME) spent several years conducting consultations with seminary faculty for the purpose of exploring how "multifaith education" might be defined. By 2008, CME had come to describe it as "the phenomenon of learning about faith traditions other than the faith tradition of the learner"—regardless of the motivation, subtext, or theological underpinning for that learning. (Thus, "teaching Christians about Islam in order to be more effective at converting Muslims" and "teaching Christians about Islam in order that they might be more competent at forming faith-based partnerships for social action" are both instances of "multifaith education.") The next step was to investigate how multifaith education was playing out.

In 2009 CME undertook a first-of-its-kind investigation of approximately one-half of the accredited U.S. Christian, Jewish, Muslim, Buddhist, and multireligious institutions then training religious leaders, in order to take a "snapshot" of how such institutions were educating religious leaders for service in a religiously diverse world.[3] The resulting report, *Beyond*

---

2. From 1999 through 2013, I was an occasional consultant by Auburn Theological Seminary's Center for Multifaith Education, designing and implementing colloquia, conducting research, and writing reports and educational materials. I designed and facilitated a multifaith education program underwritten by Trinity Grants (NYC), 2003–2005. As a consultant to the National Council of Churches, I recruited authors for a special issue of the journal *Teaching Theology and Religion*, which focused on educating religious leaders for multifaith contexts. I was the founding instructor for the Worldviews Seminar—an intensive introduction to America's religious diversity conducted annually 2002–2012, based at the University of Michigan-Dearborn but also including students from nearby Ecumenical Theological Seminary. From February 2008 through June 2011 I was an instructor for the "Multifaith Track" of New York Theological Seminary's Doctor of Ministry program. Since 2011, my work at Hartford Seminary has included the development of programs and courses aimed at improving multireligious literacy and skills for leadership in multifaith contexts.

3. As a consultant to Auburn Theological Seminary's Center for Multifaith Education, I was the lead researcher for this study and a principal author of the final report.

World Religions: The State of Multifaith Education in American Theological Schools,[4] asserted four key findings:

1. Contrary to common perceptions, many American seminaries were offering an impressive range of academic course offerings about other faith traditions. Only 14 percent of the courses we investigated used a traditional "world religions" approach (i.e., survey of five or more faith traditions in a manner not unlike courses one might find in an undergraduate school catalogue). We acknowledged that the traditional world-religions survey course is not without merit; but the plethora of other approaches delighted us!

2. Islam and Judaism were the most represented religions taught about in the academic course offerings we discovered in the schools we investigated—and at roughly equal levels.

3. Theology was the most common frame for learning about other faiths in the seminary classroom.

4. Multifaith education was included in early 21st century American theological school curricula for one of three key reasons:

   a. A school might believe that multifaith education makes better religious leaders—that having a working knowledge of other religions would allow clergy to minister more effectively in multifaith contexts.

   b. A school might be convinced that multifaith education strengthens faith—that learning about and from other religious traditions helps a religious leader-in-training grow in his/her own religious convictions and practice.

   c. A school might be convinced that multifaith education will make a student more adept at proselytizing—more effective at converting adherents of other religions to that student's (and, presumably, that school's) own tradition.

If we were to conduct a similar survey today, we would note that some of the courses we highlighted as exemplary are no longer being taught; some of the programs we celebrated as cutting-edge have been scaled back or eliminated. Yet, because other institutions have added or expanded interfaith offerings, I believe that the general thrust of these findings would still prevail; I am also certain that we would be celebrating some new trends.

As evidence of one new trend, we would, for example, note that the number of seminaries at which a professor has "interfaith" (or a related

---

4. http://www.auburnseminary.org/seminarystudy.

term) in her title has expanded sufficiently enough that the American Academy of Religion now has an Interreligious and Interfaith Studies Group. Andover Newton Theological School's Center for Inter-Religious and Communal Leadership Education is directed by Jennifer Howe Peace, Assistant Professor of Interfaith Studies; at Claremont School of Theology, Najeeba Syeed is Assistant Professor of Interreligious Education; Yehezkel Landau was for several years Associate Professor of Interfaith Relations at Hartford Seminary, where I serve as Faculty Associate in Interfaith Studies. This list continues to grow.

As evidence of a second new trend, we might recall that in a 2009 essay, "On Teaching Islam and the Future of Christian-Muslim Relations," Amir Hussain reflected on possibilities for teaching Islamic theology in Christian North American theological schools. His primary concern was for the development of partnerships between theological schools with long experience in the formation of leaders and Muslim communities with no seminaries of their own.[5] In fact, during the past two decades, a number of Christian seminaries have admitted the occasional Muslim student.[6] I was fortunate to have been mentored by Ibrahim Abu-Rabi'—who, when he came to Hartford Seminary in 1991, became the first Muslim to serve as a full-time professor at a U.S. Christian theological school. But now, by virtue of Henry Luce Foundation grants, several historically Christian seminaries have added a Muslim to their faculty. To name three: Jerusha Tanner Lamptey is at Union Theological Seminary in New York City; Zeyneb Sayilgan is at Virginia Theological Seminary; and, uniquely, Celene Ayat Lizzio holds a joint appointment at Andover Newton Theological Seminary and Hebrew College. Seminary professors now enjoy multifaith collegiality in the broader academy that was barely possible in 2009.

MULTIFAITH EDUCATION MODELS AND METHODS

Thus having moved far beyond defining multifaith education, and having made clear that multifaith education is happening in many places, the next pressing question was exactly *how* it was happening. In 2010, Auburn surveyed forty seminary faculty about their pedagogies of multifaith education—and again I was the lead researcher. When asked about their preferred

5. Hussain, "On Teaching Islam," 81–92.

6. I personally encountered this phenomenon in courses I offered at the General Theological Seminary (NYC), Ecumenical Theological Seminary (Detroit), and New York Theological Seminary (NYC)—which actively recruited Muslims for its Doctor of Ministry program.

teaching methods, our respondents expressed near equal enthusiasm for collaborative-group learning (68 percent), direct lecture (63 percent), and experiential learning, such as site visits (61 percent). In teaching *about* a religious tradition, 85 percent said that beliefs and practices were given roughly equal attention. Comparative-religion approaches were favored over others, with a history-of-religions methodology coming in second. More than half of our respondents described their courses or programs as "subject-centered" (i.e., they honor the material over the individual student); 37 percent described their courses or programs as "learner-centered" (focused on the interests, needs, capacity, and previous knowledge of the learners); only 9 percent were "problem-based" (using case-study method or a pragmatic focus). This may sound rather ordinary. However, our respondents also submitted a wealth of "multifaith teaching tactics"—some of which can be found in a special issue of *Teaching Theology and Religion* or archived on the Auburn website[7]—which are distinctively creative.

And we need creative approaches to multifaith education. In recent years, I have done much teaching of second-career students. I know that a respectful, accepting learning environment takes account of the fact that adults learn through various modes: the experiential, personal involvement mode; the watching-and-listening mode; the logical analysis and systematic planning mode; and, the hands-on mode. To the extent that the material and the schedule allow, I do my best to provide for all four.

But what multifaith education practices are most effective? What competencies should we be cultivating in our students for a religious leadership in multifaith contexts? What knowledge and skills make possible one's ability to lead one's community in elegant practice of interfaith hospitality and collaboration? I believe that, at its best, education for leadership in religiously plural contexts has eight attributes.

1. Effective education for interfaith hospitality and collaboration begins with lessons in theologies of religious manyness. In 2011, I coined the term *religious manyness* to name a situation provoking a theological response, and have used it quite a lot since then in my writing, teaching, and public lecturing.[8] Why not just speak of *religious diversity*? In fact, I do, sometimes. However, particularly in educational institutions, *diversity* may denote more than merely the state of variety; it often connotes a stance of promotion of respect for difference, of provision of a safe and nurturing environment for the exploration of differences. To say "religious diversity"

---

7. Mosher, *Teaching Theology*. See also http://www.auburnseminary.org/mfpedagogy.

8. See, for example, Mosher, *Toward Our Mutual Flourishing*, particularly pages 3–4.

would thus imply a degree of activism toward acceptance, rather than a mere naming of a state of affairs. To the contrary, *religious manyness* names a state of affairs, a *construction zone for theology*, to borrow a phrase from Terrence Tilley.[9]

And if we are to encourage hospitality and collaboration in "the multifaith and multicultural context of contemporary society"—a zone characterized by religious manyness—we must be sure they have a theology, i.e. ,a faith-based rationale, that makes it possible for interfaith hospitality and collaboration to be construed as acts of faithfulness.[10] As a first step toward embrace or construction of an openhearted theology of religious manyness, I begin by defining *religion* as does Byron Earhart: as "a distinctive set of beliefs, rituals, doctrines, institutions, and practices that enables the members of that tradition to establish, maintain, and celebrate a *meaningful world*."[11] By defining religion phenomenologically, in terms of worldview, I can then assert that everyone has a religion (even if they do not call it that)! *Everyone* has a means for making sense of the world—even those among my students whose approach is eclectic or not easily labeled! I then call my students' attention to Roman Catholic theologian William Portier's assertion that inquiries are always "perspectival, i.e., located somewhere"; that "when they ask questions, questioners stand somewhere."[12] I therefore insist that my students name or explain their own religious *location*, that they describe where they *stand*. I then guide them in searches of their location's texts, traditions, practices, or doctrines for whatever might undergird interfaith hospitality and collaboration—whatever will support interfaith hospitality and collaboration as something to be undertaken *because of* (rather than *in spite of*) their religion-location; that is, whatever will allow interfaith hospitality and collaboration to be construed as acts of faithfulness. Indeed, cultivation of multifaith cooperation cannot succeed if it be not construed as a social good and an act of faithfulness. But "cooperation" is not always the goal of multifaith education.

2. Effective education for interfaith hospitality and collaboration encourages deepening of one's knowledge of (thus ability to talk with confidence about) one's own beliefs and practices. Closely related to having worked out a theological rationale for interreligious hospitality and collaboration is the cultivation of sufficient "appreciative knowledge" (Eboo

9. Tilley, *Religious Diversity*, 47–50.

10. Here, I am borrowing a turn of phrase used by Lochhead in his *The Dialogical Imperative*, 40.

11. Earhart, *Religious Traditions*, 7; emphasis mine.

12. Portier, *Tradition and Incarnation*, 5.

Patel's term) about one's own religion. Presumably, U.S. theological schools are promoting such knowledge across their curricula.

3. Effective education for interfaith hospitality and collaboration favors experiential learning. Effective systems for learning about religious diversity experientially are many. Here are three:

- *The weeklong immersion seminar* featuring one or more site-visits per day. I have used this model at four institutions during the past two decades. The intensity of the schedule builds excitement; but it can also overwhelm. And because it allows little possibility for homework during the class-meeting week, participants must be willing to complete reading and writing assignments after the face-to-face portion of the seminar adjourns.

- *The spiritual pilgrimage,* for which students meet for a weekday (or weeknight) two- or three-hour information session on a particular religion, then—on the following weekend—pay a visit (as a group) to a house of worship representative of that religion; preparatory reading and follow-up writing are part of the week-by-week rhythm of the course. A semester might include six of these pairs of classroom and onsite learning experiences.

- *The contextual approach,* by which the class is embedded in an overarching experience. For example, the Seminary Consortium on Urban Pastoral Education (SCUPE) used the 2015 Parliament of the World's Religions as its "textbook" and classroom. Students met with their professors for orientation on the day before the Parliament opened, and for a wrap-up session on the day after the Parliament adjourned. On the days of the Parliament itself, they attended sessions of their choosing and engaged other attendees in conversation, coming together in the evening to share and reflect on their experiences. These reflections, in turn, informed the SCUPE workshop presented on the Parliament's final afternoon.

Whatever the actual schedule, I do love field-trip driven courses. I think that site-visits are an ideal way to explore a "theological construction zone"—that is, "a distinctive cultural site" in which to construct a theology of religious difference. In fact, in all of my teaching on multifaith concerns, I include site-visits whenever possible, even in courses that would not necessarily demand a field trip. For a course having much to do with literary theory, close reading, and analysis of sacred texts, an early session was given over to a field trip to a well-known landmark in order to consider architecture as critical interpretation of space and purpose—and to engage in some preliminary "close reading" of this structure and its relation to the city in which it stands.

However, such experiential pedagogy is not without its detractors and I admit that caution is advisable—a point made by Marianne Moyaert in her essay *Inappropriate Behavior? On the Ritual Core of Religion and Its Challenges in Interreligious Hospitality*.[13] In short, when it comes to site-visits for the purpose of understanding other people's beliefs and practices, time must be made for preparation and debriefing—apart from the site-visit itself. Time in preparation is well spent. Students need coaching in "how to be a perfect stranger" (how to be a polite visitor to a strange, perhaps even off-putting, domain). Preparation includes attention to how such a visit can be construed as an act (rather than a violation) of faithfulness to one's own tradition; it includes a reminder of the distinction between idol and icon, and a lesson in how to ask a clarifying question. Debriefing (which sometimes take the form of "putting out fires") is essential; without it, a site-visit can do more harm than good.

4. Effective education for interfaith hospitality and collaboration takes a phenomenological approach. That is, it will be more concerned with a religion's present lived reality than the complexities of its early history. The phenomenological approach prefers to let each religion be appreciated on its own terms. It acknowledges that a given category (having a sacred text, for example) may be of major importance in one religion, but, while it may be present in other religions, its role there might be minor, or at least quite different. It recognizes that while all religions provide answers to worldview questions (such as "How did the world come to be?" or "What is the nature of humanity?" or "What is wrong, and how can it be fixed?" or "What happens when we die?"), a religion need not answer all of them.

5. Effective education for interfaith hospitality and collaboration encourages understanding of each religion's own multiplicity of expressions—thus the reality of intra-religious complexity. Spending some time in this domain should reduce the impulse to expect our neighbors of other faiths to provide us with simple answers to complex questions—questions such as "What is the role of women in your religion?" or "What does your religion teach about what your attitude should be toward people of other religions?"

6. Effective education for interfaith hospitality and collaboration encourages both formal and functional comparison-making, paired with an attitude of delighting in the differences. And much of the dialogue involves the deepening of understanding of the difference between formal and functional comparisons. The Qur'an and the Bible both are "books"; that

13. Moyaert, "On the Ritual Core of Religion."

is a formal comparison. But considering a functional comparison might be more enlightening: a syllogism such as "the Qur'an is to Muslims as Jesus is to Christians," for example; or "Mary is to Christians as Muhammad is to Muslims," in that each is a "bearer of the Word," for another.

7. Effective education for interfaith hospitality and collaboration is dialogical. As important as site-visits can be, it is crucial that students understand that site-visiting is not *dialogue*; it is *encounter*. Encounter is a useful step toward dialogue, but dialogue (as social scientist Daniel Yankelovich defines it in his *The Magic of Dialogue*) is a transformative activity—a constellation of strategies employed for the purpose of strengthening relationships or solving problems, and usually entailing multiple sessions. It is also a powerful teaching mode.

As a phenomenologist—one who would prefer to let each religion be appreciated on its own terms, I have become quite fond of *comparative theology*, as defined by Francis Clooney. For Clooney, comparative theology is an endeavor which "combines tradition-rooted theological concerns with actual study of another tradition."[14] When possible, I like to teach about another religion "dialogically"—in conversation with its practitioners. Thus, following Clooney, I define *dialogical comparative theology* as an endeavor in which tradition-rooted theological concerns are combined with actual study of another tradition in a manner that is dialectical (that is, making use of reciprocal discourse) for the purpose of gaining clarity—thus is transformational.

Closely related to *dialogical comparative theology* is the dialogical study of sacred texts. Approaches include the use by Andover Newton and Hebrew College of *havruta* (scripture study in pairs—in their case, a Christian seminarian paired with a rabbinical student); or the many instances of the employment of the method known as Scriptural Reasoning. My students in *Christian-Muslim Encounter: the theological dimension* love to study Bible and Qur'an together, using methods and materials borrowed from the Building Bridges Seminar. Imagine them huddled in twos or threes, reading aloud to each other the Fatiha and the Lord's Prayer, sharing how they were taught these texts as children and how they function in their daily lives now, and answering each other's questions about the meaning of a particular word or phrase. Imagine them studying Psalm 19 alongside a Quranic passage with similar themes [Sūrah al-Rūm (30):19–30]; or poring over the Quranic account of the birth of Jesus alongside the account in the Gospel of Luke.

14. Clooney, *Comparative Theology*, 10.

The dialogical, comparative study of formulaic birth narratives is interesting, but during a recent class, as we discussed what our textbook had to say about narrative theology and creedal formulas in Christianity and Islam, we went in a different direction: we began by reading aloud a story almost every Muslim would have heard since childhood. Known as the Hadith of Gabriel, it recounts an interrogation of the Prophet Muhammad by a mysterious "traveler" (who turns out to be the Angel Gabriel) in front of the Prophet's disciples. This was followed by a recitation of the Prologue to the Gospel of John ("In the beginning was the Word . . ."). The class then proceeded to compare these two narratives. Beyond style (one was catechetical; the other, didactic), students noted that the Christian narrative conveyed core doctrine only, whereas the Islamic narrative encapsulated core practices as well as core beliefs, and asserted the religion's foundational ethical principle—without which the value of the beliefs and practices collapse. It was a rich and prolonged exchange. Such discussions have the potential to (and often do) transform!

8. Effective education for interfaith hospitality and collaboration includes the teaching of concrete skills and strategies for facilitating interfaith hospitality and collaboration. As fascinating as multifaith literacy is to me— as much as I delight in learning and teaching others about how Zoroastrians name the Ultimate, or how the Bahá'í calendar is constructed, or how Sikhs worship—it is abundantly clear to me that other skills are necessary for truly effective multifaith cooperation. Therefore, my courses aimed at enhancing religious multilingualism include lessons on concrete skills for leadership in multifaith contexts.

I might begin by introducing my colleague Yehezkel Landau's "Twenty Attributes of Effective Interfaith Leadership"—described in detail in his Doctor of Ministry thesis[15] and distilled by me, with his permission, into an outline useful as a classroom discussion prompt. Effective interfaith leadership, Landau asserts, draws upon five areas of knowledge or awareness:

1. Informed understanding of the beliefs and practices of the faith traditions represented;

2. Awareness of how sacred scriptures function in each tradition;

3. Knowing the difference between a faith tradition, as it is understood and practiced by believers, and the historical and cultural contexts in which it developed and is lived today;

4. Psychological awareness of how negative feelings, often suppressed and unconscious, operate in human relationships;

15. Landau, "Interfaith Leadership Training."

5. "Emotional intelligence," by which he means being in touch with one's own feelings, including fear and anger, and knowing how they are aroused.

Effective interfaith leadership, Landau continues, requires eight skills:

1. Capacity for self-criticism;

2. Capacity for appreciative listening without judgment or investment in any outcome;

3. Ability to communicate constructively, even when disagreeing, without verbal violence or belligerence;

4. Ability to monitor, and respond to, group process and dynamics;

5. Ability to facilitate religiously diverse groups, acting as a teacher, guide, and evocative questioner depending on the circumstances—i.e., the ability to combine *instructional* and *elicitive* styles of teaching;

6. Ability to lead, or co-lead, comparative scripture study;

7. Ability to design and lead interfaith worship or devotion;

8. Grasp of methods and techniques for conflict transformation.

Finally, he says, effective interfaith leadership depends upon seven personal qualities:

1. Faithful discipleship in one's own tradition, in tandem with openness to the spiritual treasures of others;

2. Self-confidence in leading and motivating others, combined with genuine humility;

3. Open-mindedness and flexibility;

4. Open-hearted hospitality—described in terms of "empathy" and "compassion";

5. Patience—that is, the ability to stay calm under pressure;

6. Creative imagination;

7. A sense of vocational commitment to interfaith work.

Some of the items on this checklist must await their cultivation in other venues. Others, however, will be addressed during the seminar at hand, through sessions on skills and strategies such as Fierce Conversations methodology and other approaches to conflict transformation;[16] or the Hoshin

16. Scott, *Fierce Conversations*.

Kanri approach to project sequencing;[17] media training (why and how to craft a fifteen-second elevator speech or a seven-second soundbite; why and how to stay on message); or best practices in interfaith entrepreneurship.[18] As a practitioner of Engaged Buddhism might say, without *upaya* (skill in means) and *prajna* (wisdom), your *karuna* (compassion) can only take you so far. The development of skill in means moves us from multifaith understanding to effective activism, to the creation and cultivation of multifaith circles of virtuous collaboration.

In courses aimed at cultivating leadership skills for multifaith contexts more than at increasing students' multireligious literacy *per se*, I have found case study methods to work well. Work with case studies can provide for watching-and-listening, for logical analysis and systematic planning, and even for hands-on involvement. I am partial to certain cases developed by Harvard's Pluralism Project—not only because they are well-formulated, but because they showcase the tribulations of people in my personal circle of friends.[19] But for cases appropriate to the training of religious leaders, I turn as often to films such as Unity Productions Foundation's *Talking Through Walls* (about the challenges of getting permission to build a mosque);[20] Daniel Schipani's book, *Multifaith Views in Spiritual Care*;[21] and Scarboro Missions' resources for interfaith trainings for chaplains.[22]

---

17. *Hoshin Kanri* is Japanese for "ship in a storm" or "compass needle"; that is, guidance for traveling in the right direction. It offers a method for project sequencing (once a project is defined) and for gaining feedback about one's project sequence plans before project execution commences. For an introduction to this methodology, see Colletti, *The Hoshin Kanri Memory Jogger*.

18. By interfaith entrepreneurship I mean models and strategies for freelance work and the launching of personal professional initiatives in the arena of interreligious concerns. In addition to offering myself as a role model, I might highlight the work of other entrepreneurs—among them Frank Fredericks, founder of World Faith, which brings together religiously diverse young people to work together on development issues (worldfaith.org); Ruth Broyde Sharone, founder of Festival of Freedom (http://minefieldsandmiracles.com/Bio.html); Eboo Patel, founder of Interfaith Youth Core (https://www.ifyc.org/); Samir Selmanovic, founder of Faith House Manhattan (http://www.faithhousemanhattan.org/), or Tiffany Puett, founding director of the Institute for Diversity and Civic Life (http://diversityandciviclife.org/).

19. Harvard University Pluralism Project's Case Study Initiative, http://pluralism.org/casestudy.

20. http://www.upf.tv/films/talking-through-walls/.

21. Schipani, *Multifaith Views*.

22. http://www.scarboromissions.ca/interfaith-dialogue/curriculum-resources/workshop-outline-for-chaplains-and-spiritual-caregivers.

ASSESSING PROGRESS TOWARD INTERFAITH RELATIONS COMPETENCE

Whatever our mode of instruction or course content, one of the current challenges for multifaith education is assessment, not only of "multireligious literacy" but also (and perhaps more importantly) "interfaith literacy"— which, Eboo Patel asserts, is necessary in order for interfaith cooperation to become a social norm. Interfaith literacy, as he sees it, has four aspects:

1. Appreciative knowledge of religions(s) (our own; those embraced by others);

2. A theology of (i.e., faith-based rationale for) interfaith cooperation;

3. Knowledge of the history of interfaith cooperation;

4. Knowledge of shared values between and across different religions.[23]

One of my ongoing projects is the construction and refinement of matrices for assessing competencies for leadership in multifaith contexts: development of the requisite leader attributes, of spiritual caregiving skills, and of sufficient multi- and interfaith competencies. Having delineated relevant and necessary categories of learnings, how might we best describe the benchmark for each? Milestones? The capstone? My students have found it an eye-opening experience to work with these matrices as they strive to become more effective purveyors of interfaith hospitality, more adept facilitators of multifaith cooperation.

BIBLIOGRAPHY

Albanese, Catherine L. *America: Religions and Religion.* 4th ed. Belmont, CA: Thomson Wadsworth, 2007.

Appiah, Kwame Anthony. *Cosmopolitanism: Ethics in a World of Strangers.* New York: Norton, 2006.

Ashley, Willard W. C. *Learning to Lead: Lessons in Leadership for People of Faith.* Woodstock, VT: Skylight Paths, 2012.

Berthrong, John. *The Divine Deli: Religious Identity in the North American Cultural Mosaic.* Maryknoll, NY: Orbis, 1999.

Borelli, John, ed. *A Common Word and the Future of Christian-Muslim Relations.* Washington, DC: Prince Alwaleed Bin Talal Center for Muslim-Christian Understanding, Georgetown University, June 2009.

Chittister, Joan. *Welcome to the Wisdom of the World and Its Meaning for You: Universal Spiritual Insights Distilled from Five Religious Traditions.* Grand Rapids: Eerdmans, 2007.

23. See Patel with Scorer, *Embracing Interfaith Cooperation* DVD, Session 2.

Clooney, Francis X. *Comparative Theology: Deep Learning across Religious Borders.* Hoboken, NJ: Wiley-Blackwell, 2010.

Coletti, Joseph. *The Hoshin Kanri Memory Jogger.* Salem, NH: GOAL/QPC, 2013.

Earhart, H. Byron, ed. *Religious Traditions of the World: A Journey through Africa, Mesoamerica, North America, Judaism, Christianity, Islam, Hinduism, Buddhism, China, and Japan.* San Francisco: HarperSanFrancisco, 1992.

Eck, Diana L. *A New Religious America: How a "Christian Country" Has Become the World's Most Religiously Diverse Nation.* San Francisco: HarperCollins, 2001.

Fisher, Mary Pat. *Living Religions.* 4th ed. Upper Saddle River, NJ: Prentice-Hall, 1999.

Landau, Yehezkel. "Interfaith Leadership Training at Hartford Seminary: The Impact of the Advanced 'Building Abrahamic Partnerships' Course." DMin thesis, Hartford Seminary, 2013.

Lochhead, David. *The Dialogical Imperative: A Christian Reflection on Interfaith Encounter.* Maryknoll, NY: Orbis, 1988.

Mabry, John R., ed. *Spiritual Guidance across Religions: A Sourcebook for Spiritual Directors and Other Professionals Providing Counsel to People of Differing Faith Traditions.* Woodstock, VT: SkyLight Paths, 2014.

McCarthy, Kate. *Interfaith Encounters in America.* New Brunswick, NJ: Rutgers University Press, 2007.

Mosher, Lucinda. *Faith in the Neighborhood: Belonging.* New York: Seabury, 2005.

———. *Faith in the Neighborhood: Loss.* New York: Seabury, 2007.

———. *Faith in the Neighborhood: Praying: The Rituals of Faith.* New York: Seabury, 2006.

———, guest ed. *Teaching Theology & Religion* 16/4 (October 2013).

Mosher, Lucinda Allen. *Toward Our Mutual Flourishing: The Episcopal Church, Interreligious Relations, and Theologies of Religious Manyness.* New York: Lang, 2012.

Moyaert, Marianne. "On the Ritual Core of Religion and Its Challenges in Interreligious Hospitality." *Journal for the Academic Study of Religion* 27/2 (2014) 222–42.

Moyaert, Marianne and Joris Geldhof. *Ritual Participation and Interreligious Dialogue: Boundaries, Transgressions and Innovations.* London: Bloomsbury Academic, 2015.

Niebuhr, Gustav. *Beyond Tolerance: Searching for Interfaith Understanding in America.* New York: Viking, 2008.

Patel, Eboo. *Sacred Ground: Pluralism, Prejudice, and the Promise of America.* Boston: Beacon, 2012.

Patel, Eboo, with Tim Scorer. *Embracing Interfaith Cooperation: Eboo Patel on Coming Together to Change the World.* New York: Morehouse Education Resources, 2012.

Portier, William. *Tradition and Incarnation: Foundations of Christian Theology.* Mahwah, NJ: Paulist, 1994.

Sacks, Jonathan. *The Home We Build Together: Recreating Society.* New York: Continuum, 2007.

Schipani, Daniel S., ed. *Multifaith Views in Spiritual Care.* Kitchener, ON: Pandora, 2013.

Scott, Susan. *Fierce Conversations: Achieving Success at Work and in Life One Conversation at a Time.* New York: Berkley Trade, 2004.

Smart, Ninian. *Worldviews: Crosscultural Explorations of Human Beliefs.* 3rd ed. Upper Saddle River, NJ: Prentice-Hall, 2000.

Steinkerchner, Scott. *Beyond Agreement: Interreligious Dialogue amid Persistent Differences*. New York: Rowman & Littlefield, 2010.

Tilley, Terrence. *Religious Diversity and the American Experience*. New York: Continuum, 2007.

Valkenberg, Pim. *World Religions in Dialogue: A Comparative Theological Approach*. Winona, MN: Anselm Academic, 2013.

Wuthnow, Robert. *America and the Challenges of Religious Diversity*. Princeton: Princeton Univers-ity Press, 2005.

Yankelovich, Daniel. *The Magic of Dialogue: Transforming Conflict into Cooperation*. New York: Touchstone, 1999.

ONLINE RESOURCES

Harvard University Pluralism Project Case Study Initiative. http://pluralism.org/casestudy.

Scarboro Missions. *Workshop Outline for Chaplains and Spiritual Caregivers*. http://www.scarboromissions.ca/interfaith-dialogue/curriculum-resources/workshop-outline-for-chaplains-and-spiritual-caregivers.

Unity Productions Foundation documentaries—among them. *Talking through Walls: How the Struggle to Build a Mosque Unites a Community*. http://www.upf.tv/.

6

Pursuing and Teaching Justice in Multifaith Contexts

—Justus Baird

INTRODUCTION

On a Friday afternoon in early October 2015, a few hours before Shabbat began, an email came to my inbox from a listserv I participate in. The listserv is composed of sixty American rabbis who are alumni of a cross-denominational rabbinic leadership program. The subject line was "Anti-Muslim rallies planned for tomorrow." Anti-Muslim organizers were using Facebook to inspire a "Global Rally for Humanity," writing that "humanity is attacked daily by radical Islam" and called for protests at local mosques. The event page for the Michigan rally described the Dearborn event as "OPEN CARRY anti-mosque pro-AMERICA rally on 10/10!"

The writer to the listserv invited members of this group of rabbis to form or join a counter–demonstration if their community was being targeted. A few rabbis replied to suggest contacting local Muslim leaders first in order to support existing efforts. Other repliers questioned whether a counter-demonstration was an effective strategy for countering such protests; perhaps ignoring them would decrease the chances that the message of the hateful protests would spread.

Then a reply came to ask whether we (American rabbis) can request that Muslims condemn the terror attacks on Jews in Israel, wondering aloud whether they (American Muslims) have a responsibility to do so.

This brief exchange over an email listserv demonstrates how multifaith engagement is always entangled in cultural and political contexts. Here, one's ability to stand in solidarity with another faith community in their moment of need is heavily influenced by perceptions about that community's stance on seemingly unrelated issues.

In another example of this entanglement, a seminary professor tells a story about a multifaith panel of local religious leaders that he had painstakingly assembled for his student body. During the event, the imam on the panel made a comment about the problem of homosexuality. The students at this liberal seminary became fixated on the comment. In debriefing with his students, the professor realized his students had trouble hearing anything else the imam had to say. Another professor, a Jewish faculty member at a mainline seminary, told a story about racial issues that were stirred up between black and white students by a difficult passage in the Hebrew Bible while they were discussing Jewish interpretations of the passage. Multifaith education always occurs among embodied teachers and students. There is no approach to cross-faith learning or engagement that can completely ignore issues like race, inequality, sexuality, and gender.

In my own work at Auburn Seminary, we focus our energy and resources on equipping leaders for what we call "faith-rooted social justice work." Because faith traditions almost by definition have particular visions for society, it is not surprising that some of their adherents strive to shape their community and society. These practices can take diverse forms, such as community development (or asset-based development), lobbying at the national level or local/state level, direct service (soup kitchens, shelters, etc.), community organizing, advocacy around issues or particular policies, re-framing of public language and messages, online petitions, street protests and other forms of direct action, movement building work, and more.

The Reverend Alexia Salvatierra, a veteran organizer in faith communities and a Lutheran pastor, coined the phrase "faith-rooted" in 2007 while working with Clergy and Laity United for Economic Justice. She used the phrase to describe a style of organizing and action work that is shaped and guided in every way by faith principles and practices. As she would later write in her book (with Peter Heltzel), *Faith-Rooted Organizing*, "Faith-rooted organizing is based on the belief that many aspects of spirituality, faith traditions, faith practices and faith communities can contribute in unique and powerful ways to the creation of just communities and societies."[1]

While a consensus definition of "faith-rooted social justice work" does not yet exist, the following characteristics are lifted up by champions of the movements:

i.   this is not merely organizing people of faith, rather it is helping people of faith dig into their religious traditions and spiritual practices as foundational to their action and advocacy work;

ii. politicians or other influencers are not targets; they are children of God, and should be treated with love and respect;

iii. the point is less about winning a battle, and more about being in the "right fight";

iv. engagement holds the possibility of transforming people at an intrapersonal level, in terms of their relationships in the community, while simultaneously addressing the social context which is creating them; and

v.   the perspectives of poor and marginalized people should be prioritized for the sake of the common good.

These practices stand on the shoulders of historical faith-rooted activism such as the civil rights movement led by figures such as Martin Luther King Jr., the Central American sanctuary movement in the U.S., and the farm workers movement led by Cesar Chavez, among many other inspiring examples of justice work that communities of faith have led and participated in. Indeed, faith-rooted justice work is not a new practice; it is an ancient one. What is new, however, is: (i) a burgeoning commitment to systematically teasing out and understanding the role faith plays in justice work vis-à-vis secular practices; (ii) new contexts and new tools to engage in faith-rooted justice, such as an increasingly multifaith American society and digital organizing practices; and (iii) a blossoming of formal education programs that strive to equip leaders of faith with specific skills, practices, and knowledge to engage in faith-rooted justice work.

Nonprofit organizations pioneered learning programs in faith-rooted justice work in the 1980s and 1990s. More recently, seminaries across the theological spectrum have begun offering certificate and degree programs with titles like MA in Social Justice, MA in Social Transformation, MA in Theology and Social Justice, and MA in Justice and Mission.[2] This blos-

1. Salvatierra and Heltzel, *Faith-Rooted Organizing*, 9.
2. For a detailed background on the development of these learning programs and

soming of educational opportunities is in part a response to interest and demand from students and from leaders of campaigns who need organizers to mobilize religious communities, and in part a move by struggling seminaries eager to develop new degree programs as the traditional Master of Divinity degree experiences continued enrollment drops.

As more and more faith leaders engage in social justice work through a religious lens, and as more and more educational institutions commit to developing learning programs focused on faith and social justice, important questions arise. What pedagogical wisdom can inspire educators in this growing field? What competencies are relevant for leadership in the field of faith-rooted social justice? How does multifaith justice work influence multifaith education, and how does multifaith education influence faith-rooted justice leadership?

This chapter intends to explore these questions. What follows is a description of the state of multifaith education for social justice as of 2016, an annotated list of leadership qualities for faith-rooted justice leadership in a multifaith context, a description of key tools in the educator's pedagogical toolbox for creating learning environments in this field, and a personal reflection about how engaging in multifaith movements for social justice impacts participants.

THE STATE OF MULTIFAITH EDUCATION FOR SOCIAL JUSTICE

Faith-*rooted* approaches to social justice grew out of faith-*based* approaches. And faith-based approaches grew out of secular social change practices. Faith-rooted social change practices emerged from a deep desire of communities of faith to ground their efforts toward improving the world in the teachings and practices of their respective religious traditions.[3]

There are a variety of sites where adherents or faith leaders engage in significant learning about faith-rooted justice work. These include (a)

---

the institutions behind them, see the report, "Educating Leaders for Faith-Rooted Justice Work" by Justus Baird (New York: Auburn Seminary, 2013) available at auburn-seminary.org/research.

3. "Faith-based approaches" refers to organizing faith communities for social change, i.e., organizing within faith communities, without rooting the technique itself in religious teachings or practice. For background on the historical development of the field of faith-rooted activism, which has roots in the fields of nonviolence and theologies of liberation, see the report "Putting Faith First: Traditions and Innovations in Organizing within Religious Communities" (Los Angeles: University of Southern California, 2012) and the book *Faith-Rooted Organizing*.

congregations with deep experience in justice work that offer an education program, such as Judson Memorial Church in New York City; (b) justice-focused religious nonprofits with an education program, such as Sojourners, Clergy and Laity United for Economic Justice (CLUE-LA) in Los Angeles, and the Religious Action Center in Washington, DC; (c) non-seminary religious leadership training programs with a focus on social justice, such as The Beatitudes Society, JOIN for Justice, and the American Muslim Civic Leadership Institute; and (d) seminaries with justice-focused educational offerings.

Educators from all of these settings envision pedagogies that combine action with reflection, praxis with theory, field experience with theological reflection. A few educational efforts have successfully integrated these two aspects of learning, but most educational programs could strive for a better balance. Even in most religious nonprofits, field experts impart their experience through apprentice-like methods or internships, with limited attention to questions of formation, spiritual practices, or theological reflection. In seminaries, theory and reflection take up much of the learning, with praxis-based learning receiving more limited attention. Educators have yet to share curricula, develop a shared educational vision, articulate competencies, debate best practices, or create standards of excellence. As a result, field practitioners routinely feel as if they have no time for reflection and are disconnected from movement theorists while seminary educators feel cut off from practitioners and rarely take into account learnings from contemporary justice campaigns. Natural allies on both sides of this divide find themselves both romanticizing and undervaluing the other.

Faith-based nonprofits (as opposed to seminaries) pioneered programs to equip religious leaders for social change work. These programs took on the form of year-long internships, short-form trainings, and fellowship programs. Until recently, such programs rarely offered theological reflection or other formation-oriented forms of education. Early pioneers with ten or more years of experience training leaders include Sojourners, CLUE-LA, the Religious Action Center, the Christian Community Development Association, a network of Jewish nonprofits that became Bend the Arc and JOIN for Justice, and the Inner-city Muslim Action Network in Chicago. In addition, community organizing groups working in faith communities, like the PICO National Network and the Gamaliel Foundation, developed not only practices for organizing but also pedagogies for training their organizers.

Seminaries are deeply committed to social justice work in their mission and language, but only a handful of seminaries exhibit a commitment to educating and equipping religious leaders with the necessary capacities or skills to carry out social justice work in congregations or other organizations. A 2007 survey by Steven Newcom (United Theological Seminary of Twin Cities, in New Brighton, MN) of sixty seminary leaders found that, while seminaries were skilled at "talking the talk," they had little to no practical training available for their students in social justice ministry. Change-making techniques, practices for applying religious teachings to contemporary social issues, and even spiritual practices that help sustain justice work were absent from most seminary courses on social justice. More recently, leading seminaries began offering field-based internships and hiring practitioners as adjuncts to address this gap.

In 2005, Charles Foster and his co-authors noted in *Educating Clergy* that "the null curriculum [of seminaries they visited]—what seemed most absent—was some attention to the dimensions of public spiritual leadership, especially those spiritual practices associated with the historical concerns for justice in both Jewish and Christian traditions . . . [I]n our surveys of students, alumni and alumnae, and faculty, only small numbers of present and former students chose 'engagement in social justice and advocacy' as one of their five most formative experiences during seminary from a list of twenty possible choices."[4]

As early as 2005, seminaries began offering new degree programs like the MA in Social Change. Such degrees are now offered by Iliff School of Theology (Denver), Denver Seminary, Starr King School of Ministry (Berkeley), Claremont Lincoln University (Claremont, CA), and the Seminary Consortium for Urban Pastoral Education (SCUPE, in Chicago). Other seminaries offer MA specializations, certificates, and fellowships that equip religious leaders for social change work. Such programs are offered at Wesley Seminary (Washington, DC), United Theological Seminary of the Twin Cities, Chicago Theological Seminary, and St. Paul School of Theology (Oklahoma City). There has been one national effort to encourage seminaries to adopt the specific praxis of congregation-based organizing; the Interreligious Organizing Initiative has a seminary steering committee that strives to introduce congregation-based community organizing into seminary curricula.

One important area that demands additional attention from educators is congregation-based justice work. Anecdotally, we know that many pulpit clergy are at a loss of how to introduce social justice practices to their congregation. Other clergy have tried out one or more methodologies but have not found a sustainable approach for their congregation. Pulpit clergy feel much more confident in their pastoral and preaching skills than in their

4. Foster et al., *Educating Clergy*, 285–6.

social justice leadership skills. Many congregational leaders desire to bring such work to their congregation, but fear the repercussions, e.g., alienating particular congregants. In some cases, the motivation for engaging in justice work may be rooted in a desire to revive a weak congregation. Among pioneers of faith-oriented justice work, controversy exists about the most effective, and most faith-rooted, ways to work in and with congregations. Faith-based organizing groups like PICO, Gamaliel, and the Direct Action and Research Training Center (DART) are generally committed to particular forms of community organizing as the primary tool for pursuing justice. Some models require participation of the entire congregation, some focus on the role of clergy, and other models work with small groups of motivated congregants within a congregation. Congregational leaders rarely have the time, energy, or background to survey a variety of approaches, identify which ones are most likely to succeed in their setting, and try them out.

To improve the field of multifaith education for social justice, educators and institutions could invest in activities such as:

i. Studying and researching the needs of religious leaders with respect to their social justice leadership. What do leaders in the field say they need? What are the outcomes of existing education programs? What assessment tools can help analyze faith-rooted justice leadership?

ii. Exploring models for social justice work in congregations. What can we learn from various faith communities to improve our understanding of how congregational communities can successfully engage issues of social and economic justice? Are certain models more likely to succeed in particular congregational settings?

iii. Convening educators from seminaries and religious justice-oriented nonprofits to strengthen the ties between and among leaders within these two communities.

iv. Piloting education programs for current and emerging faith-rooted justice leaders that marry action and reflection modalities.

DESIRED LEADERSHIP TRAITS
FOR FAITH-ROOTED SOCIAL JUSTICE LEADERSHIP

The faculty team at Auburn Seminary developed a list of leadership traits or criteria that we look for and strive to inculcate in the leaders we equip and support. The list was developed through deep reflection and discussion, not through formal research.

Educators sometimes discuss learning goals in terms of content or competencies. Does faith-rooted justice leadership demand one type of learning over another? Identifying qualities that are important for leadership in this field is one way to explore the question of what type of learning educators should prioritize.

The language used in the list of leadership qualities for faith-rooted justice work is intentionally colloquial. The list strives to articulate what we believe to be important about religious leadership related to multifaith social justice work.

- Content and Credibility. Has a compelling message. Has a personal narrative that fits the work. When you sit with the person, you sense her or his authenticity.

- Constituency. A strong reputation that can serve as a foundation to build upon. Or a growing following to engage. Or an institution/program to leverage that provides a platform to stand on.

- Commitment to the Movement. Committed to public faith-rooted justice work. Whether a solo-artist or multi-talented generalist, she or he wants to be "in the kitchen" of multifaith movements for justice. Plays well with others.

- Ambitious *and* Coachable. Has started down the path to self-awareness in some form or fashion. Has ego strength—a healthy ego. And has sufficient humility to be coachable. Ready and eager to learn in order to better fulfill her or his calling.

- Relevant. Has something that makes you think her or his time has come, and her or his context matters for the movement. Leans in to a multifaith, multicultural America.

- Seeker of Resilience. Sufficiently stable, psychologically and emotionally, to deal with the rough and tumble world of faith-rooted justice work. Not destined to "flameout" after a short and bright episode of leadership. No martyrs. Demonstrates a commitment to wholeness and resilience: curious about practices that sustain self and community for the long haul.

- Faithful Strategist. A faithful and smart strategist: knows when to lead with love, when to pick a fight, and when to duck. A closer. Courageous in the face of conflict, yet gracious is his or her approach toward controversial issues. No "litmus test" on particular issues, but no mean-spirited behavior toward those who see it differently.

- A Little Charisma. That spice that draws you in. A unique soul. May have a "crazy" factor—crazy like a fox.

- Entrepreneurial. Creatively applies the wisdom of tradition to the challenges of today. Sees failure as a great learning tool. Able to lead others through the unknown. Is "religious about the right things"—making an impact, not about tactics or methods.

A PEDAGOGY TOOLBOX
FOR TEACHING MULTIFAITH SOCIAL JUSTICE

Myles Horton, founder of the Highlander Folk School, once said educators "are the expert in *how* they're going to learn, not in *what* they're going to learn."[5] Pedagogies are the tools in the educator's toolbox. The following nine pedagogies are not unique to multifaith education or to social justice leadership learning. However, after years of working with thousands of leaders of faith, from teens and seminarians to elite practitioners, these pedagogies have proved their value again and again in multifaith settings. The art of the educator is in sensing which methods to employ with any particular group of learners in any particular moment.

Applied Theology

What do ancient religious teachings have to say about twenty-first century justice issues? Investigating religious teachings that speak to contemporary issues of social justice is a critical part of faith-rooted justice work. In some cases, religious teachings are a core part of public narratives around a particular issue, such as LGBT equality or climate change. In other cases, religious teachings may seem more tangential, such as those concerning the role of money in the political system. But for all issues of social justice, inviting leaders of faith to ground their attitudes and approaches to individual issues in the teachings of their tradition, and to be guided by those teachings (exegesis rather than eisegesis), is a critical practice of faith-rooted justice work. It is also an important pedagogy of multifaith education, one in which people from different faith backgrounds discover shared values and divergent teachings from multiple traditions on an issue they care about.[6]

---

5. Horton and Freire, *We Make the Road*, 162.

6. For an example, see "Lo$ing Faith in Our Democracy," a multifaith applied theology report that weaves together the voices of theologians from mainline Protestant, Catholic, Evangelical, and Jewish traditions on the role of money in the American

Case Study Methods

Case study learning was pioneered in the early twentieth century at Harvard Business School as a way to train future business leaders for the messy and complex realities of the business world. As Louis Barnes, Roland Christensen, and Abby Hansen wrote:

> A good case is the vehicle by which a chunk of reality is brought into the classroom to be worked over by the class and the instructor. A good case keeps the class discussion grounded upon some of the stubborn facts that must be faced in real life situations. It is the anchor on academic flights of speculation. It is the record of complex situations that must be literally pulled apart and put together again for the expression of attitudes or ways of thinking brought into the classroom.[7]

In a sense, case study methodologies are well known to religious communities. The use of cases in the development of religious law and the use of reality-based narratives as sources of wisdom (such as parables for Christians and *midrash* for Jews) is so common that religious traditions simply would not exist as they do today without the use of case learning methods.

Case study learning methods are attractive to educators engaged in multifaith education or justice education. Cases bring a "third party" into the room that learners can consider, debate with, and point to, without attacking another learner. Cases allow difficult truths and stereotypes to enter the discussion (in the form of behaviors or attributed sayings in the case) without being attached to the educator or learner. Cases invite learners to reflect on whom they are identifying with in a particular narrative and to examine those preferences. Cases focus on particulars, rooted in a community context, and offer the learner concrete examples of practiced faith that instill a sense of how diverse each tradition can be.[8]

Experimental Ritual and Worship

All too often, facilitators of multifaith gatherings (especially justice-oriented gatherings) either ignore ritual and worship or engage in ritual and worship that is boring or mildly offensive. Leaders often start with representational

political system, available at auburnseminary.org.

7 Barnes, Christensen, and Hansen, *Teaching and the Case Method*, 44.

8. The case study initiative at the Pluralism Project at Harvard University maintains an excellent set of cases of leadership through multifaith calamities for use by educators.

approaches in which one person from each tradition represented in the group takes a turn. The "least common denominator" approach of identifying something non-offensive or "universal" from each tradition creates a bland ritual mix that is not spiritually engaging to adherents of particular faith traditions nor to non-adherents, like a potluck to which everyone brought plain rice, pasta, and tortillas.

Instead, educators and leaders are encouraged to experiment with approaches to ritual and worship in multifaith settings. Steps in this process include creating a small working group of leaders who love worship and ritual and have strong working knowledge of the traditions that will be present; challenging them to be playful and experimental; and reminding them that the goal is not to put any tradition on display, but instead to create meaningful and worshipful moments for a diverse group. My colleagues who teach in this area offer best practices such as the following:

- preferring techniques that feature participation over frontal facilitation;

- considering creative language to describe God or the divine;

- standing in the depth of one's particular faith and claiming a practice from that particular tradition;

- making sure the planning team represents key groups that will be present;

- making the experience beautiful (i.e., respecting the space, playing with darkness and light, using poetry, candles, or any objects that creates beauty in the space); and

- creating conditions for vulnerability and intimacy with participants.

One ritual that has worked well with leaders we support has been "the clearing."[9] Modeled metaphorically off of the image of the clearing from Toni Morrison's novel *Beloved*, the "clearing" is a ritual and worship time we use to open and/or close a gathering. Participants are invited to bring an object of significance to them and to tell a very brief story about the object. The objects are placed on a beautifully appointed low table in the center of the circle, and the objects remain on the table during the gathering until the closing session when they are removed. The objects might represent a formative memory from one's faith tradition, the people a leader serves, a struggle one holds close, or even a dream yet to be pursued.

9. This approach was developed by my Auburn Seminary colleague Lisa Anderson.

Faith-Alike Groups

Put learners into faith-alike circles in the midst of a diverse gathering. For instance, in a multifaith setting, this would mean putting Jews into their own group, Catholics into their own group, and Hindus into their own group. In ecumenical settings, this might mean putting conservative evangelicals into a group, Orthodox Christians into a group, and Presbyterians into a group. Whatever the grouping, the purpose is to create a space in which learners who share one aspect of a faith identity have a place to reflect with peers from a similar faith community on their experience in the larger setting. For example, during intense Jewish-Christian dialogue trips for seminarians to Israel and the West Bank, we created regular times for the rabbinic students to caucus and the Protestant seminarians to caucus. These faith-alike moments in multifaith educational settings create critical spaces for learners to feel at home, share language, and perhaps most importantly, remember that there is diversity within their own faith community.

Fieldwork Embedded in a Community

Like pastoral skills, faith-rooted justice skills are best learned through a rhythm of action and reflection (the methodology of Clinical Pastoral Education and many other educational programs). Working with teams of practitioners embedded in living communities, as a faith voice that is part of an effort to pursue justice, is a critical learning method. Many aspects of multifaith engagement in justice work can only be learned in the field.

Leadership Assessments

Many academic and professional assessment tools exist to evaluate leadership capacity or analyze leadership practices. After reviewing many such tools, my colleagues and I felt drawn to a strengths-based approach to leadership learning. We developed our own assessment tool to better understand the leadership potential and needs of the senior leaders that joined our national fellows program. Some sections in the assessment focus on multifaith engagement, including questions like these:

i.   How satisfied are you with the degree of faith-rootedness of your work?

ii. If you could develop a new alliance with one faith leader or institution, who would it be?

iii. Describe the personal relationships you have with members of other faith communities that keep you informed and honest.

iv. To what degree do you intentionally develop relationships with people you disagree with?

v. How effective are you at crossing faith divides within a particular tradition and across traditions?

After asking leaders to complete written responses, we conduct an in-person interview with the leader to explore their responses. Intentional conversations about a faith leader's commitment to and experience with multifaith engagement, in response to questions like these, create a reflective space for both learner and educator.

Peer Consultations

Peer consultations are facilitated moments for learners to share leadership challenges in a small group setting and to receive thoughtful reflection from peers in response. In multifaith settings, peer consultations can ignite deep relational ties as learners realize that their peers from other faith communities have thoughtful guidance to offer. Learners begin to see their peers of other faiths as resources for growth. Expressing vulnerability in safe settings allows relationships to deepen quickly.

Role-Playing and Simulation

Recently I was invited to guest teach at a flagship mainline Protestant seminary about American Jewish attitudes toward the Israeli-Palestinian conflict. Knowing that it was unlikely the seminarians would remember anything I said in a lecture, I used a role-play. With advance warning prior to the class, I invited the students to role-play an interfaith clergy council meeting at which a rabbi had requested that the group endorse a petition against Boycott Divestment Sanctions (BDS). By putting themselves in the heads, hearts, and bodies of a future clergy person wrestling with a real-world problem, these seminarians were able to learn more deeply. At Auburn, the most popular multifaith trainings include media and organizing trainings, both of which feature role-play and simulation as core methodologies. In the media training, learners go on camera to practice their new media skills in front of peers. In the organizing training, learners experiment with new tactics in a simulation game of an actual campaign. These pedagogies, especially in multifaith settings, allow learners to take on new identities and create an atmosphere of playfulness that enhances learning.

Text Study

Text study in a multifaith environment allows learners to share from their own tradition while learning about someone else's. While formal methods like Scriptural Reasoning exist, educators should feel empowered to engage informal methods as well. Text study methods are at their best when they feature small group learning. It is critical to include knowledgeable representatives of the traditions being explored in the planning to help select appropriate texts and inform the planning group about cultural approaches to text learning. For instance, while many people from active Jewish learning backgrounds may be comfortable "digging into" a sacred text, learners from other religious backgrounds may be more reticent to challenge a text or an interpretation of it. Focusing texts on a particular topic invites exploration of shared values and divergent teachings. Asking learners to share how a particular text shapes their attitude toward an issue invites reflective practice. At a multifaith gathering of elite faith-rooted justice leaders, we explored texts from the Jewish and Christian canons about the "breastplate of judgment" (*choshen mishpat*) that the high priest was instructed to wear. After the study, the leaders reflected on what practices and tools they use to stay connected to the divine and to stay grounded in their tradition.

REFLECTIONS ON THE IMPACTS ON PARTICIPANTS IN MULTIFAITH MOVEMENTS FOR SOCIAL JUSTICE

How does active engagement in multifaith movements for social justice impact participants? The following reflections are my own emerging hypotheses of how the faith formation and learning of participants in multifaith movements for social justice are impacted.

Engaging in social justice advocacy and action in a multifaith context compels one to develop an operational theology of difference, consciously or subconsciously. A shared mutual purpose of pursuing some small project that might improve the world—this common mission establishes a foundational connection and pre-supposes an overlapping worldview. Whatever theologies I espouse in my head, I have developed some form of an operational theology of difference when I pursue justice alongside peers of other traditions.

Pursuing social justice across faith lines develops relationships that are likely to lead to behaviors of solidarity, that is, noticing when one faith community is under threat in the public square and offering support or standing up for them in response. A "we-ness" has been created that can lead to a capacity to withstand tension that arises between faith communities and to respond to injury with grace instead of defensiveness.

Working alongside justice-pursuing leaders of other faiths inspires participants to be faithful to their own religious tradition and to root their work in that tradition. When my peer across faith lines explains why she is committed to work on climate change, racial injustice, or poverty, I reflect on why I am called to such work. And I become reflective about what contribution my own faith tradition can offer as we try to shape solutions to the problem. Being called upon as a representative of a particular faith tradition in a multifaith context calls me to wear my faith identity with pride, speak on behalf of my faith tradition with confidence, and imitate the role models in my tradition who have inspired me. I am drawn to learn more about my own tradition when peers ask me about my faith.

Maintaining working relationships with colleagues from multiple faith traditions stimulates the development of language and habits of inclusivity and curiosity. These ongoing relationships threaten majority mindsets and host-guest relationships, replacing them with partnerships. I learn to build spaces that are authentically welcoming, rather than spaces that are dominated by the culture of a particular tradition or ones that feature an eclectic mishmash of ritual *tchotchkes*.

Is wandering into and out of deep relationship with religious others an important part of our faith development? It is possible that certain personalities, or learners at certain phases of faith development, are more drawn to multifaith environments and are able to learn more deeply in the presence of the religious other—and that other personalities, or learners at different stages of faith formation, are able to grow more effectively in a religiously homogenous environment.

There is an "Americanness" to these reflections. My own work has included significant, ongoing experiences in multifaith settings in the regions of Israel/Palestine, Northern Ireland, and Cape Town. The dynamic between faith communities, especially around social justice work, is unique in each of these regions and significantly different than in the United States. At the same time, the ever-increasing globalization of culture of our era means that some narratives (e.g., terrorism, extremism, climate change) are well-understood across regions. And there is hunger in these regions, at least among the communities Auburn Seminary is in relationship with, to learn from the American experience of faith communities coming together on particular issues of justice to heal and repair the world.

CONCLUSION

Social justice work, in various forms of action and advocacy, is an increasingly important setting for multifaith learning and encounter. Equipping leaders for religious leadership in a multifaith world requires educators to consider what content and competencies leaders will need to thrive in pursuing social justice in multifaith contexts. Pedagogies that are used by educators for social justice leadership may be of use to multifaith educators, and practices used by educators in multifaith settings may be valuable to educators focused on equipping leaders for faith-rooted justice work. Educators and institutions in these fields are encouraged to increase the amount of research, collaboration, and shared learning for the benefit of the leaders we serve and the communities we live in.

BIBLIOGRAPHY

Barnes, Louis B., C. Roland Christensen, and Abby J. Hansen. *Teaching and the Case Method: Text, Cases, and Readings.* Boston: Harvard Business School Press, 1994.

Foster, Charles, et al. *Educating Clergy: Teaching Practices and Pastoral Imagination.* San Francisco: Jossey-Bass, 2006.

Horton, Myles, and Paulo Freire. *We Make the Road by Walking: Conversations on Education and Social Change.* Philadelphia: Temple University Press, 1990.

Salvatierra, Alexia, and Peter Heltzel. *Faith-Rooted Organizing: Mobilizing the Church in Service to the World.* Downers Grove, IL: Intervarsity, 2014.

7

Spiritual Formation in a Multifaith World

—Ruben L. F. Habito

That spiritual formation is a vital aspect in the training of pastors/ministers, educators, and other leaders of religious communities is a matter no one will dispute. There are varying formats by which this is undertaken in theological schools and seminaries preparing persons for religious leadership. This chapter will address the question of what a multifaith context can bring to spiritual formation, and what a difference it makes.

The essay begins by asking what "spiritual formation" is about, describing some multifaith perspectives on the question. It then continues with some theological considerations on how Christians may approach and relate to members of other religious traditions constructively and meaningfully from the standpoint of Christian faith, insofar as these have implications for spiritual formation. Next it will describe and suggest pedagogical strategies that may be employed in the classroom or in small group settings that may enhance, deepen, and expand horizons of spiritual formation. I conclude with some caveats, and overall reflections on spiritual formation in a multifaith context.

WHAT IS SPIRITUAL FORMATION?— MULTIFAITH PERSPECTIVES

There is a way of using the term "spiritual" in much of Western culture and Christian discourse that tends to oppose it with "the material" or "physical" or "bodily" aspect of our being. Plato's *Phaedo,* a discourse recounting the death of Socrates and expounding arguments for the immortality of the soul, is a classic document that describes this dualism between soul and body, spiritual and material, rational and sensual aspects of existence. The influence of this way of thinking continues up to our present day.

Although Christian tradition emphasizes the resurrection of the body as a central teaching about human ultimate destiny, the dualistic frame of mind that views the body as a prison of the soul, with the latter being immortal and the former subject to corruption, became a predominant view of the afterlife among Christians.

With this declared opposition between "spirit" (πνευμα) and "flesh" (σαρχ) found in Christian scriptures, "being spiritual" has all too often been associated with an attitude of neglect of, and even disdain for, things of the body. The ideal of a "spiritual person" is thus taken to be one that is disembodied, otherworldly, angelic, concerned with "things that are above," and not with earthly matters.

There is, however, a theme at the heart of the Christian Gospel message itself that cuts through and challenges this attitude of disdain for the bodily, the material aspect of our being. The Good News is precisely that "The Word *was made flesh* (σαρχ εγενετο), and dwelt among us" (John 1:14). In other words, it is this very flesh, this very same mortal, finite, vulnerable body of ours that God has assumed, and has come to inhabit, as God took on the fullness of our humanity in Jesus Christ. In 1 Corinthians 6:19–20, Paul reminds us, "Do you not know that your body (σωμα) is a temple of the Holy Spirit within you, which you have from God, and that you are not your own? For you were bought with a price; therefore glorify God in your body."

Other passages convey an ambivalent attitude toward the body in Christian scriptures. In surveying the various forms of Christian spirituality throughout much of Christian history to the present, the negative attitudes toward the body and materiality have prevailed over the contrasting and yet more important message of Scripture regarding the holiness, the giftedness of this body of ours, the Divine dwelling therein. In recent years the need to reclaim this dimension of the holy in our bodily way of being has come to be repeatedly emphasized by more and more authors writing on Christian life and spirituality.[1]

Is there a way of understanding the term "spiritual" that does not necessarily fall into a dualistic mindset, that is, in opposing the realm of the spiritual with that of the physical or material? There is a multi-volume series on *World Spirituality: An Encyclopedic History of the Religious Quest*, published by Crossroads over many years, which includes titles such as *Hindu Spirituality*, *Buddhist Spirituality*, *Jewish Spirituality*, *Christian Spirituality*, *Islamic Spirituality*, *African Spirituality*, and others. In order to find a way of using and understanding the term "spirituality" that could provide a common ground shared by all the volumes, as well as allow for the particularity and distinctiveness of each of the traditions represented, the editors have offered a working definition for the term in the common preface found in each of the volumes:

> The series focuses on that inner dimension of the person called by certain traditions 'the spirit.' This spiritual core is the deepest center of the person. It is here that the person is open to the transcendent dimension; it is here that the person experiences ultimate reality. This series explores the discovery of this core, the dynamics of its development, and its journey to the ultimate goal. It deals with prayer, spiritual direction, the various maps of the spiritual journey, and the methods of advancement in the spiritual ascent.[2]

This "working definition" calls our attention as we explore the horizons of spiritual formation for theological education in a multifaith context: "the spiritual" is the deepest center of the human being, where we humans are open to the transcendent dimension. How does this play out in particular religions?

In the Hindu tradition, the term used to refer to ultimate reality is *Brahman,* a gender-neuter noun form coming from the Sanskrit verb *brh,* which means "to expand," "to grow bigger and bigger." In its lexical meaning, *Brahman* is therefore "that which keeps on ever expanding" or "that which keeps just getting bigger and bigger"—in short, that which is bigger than anything we can ever conceive of in our minds. This of course resonates deeply with the Christian theological statement about God as "that than which nothing greater can be thought" (Anselm of Canterbury)— *Deus semper maior* ("God is always more [than whatever we humans can

---

1. See Consiglio, *Soul, Spirit and Body;* Fox, *Sins of the Spirit;* Ryan, *Reclaiming the Body;* Paulsell, *Honoring the Body,* among notable examples.

2. Cousins, *World Spirituality,* xii.

imagine!]"). This transcendent reality referred to as *Brahman*, the ground, the source, the sustainer of all that exists, is beyond all description, beyond all humanly attributable qualities (*nirguna*) no matter how sublime, beyond all conceptualization, and yet manifests itself in a variety of forms (*saguna*).

What is important to note is that in this tradition, this ultimate reality referred to in this way is one with *Ātman*, a term used to refer to the innermost core of the human being, the (true) Self (sometimes also translated as "the Soul"). This term *Ātman* is etymologically linked to the term for "breath," and is akin to the German *atmen* ("to breathe") and *Atem* (the breath), as well as the Dutch *ademen* ("to breathe") and the Old English *æthm* ("breath"). The well-known dictum that is said to summarize the core message of the Hindu tradition, called *Sanātana Dharma* (Eternal or Unchanging Truth) by many of its adherents, is the affirmation of the identity of *Ātman* with *Brahman*, as put forth in the formula "*Brahman* is no other than *Ātman*, *Ātman* is no other than *Brahman*." *THAT thou art. I am THAT.*

What this is saying, in effect, is similar to what the working definition of "the spiritual" affirms. That is, the innermost core of the human person, the deepest center of our being, is where we are open to and actually encounter "the transcendent," in the particular way it is articulated in this tradition. "Spiritual formation" in this context then would entail the process by which a person grows in the awareness and knowledge of the transcendent *Brahman* in coming to know one's own *Ātman*. In coming home to the core of one's being, one encounters the Infinite reality manifested therein, such that one's day-to-day life is enlightened and empowered by this living knowledge of the Infinite that permeates every aspect of one's being.

There are three paths in the Hindu tradition by which union with the Infinite is accomplished and brought to fruition. These can be understood as three different approaches to "spiritual formation" in this tradition—the way of ritual action (*karma-mārga*), the way of knowledge (*jñāna-mārga*), and the way of devotion (*bhakti-mārga*). These three modes of spiritual cultivation toward union with the Infinite are carried out with detailed prescriptions in various philosophical/theological schools as well as communities of devotion (centered on one of the divinities in the Hindu pantheon understood to be a particular manifestation or embodiment of the One unchanging *Brahman*).

In the East Asian religious traditions, notably Confucianism and Daoism (and to some extent, in East Asian developments of Buddhist tradition) ultimate reality is often referred to as *Dao* (also transcribed as *Tao*) 道 (*Dōā* in Japanese, *Do* or *To* in Korean), translated as "the Way." The *Dao De Jing* (*Tao Te Ching*), a well-known treatise expounding on this notion of ultimate reality in its relation to the universe, to the natural world, and to human life, opens with the enigmatic statement that "the Way that can be followed is not the Eternal Way, the Name that can be named is not the Eternal Name; (the) Nameless is the origin of Heaven and Earth." There is a double meaning in the key Chinese term that enables the first sentence to be rendered also as "The Way that can be spoken is not the Eternal Way." In short, it is a statement about the transcendent, unknowable, unnamable nature of ultimate reality. Being transcendent, beyond language, beyond our grasp, the Dao also permeates through everything in the existing universe, as the immanent principle of order and harmony in nature and in human society.

Another central concept in East Asian traditions is Qi (also written as Chi) 気, which means "air" or "breath." Qi is the principle that sustains life, and is the power or energy that governs movements, as well as determines health and harmony in living beings. East Asian sages throughout history have developed ways of harnessing, regulating and balancing the power of Qi through martial arts, medicinal practices such as acupuncture, acupressure, and massage, and also psycho-physical exercises as Tai Chi Chuan (太極拳), whereby human beings learn to attune to this power and put themselves in alignment with its movements and directions.

There is an intimate relationship between these notions of Dao and Qi, expounded in various ways by philosophical schools that emerged through the centuries (philosophical Daoism, Neo-Confucian philosophy, etc.). "Spiritual formation" in East Asian traditions thus entails and includes these various practices of aligning oneself with the Way, regulating the flow of Qi, and harnessing its energies toward the maintenance of health and harmony in individual human lives and in society as well.

In looking at the Buddhist traditions, we find a wide variety of developments over its two and a half millennia of history, and thus need to be specific in noting to which form or to which school of Buddhism we are referring.[3] This is not the place to go into detail on this matter, but I will attempt to offer a very rough and admittedly woefully limited summary for our purposes here.

At the foundations of the Buddhist traditions is the awakening experience of the man Gautama, the Buddha (Awakened One), and the way of life and view of the world ushered forth by that experience. This experience is understood as liberating human beings from the suffering and dissatisfactory condition of our finite existence, enabling us to arrive at a place of peace that enables us to overcome the fear of death and the dissatisfaction with the human condition as a whole. It is a place of deep inner peace whereby all

3. See the two volumes on *Buddhist Spirituality* in the Crossroads series, cited above, footnote 2, for particulars.

the delusions and misgivings, all the things that cause suffering and dissatisfaction, have been extinguished and put to rest (a state called *nibbāna*, or *nirvāna* in Sanskrit). The Buddha's followers (*sangha*) through the ages have followed his teachings (*dharma*) seeking this awakening for themselves and for others, and have developed various spiritual practices geared toward the realization of this awakening.

The Buddha's own instruction to those followers who asked him, "Sir, please teach us how to come to awakening also," can be summed up in two words: "Stop, and see!" In Pāli, the language in which the early teachings of the Buddha have been handed down to us, the words are *samatha,* which means "stopping the discursive activities of the mind, and letting it come to rest," and *vipassanā,* which means "seeing clearly into the nature of reality," or "seeing things just as they are, without delusion or obstruction," which brings about genuine wisdom that empowers a life of compassion. We can see these two aspects contained and cultivated in the different forms of meditative practice developed by the various Buddhist schools through the ages.

Buddhist spiritual formation is geared toward a life of awakening, wisdom, and compassion, following in the footsteps of the Buddha. It begins with Right Conduct (*sīla*), which means living responsibly in doing no harm, doing what is good, and purifying one's heart and mind. With this in place, one is thus able to engage in the practice of Concentration (*samādhi*), which corresponds with "calming the mind," and the cultivation of Wisdom (*paññā*), which corresponds with "seeing things as they are," as described above. Keeping the mind from being preoccupied with outward phenomena that come through the senses which cause one to be dispersed in different directions, and instead letting the mind turn inwards to the core of our being, and remain in stillness therein, leads to this experience of awakening. This is an experience whereby one sees into a realm that is beyond words, a realm that is "transcendent," i.e., beyond what is accessible to the six senses, a realm not accessible to the subject-object modality of consciousness, and yet has definite cognitive implications that bear on the world of phenomena. Key Buddhist terms (*nirvāna, śūnyatā, dharmakāya*) used to designate this realm of awakening are thus terms referring to this "transcendent" dimension. In short, here we see the twofold movement of "turn to the innermost core of our being" and "encountering and experiencing the transcendent" as key facets in Buddhist spiritual formation.

In Judaism, one could frame spiritual formation in the context of life lived in fidelity to the Covenant with the Living God, the God of Abraham, Isaac, and Jacob.

> But this is the covenant that I will make with the house of Israel
> after those days, says the Lord: I will put my law within them,
> and I will write it on their hearts; and I will be their God, and
> they shall be my people. (Jer 31:33)

Living this covenant in one's individual life and in the life of the community entails various particular practices involving acknowledgement of the presence of Divine Reality through worship (individual and communal), observance of Shabbat (Day of Rest), and other stipulations pertaining to food, behavior, human relationships, and other aspects of day to day human life, as laid down in the Books of the Torah. Needless to say, varying approaches with regard to particulars involved exist among Jewish followers, based on whether one takes an Orthodox, Conservative, Reformed, Reconstructionist, or other position in the matter.[4]

In Christian tradition, the term "spirit," from which "spiritual" is derived, comes from the Latin *spirare*, which means "to breathe." To "inspire" is thus "to breathe into," to "expire" is to be in a state where the breath has left, and therefore to die. *Spiritus* in Greek is *pneuma* (πνευμα), and in Hebrew *rūah* (רוּח), which in frequent Scriptural usage is associated with "Breath of God." Without going into a detailed analysis and exegesis of the many occurrences of the term, the point here is that "to be spiritual" is to be intimately steeped in the Breath of God, the Holy Spirit.[5] In this context, "spiritual formation" is no other than the process of continued deepening in a life of intimacy with the Spirit of God that works in us, bearing forth its fruits in our lives. "The fruit of the Spirit is love, joy, peace, patience, kindness, generosity, faithfulness" (Gal 5:22).

St. Augustine's dictum that God is "more intimate to me than my innermost, and higher than my uppermost" (*intimior intimo meo et superior summo meo*) (*Confessions* 3.6.11) is at the heart of Christian tradition in locating where to find God in our lives. It is in this "deepest center" of our being (immanent), which is at the same time also "beyond all that we are" (transcendent). This is the Triune God, Creator, Redeemer, and Sanctifier, who draws us closer and closer to intimacy in this Divine trinitarian embrace, vivifying and sustaining us in the Spirit. For Christians then, "spiritual formation" is this process of growing ever more deeply in intimacy with the Triune God, drawn by the Spirit (Breath) of God. We will look at some particular aspects of this in our third section.

---

4. See the two volumes on Jewish spirituality in the Crossroads series, cited above, footnote 2.

5. See Thistleton, *The Holy Spirit in Biblical Teaching*.

At the foundations of Islam is its declaration of faith, the first of its Five Pillars: *There is no God but God (Allah), and Muhammad is his prophet.* The other four pillars then consist in the way of life that is consonant with having made this affirmation of faith in the One God and his prophet Muhammad: prayer, help toward the needy, self-purification through fasting and other disciplines, and pilgrimage (to Mecca, as one is able). Practicing the Five Pillars is the way for human beings to live in total submission to the One God, which is the central teaching of this faith tradition.

Spiritual formation can be described as the strengthening and deepening of one's faith conviction that God alone is Sovereign, Master, and Deity, upon whom one must entrust one's entire life. This entails an attitude of total obedience to God's commands in everything that pertains to human life, desisting from what is prohibited or disapproved, and following what is mandated or prescribed. A person who excels in living a life of total submission to God thus attains a state of holiness and godliness in harmonizing all of one's thoughts, words, and actions with the will of God.[6]

These multifaith perspectives on the terms "spiritual" and "spirituality" provide us with ways of understanding spiritual formation that does not necessarily entail a dualistic mindset opposing the spiritual with the corporeal or material, but take it as a holistic process involving the integral human person, in touch with the core of one's being and in relation to ultimate reality, and in relation to self, society, and the natural world.

THEOLOGICAL CONSIDERATIONS IN APPROACHING RELIGIOUS OTHERS

The very fact that we live in a globalized, multifaith society brings before us key questions that Christians are called to address. How are we to relate to those from other religious traditions from a standpoint of Christian faith? This is the question pursued in an area in systematic theology known as "theology of religions," the endeavor of faith seeking understanding of the Religious Other in our midst. On this theme, voluminous tomes have been written in the last few decades, and this is not the place to offer a summary or even a review of these developments.[7] Providing adequate and effective guidance of students toward framing a viable theological stance that will serve to ground their understanding of Christian life and ministry in the

6. For particulars, see the two volumes on Islamic Spirituality in the Crossroads series, footnote 2.

7. For a treatment of the various approaches in theologies of religions, see Knitter, *Introducing Theologies of Religion.*

light of contemporary realities, especially referring to its multifaith context, is a vital and indispensable component of seminary education whose aim is to form effective religious leaders in today's world.[8] The task is to provide resources for a viable theological framework in situating Religious Others in the context of Christian faith that, at the same time, will motivate both a constructive attitude grounding dialogical engagement toward mutual learning and cooperative efforts with members of other faith traditions.

The Biblical witness presents an ambivalent picture on this matter. Some texts like John 14:6 ("I am the Way, the Truth and the Life. No one comes to the Father except by me") and Acts 4:12 ("Salvation is found in no one else, for there is no other name given under heaven for humankind by which we must be saved") used by many Christians as "proof-texts" to show the exclusivity of Christianity and thus to look at Religious Others from this superior vantage point. On the other hand, passages like John 1:1–9 ("In the beginning was the Word . . . the true Light, which enlightens everyone, was coming into the world") and Acts 17:22–31 ("The God who made the world and everything in it . . . is not far from each one of us . . . we too are his offspring") and many others, convey the message of God's self-revelation to all humanity, and God's will to save all of Creation.[9]

In looking at past Christian history, David Lochhead lists different kinds of attitudes that have marked the way Christians related to Religious Others: isolation, competition, hostility, and partnership.[10] Of these, the author argues, only the last remains a viable one for Christians, and gives theological grounding for his claims. The book's central claim, reflected in the title, is that to be Christian is to be held accountable to how we embody the "dialogical imperative" in our own lives. Lochhead provides solid Scriptural and traditional arguments for his thesis. In short, this dialogical engagement with the Other is the way God has dealt with us, God's own people throughout our collective history, and it is this kind of engagement that we are also called to take vis-à-vis the Other in our midst.

Lochhead takes the theology of his mentor, Karl Barth, as his framework for developing his thesis. As is well-known, Barth makes a distinction between Religion and Revelation, describing the former as the human attempt to reach God, whereas the latter is the initiative by God to reach and communicate with us humans. The latter is a free gift of grace that God continues to give us human beings, whereas the former is a result of sin

8. See Brockman, et.al, *The Gospel among Religions*, for an example of a textbook and reader designed for seminary education.

9. See ibid., 47–53, for a reflective analysis of some of these passages.

10. Lochhead, *The Dialogical Imperative*.

and unbelief, with the repeated attempts by human beings to be "like God" and thereby motivated by human pride (*hubris*). The narrative of the failed Tower of Babel illustrates the outcome of such human attempts, which lead only to idolatry. Barth identifies Revelation with the fullness of the self-revelation of God in Jesus Christ, and as transmitted to the rest of humankind through the Bible. In making this identification, Barth also is making a sharp critique against those who call themselves Christian, but who have identified their Christianity with particular forms in the cultural, social, and political order in ways that are idolatrous. In this he was of course critiquing Christians during the Nazi era who were easily swayed by the powerful social and political waves of the time.

Barth's theological framework has been read by many as providing the basis for an exclusivist stance vis-à-vis Religious Others, a position denying any truth or salvific efficacy in religions other than Christianity. Such a theological position justifies a stance of rejection or condemnation of Religious Others, or at least of regarding them as subjects of renewed Christian evangelical efforts toward conversion and baptism. However, Lochhead, while acknowledging his indebtedness to Barth, takes his mentor's theological framework and refocuses the discourse on Revelation, asking the question: Can there be Revelation also in those traditions other than Christian? Based on Barth's own theological understanding of the sovereignty of God over all creation, who in their right mind can say "No," as if to speak in God's own name? In short, while fully accepting the Christian claim of the definitive and unique nature of God's Self-revelation in Jesus Christ, if we also accept that God *is* God, know our place as humble creatures of a loving God, and grant God the full power and right to be God, then *only* a stance of *openness to the possibility* that throughout human history God may have also Self-revealed to other traditions and to human beings outside the Christian fold would be a viable position to take.

How then do we determine if such a "possibility" has become an actuality? How can we know whether something that we encounter from outside of the Christian fold is in fact from God's own Self-revelation, that is, God's own Word as coming to us from the world that is God's creation? Lochhead proposes a fourfold set of criteria: First, it must cohere with the witness of the Word of God as found in the Bible, not just based on so-called "proof texts," but seen in the entire context of the Scripture as conveying its overall message of the goodness of God and God's love for all of creation. Secondly, it must be seen in continuity with, and not contradictory to, the confessional witness of the Church as the people of God on pilgrimage in history. Thirdly, the Word of God spoken outside of Scripture and the Church must be discerned based on the fruits in the context of which it is spoken: does it bring about the fruits of the Holy Spirit, in "love, joy, peace, patience, kindness, generosity, faithfulness" (Galatians 5:22), rather than their opposite? And fourthly, it must be judged based on its effects on the Christian community, that is, whether or not it enables Christians to be more faithful Christians, celebrating and being grateful for the gifts of the Spirit.[11]

In sum, Lochhead, taking a Barthian theological framework and focusing on the notion of Revelation, is not only clearing the way for an active engagement with Religious Others; he is in fact saying that it is an *imperative* for Christians to do so, if they are to be faithful to the Word of God themselves.

From another direction, the Roman Catholic Church's Second Vatican Council issued a landmark document, *Nostra Aetate*, paving the way for and encouraging Catholic Christians toward active engagement with Religious Others. Referring to religious traditions other than Christian, the following passage indicates *Nostra Aetate*'s overall thrust:

> The Catholic Church rejects nothing that is true and holy in these religions. She regards with sincere reverence those ways of conduct and of life, those precepts and teachings which, though differing in many aspects from the ones she holds and sets forth, nonetheless often reflect a ray of that Truth which enlightens all men [and women]. Indeed, she proclaims, and ever must proclaim Christ 'the way, the truth, and the life' (John 14:6), in whom men [and women] may find the fullness of religious life, in whom God has reconciled all things to [God]self.[12]

The phrasing "rejects nothing that is true and holy" becomes the heuristic principle for Catholics, and all Christians as well, to go out and discover all that is true and holy in other religions as reflecting "a ray of that Truth that enlightens all." This is read as the mandate to engage with Religious Others in order precisely to bring forth what is true and holy that comes from the same God that is revealed to us in Jesus Christ.

Another angle of a constructive approach to Religious Others is suggested by United Methodist Bishop Scott J. Jones in his work *Evangelistic Love of God and Neighbor*. As his title indicates, the author takes the evangelistic love of God and neighbor as the primary mandate of Christians, called to witness and discipleship in Jesus Christ. In this regard, taking Religious Others as neighbors one is called to love in the way that God loves us, that is, unconditionally, entails attitudes of wanting to learn about and understand

11. Lochhead, *Dialogical Imperative*, 38–39.

12. *Nostra Aetate*, No. 4.

and engage them with the open heart of Christ, and avoiding the simplistic attitude of Christian proselytism.[13]

Still another angle for a constructive, fruitful Christian approach that may provide a guideline in avoiding an attitude of superiority, but rather assuming one of humility, is offered by Pentecostalist theologian Amos Yong, many of whose works are devoted to this theme of Christian ways of relating to Religious Others.[14] In his *Beyond the Impasse: Toward a Pneumatological Theology of Religions,* Yong examines the whole arena of Creation and human history as the field of the activity of the Holy Spirit, who was sent by the Father and Creator of all, as a testimony to the Word that came in the fullness of time. Everything that is good and true and holy that is found in Creation and in humanity, including what can be found in religious traditions other than Christian, is thus attributed to this activity of the Divine Spirit working in our midst. Christians are thus called to be open to the various ways this activity is manifested, and thus ever continue to witness to the glory of the Triune God.

Yong also considers the theme of hospitality, emphasizing the Christian mandate to welcome and be hospitable to the stranger, the outsider, and the marginalized among us.[15] In so doing, we are welcoming the Divine Presence in our midst. But he goes a step further with the proposal that, in relating to the Religious Other, Christians take not just the role of the one extending the hospitality, but we also put ourselves in the place of the one receiving the hospitality. In this shift of positions, Christians may be able to encounter God from a position of weakness rather than of worldly power. This shift can have important implications for Christian spiritual formation.

There are many other recent works in theology of religions that can serve as resources for framing a viable, constructive approach in relating to Religious Others, and above I have offered only a sketch of some approaches that can support spiritual formation in a multifaith context.

PEDAGOGICAL STRATEGIES FOR SPIRITUAL FORMATION IN A MULTIFAITH WORLD

Christian spiritual formation, as briefly described above, can be understood as the process whereby we humans grow in loving intimacy with the Triune God, moving us to live our lives as a vehicle of that Divine love toward all

13. Jones, *Evangelical Love of Neighbor,* especially chapter 7, "Evangelizing Persons of Other Religions."

14. Yong, *Hospitality and the Other;* and also Yong, *Beyond the Impasse.*

15. Yong, *Hospitality and the Other.*

those we encounter in our day to day existence. It entails the practice of spiritual disciplines including contemplative prayer, the reading of God's Word reflectively and prayerfully in a way that enables us to experience it directly as addressing us in an intimate and bodily way (Lectio Divina), and other practices such as fasting, keeping Sabbath, hospitality, communal worship, and so on.[16]

What I suggest here is that the practice of these spiritual disciplines is tremendously enhanced and opened to new horizons as they are conducted with intentional reference to and keen awareness of a multifaith context. The theological presupposition underlying this statement is the acceptance of the possibility that the revelatory Word of God may be encountered through the mediation of texts, teachings, rituals, and most importantly, the person of the Religious Other in our midst. In actively testing this possibility, it is important to proceed with an openness of heart, but also with caution, advisedly in community with other spiritual practitioners who will help and support one another along the way in their individual and communal discernment. Contemplative prayer is a spiritual discipline thought for too long a time to be mainly for those called to the monastic life, and thus it has not been part of the offering in mainline Christian practice. More and more people in our contemporary world, including many Christians who seek guidance in leading a deeper spiritual life and are not finding it in their own churches, are turning to Asian, mainly Hindu or Buddhist, forms of meditative practice, led by an inner spiritual thirst. One trend that has been noted is that a good number of Jews and Christians who come to engage in Hindu or Buddhist spiritual practice arrive at a rediscovery and renewed appreciation of the contemplative traditions within their own Jewish or Christian religious heritage.[17] Much more could be said about this theme of enriching Christian contemplative prayer by way of learning from Asian traditions, but here I simply refer the interested reader to explore the numerous books already available on this theme.[18]

For Christians, reading the Bible in the mode of Lectio Divina is a way of listening from the depths of one's being (the "spiritual core") to the

16. For resources that offer very helpful guidelines in various forms of spiritual disciplines for class and educational use, see Thompson, *Soul Feast*, and Bass, ed., *Practicing the Faith*.

17. See Kasimov, Keenan and Keenan, *Beside Still Waters,* for a collection of such accounts by Jews and Christians.

18. Healy, *Entering the Cave of the Heart*; Habito, *Living Zen, Loving God;* Stabile, *Growing in Love and Wisdom*; Habito, *Zen and the Spiritual Exercises*, are among examples that present ways by which Christians may practice and learn from Hindu, Zen Buddhist, and Tibetan Buddhist meditative practices toward enriching their own Christian life and faith, among many other works that can be noted in this regard.

Word of God, in a way that may enable one to embody that Word in one's own life, in all one's thoughts, words and actions, as individuals and in community with other practitioners.[19] How may a Christian approach scriptures of other religious traditions? One may of course read scriptures of different religious traditions, including one's own, for their literary value, their intellectual content, their cultural interest, and so on. However, a proper "religious reading" of scriptural texts, as the spiritual practice of Lectio Divina is a prime example, is qualitatively different from the kind of reading human beings normally do as an intellectual or cultural activity, the kind that Paul J. Griffiths refers to as "consumerist" reading.[20]

Rephrasing the question, then, may a Christian approach a scriptural text of another religious tradition in the manner of Lectio Divina? This is a delicate issue that needs to be examined with care and caution, and one cannot simply presume that every religious text that is declared by their adherents to be so can be taken as "religious reading" by Christians, on par with their reading of the Bible. It may be helpful as preliminary knowledge to learn how devotees of other traditions regard and relate to their own scriptural texts, to appreciate the value of these texts *as religious texts* for others.[21] Approaching these texts with the question of whether these texts may also be a vehicle of encounter with God as revealed in Jesus Christ can then be a starting point for a spiritual adventure. In this regard, I recommend following the lead of others who have made such explorations and shared their discoveries in their published writings. In particular, volumes in the series edited by Catherine Cornille, entitled *Christian Commentaries on Non-Christian Sacred Texts,* offers valuable insights into the *Bhagavad-Gita* and other Hindu religious texts, and Buddhist texts such as the *Dhammapada* and the *Heart Sutra,* among those already published (and more are due to come over the next few years).[22] Yung Suk Kim's guide to reading the *Tao Te Ching (Dao De Jing)* for Christians is also an insightful volume for such possible encounters.[23] Christians reading Jewish Scriptures as Jewish Scriptures, and not as the Christian "Old Testament," is a venture with its own particular challenge,[24] not to mention Christian ventures into reading the Qur'an and other Islamic texts.[25]

19. Hall, *Too Deep for Words,* 36–56.

20. Griffiths, *Religious Reading,* 44–45.

21. Coward, *Experiencing Scripture in World Religions.*

22. Cornille, *Christian Commentaries on Non-Christian Texts* series.

23. Kim, *Why Christians Need to Read the Tao Te Ching.*

24. See Knight and Levine, *The Meaning of the Bible,* as a helpful guide.

25. See Lodahl, *Claiming Abraham.*

Encountering persons of other religions with a spirit of openness and neighborliness has led many Christians to life-transforming experiences. Interreligious friendships that come to mature out of encounters with Religious Others is being noted by more and more voices as a locus for encountering the living God.[26] To help pave the way for such encounters to happen, a helpful pedagogical strategy is to make an approach and engagement with persons of other faith traditions a task or even a requirement for class credit. The assignment is two-faceted: one is a visit to a religious center of another faith tradition, with respectful attendance at the service being conducted; another facet is an in-depth interview with a person from that faith community, asking questions that may hopefully elicit heart-to-heart conversations with the interviewee. Having given such assignments in my own classes for many years now at Perkins School of Theology, Southern Methodist University, a theological school preparing students for Christian ministry, I could write an entire volume on the rich fruits students have received from such encounters as I read their reports (also part of the assignment). Here, given the limited space, I can only give a brief summary and note some of these fruits as they relate to spiritual formation, inviting readers of this essay to venture into such encounters for themselves.

Students who visited a Jewish synagogue and met and interviewed members of the congregation reported an enhanced appreciation of the Sabbath, and resolved to incorporate this practice in their own Christian lives and ministry.[27] Students who visited a mosque and interviewed Muslim devotees during the period of Ramadan were inspired by the earnestness of those who engaged in religious fasting, and were duly moved to engage in it themselves as a way of allowing themselves to experience total dependence on God, and also experience solidarity with countless fellow human beings in our world today who go to be hungry each night. Some of the same students also were invited to an Iftar (evening meal when Muslims end their daily fast during Ramadan), and were moved by the spirit of giving and of service of their hosts. Their encounter with devoted Muslims led to a resolve in them to also observe fasting in a Christian spirit as taught in the Gospels, as well as to strengthen their resolve to be of service to others in a variety of ways in their lives of Christian ministry. A similar strengthening of resolve to be of service to others especially in welcoming the poor and marginal-

26. See Fredericks and Tiemeier, eds., *Interreligious Friendships after Nostra Aetate*; Goshen-Gottstein ed., *Friendship across Religions*, for collections of essays on Interreligious Friendship.

27. For a student essay reporting on her new insights and renewed appreciation of Sabbath from her interfaith encounters, see Green, "Sabbath Rest in Abrahamic Traditions."

ized into their circles, and seeking ways of caring for them as part of their ongoing ministry, was experienced by students who had an opportunity to visit and partake of a meal at a Sikh langar, a kitchen or refectory run by volunteers and serving food for free to all those who come.

In short, these interreligious encounters served to diversify as well as intensify the spiritual formation of the students who engaged in the assignments earnestly, as they found new empowerment and confirmation in their sense of calling to a life of Christian ministry in service of the world.

CONCLUSION

There can be a tendency for those are dissatisfied, and find a lack in what their root religious tradition has to offer, to go about and "shop around" and look for "interesting" spiritual practices here and there from other religious traditions. Sometimes (too many times?) this is done without due regard to the context in which these are practiced in their original traditions, and may result in a hodgepodge of practices that may provide some kind of consumerist gratification for the individual, but does not really lead to genuine spiritual transformation. This is an attitude that can be described as "supermarket spirituality," a kind of spiritual materialism that we need to be cautioned about.[28]

It is perhaps also due to such a tendency in our multifaith global society that many faithful Christians, wary of the charge of "syncretism," remain hesitant or cautious, not to mention disapproving and critical, of an open attitude toward learning from other religious traditions, or incorporating elements from other religious traditions into Christian practice. This calls for a thorough reflection and discussion, which we are not able to engage upon here, except to refer the reader (again) to works that have addressed the issue in thoughtful and eye-opening ways.[29] If we look at the entire course of Christian history, we cannot help but acknowledge the continuing process the Christian community has undergone in interacting with its neighbors, learning from and adapting elements in their culture, belief, and practice, and appropriating these into Christian life and worldview toward the community's own enrichment. Rather than calling this "syncretism," we can understand this as a creative process called "inculturation," the adaptation of the Gospel to the gifts of human culture, considered also as gifts of

28. See Trungpa, *Cutting Through Spiritual Materialism,* for cautions against this attitude.

29. See Schineller, "Inculturation or Syncretism?" and Schreiter, "Defining Syncretism: An Interim Report," for excellent treatments of the matter.

the Holy Spirit to humanity. With due discernment and discretion, spiritual practices found to be wholesome and beneficial that we encounter in our interactions with Religious Others, given due acknowledgement and respect and gratitude to their original holders, can be welcomed and appropriated as enriching and enhancing of Christian life and practice.

BIBLIOGRAPHY

Bass, Dorothy C., ed. *Practicing Our Faith: A Way of Life for Seeking People.* San Francisco: Wiley, 1998.

Brockman, David, and Ruben L. F. Habito, eds. *The Gospel among Religions: Theology, Spirituality, and Ministry in a Multifaith World.* Maryknoll, NY: Orbis, 2010.

Consiglio, Cyprian. *Spirit, Soul, Body: Toward an Integral Christian Spirituality.* Collegeville, MN: Liturgical, 2015.

Cornille, Catherine, ed. *Christian Commentaries on Non-Christian Sacred Texts.* Grand Rapids: Eerdmans, (six volumes) 2007–2012, and more forthcoming.

Coward, Harold, ed. *Experiencing Scripture in World Religions.* 2000. Reprint, Eugene, OR: Wipf & Stock, 2013.

Fox, Matthew. *Sins of the Spirit, Blessings of the Flesh: Transforming Evil in Soul and Society.* Rev. ed. Berkeley: North Atlantic, 2016.

Fredericks, James, and Tracy Tiemeier. *Interreligious Friendships after Nostra Aetate.* Interreligious Studies in Theory and Practice. New York: Palgrave MacMillan, 2015.

Goshen-Gottstein, Alon, ed. *Friendship across Religions: Theological Perspectives on Interreligious Friendships.* Lanham, MD: Lexington, 2015.

Green, Kallie. "Sabbath Rest in Abrahamic Traditions." *Perkins Student Journal 2014–2015* 14 (Fall 2015) 87–98.

Griffiths, Paul J. *Religious Reading: The Place of Reading in the Practice of Religion.* New York: Oxford University Press, 1999.

Habito, Ruben. *Living Zen, Loving God.* Boston: Wisdom, 2004.

————. *Zen and the Spiritual Exercises: Paths of Awakening and Transformation.* Maryknoll, NY: Orbis, 2013.

Hall, Thelma. *Too Deep for Words: Rediscovering Lectio Divina.* Mahwah, NJ: Paulist, 1988.

Healy, Kathleen. *Entering the Cave of the Heart: Eastern Ways of Prayer for Western Christians.* Mahwah, NJ: Paulist, 1986.

Jones, Scott J. *Evangelistic Love of God and Neighbor: A Theology of Witness and Discipleship.* Grand Rapids: Eerdmans, 2003.

Kasimov, Harold, et al. *Beside Still Waters: Jews, Christians, and the Way of the Buddha.* Boston: Wisdom, 2003.

Kim, Yun Suk. *Why Christians Need to Read the Tao Te Ching: A New Translation and Commentary on the Tao Te Ching from a Biblical Scholar's Perspective.* Amazon Digital Services, 2013.

Knight, Douglas A., and Amy-Jill Levine. *The Meaning of the Bible: What the Jewish Scriptures and the Christian Old Testament Can Teach Us.* New York: HarperOne, 2012.

Knitter, Paul F. *Introducing Theologies of Religions*. Maryknoll, NY: Orbis, 2002.

Lochhead, David. *Dialogical Imperative: A Christian Reflection on Interfaith Encounter*. Faith Meets Faith Series. 1988. Reprint, Eugene, OR: Wipf & Stock, 2012.

Lodahl, Michael. *Claiming Abraham: Reading the Bible and the Qur'an Side by Side*. Ada, MI: Brazos, 2010.

Paulsell, Stephanie. *Honoring the Body: Meditations on a Christian Practice*. San Francisco: Jossey-Bass, 2003.

Ryan, Thomas, ed. *Reclaiming the Body in Christian Spirituality*. Mahwah, NJ: Paulist, 2005.

Stabile, Susan. *Growing in Love and Wisdom: Tibetan Buddhist Sources for Christian Meditation*. New York: Oxford University Press, 2012.

Schineller, Peter, SJ. "Inculturation and Syncretism: What Is the Real Issue?" *International Bulletin of Missionary Research* 16 (April 1992) 50–52.

Schreiter, Robert. "Defining Syncretism: An Interim Report." *International Bulletin of Missionary Research* 17 (April 1993) 50–53.

Thistleton, Anthony C. *The Holy Spirit in Biblical Teaching, through Centuries, and Today*. Grand Rapids: Eerdmans, 2013.

Thompson, Marjorie J. *Soul Feast: An Invitation to the Christian Spiritual Life*. Rev. ed. Louisville: Westminster John Knox, 2014.

Trungpa, Chögyam. *Cutting through Spiritual Materialism*. Boston: Shambhala, 2002.

Yong, Amos. *Beyond the Impasse: Toward a Pneumatological Theology of Religions*. 2003. Reprint, Eugene, OR: Wipf & Stock, 2014.

———. *Hospitality and the Other: Pentecost, Christian Practices, and the Neighbor*. Faith Meets Faith Series. Maryknoll, NY: Orbis, 2008.

8

Pastoral and Spiritual Care in Multifaith Contexts

—DANIEL S. SCHIPANI

THE TITLE OF THIS chapter intentionally suggests that pastoral and spiritual care must be viewed as somehow different but closely related. The reason for including both adjectives qualifying *care* lies with a verifiable correlation. It is the correlation between the transition in nomenclature—from "pastoral" to "spiritual" care—increasingly explicit in health care centers and educational programs, and ongoing sociocultural developments in religion and spirituality in late modern societies. Attention to the related processes of deinstitutionalization and pluralization helps us to appreciate the significance of social changes taking place in our times while also illumining the challenges and opportunities of caregiving in multifaith contexts.[1] "Deinstitutionalization" refers to the process in which the traditional religious institutions, especially Christian in identity and nature, lose control over the religious and spiritual dimensions of society and culture. "Pluralization" refers to the increasing diversity of religious and spiritual traditions and perspectives. "Multifaith" is here used descriptively to denote the presence of a plurality of faith traditions (that is, religious and non-religious, such as Humanism) in a given social context; it should not be confused with "interfaith," a term that connotes dynamic interaction between persons of different faith tradition.

---

1. Schipani and Bueckert, *Interfaith Spiritual Care*; and Schipani, *Multifaith Views*.

The content of this chapter stems from my work as a practical theologian engaged in teaching and research, as well as caregiving practice. The first part focuses on a proposed model of the human spirit. It also makes the case for the necessary place and role of an interdisciplinary approach potentially adaptable across faith traditions. The second part presents some guidelines for the holistic formation of interfaith care givers.

AN INTERDISCIPLINARY PERSPECTIVE

A Tridimensional Anthropology

I work with a theological anthropology that has biblical and, especially, Christian (Pauline) grounding.[2] Anthropologically viewed, human beings are embodied, animated, spiritual selves always to be understood contextually (family, community, larger society). A tridimensional anthropology of body, psyche, and spirit can thus be pictured structurally, as in the diagram that follows. The external full line symbolizes the self's bodily separateness; the other two lines represent the close connection of body-psyche (as appreciated from long ago, for instance, in so-called psycho-somatic pathology and medicine), and the inseparable relationship of psyche-spirit.

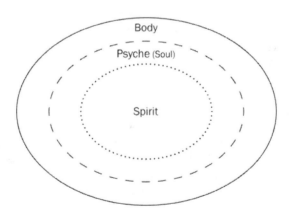

A tridimensional view of the self
(within family, social, global, cosmic contexts)

The *psychological* (dimension of) self and the *spiritual* (dimension of) self are integrated and inseparable yet they are also distinct and distinguishable. At least since Aristotle the three main, interrelated expressions of the

2. Dunn, *The Theology of Paul*, 51–78.

psychological self have been viewed in terms of thinking and knowing (cognition), feeling and relating (affection), and choosing and acting (volition). Contemporary psychology refers to those closely interrelated expressions of the psychological self as cognitive, affective, and active *registers of behavior*. All key psychological constructs—e.g., *intelligence* (whether traditionally viewed, or as emotional, social, or moral intelligence) and *personality*—are usually reflected on, and studied in terms of cognitive, affective, and volitional behaviors. Analogously, in the case of pathologies, mental and emotional disorders can be broadly defined as health conditions characterized by alterations of thinking, mood, or behavior, or some combination among those expressions of the psychological self associated with distress and/or impaired functioning.

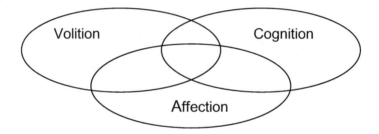

Threefold expression of the psychological self
(within family, social, global, cosmic contexts)

A Model of the Human Spirit and Spirituality

Simply stated, we are humans because we are spiritual beings. The spirit is the essential dimension of being human; hence the Judeo-Christian claim about being created in God's image, according to the words of Genesis 1:26–27. So, in terms of this model, spirituality is understood as how our spirit manifests itself in ways of searching for, experiencing ("inner" sense), and expressing ("outer" manifestations) in three interrelated domains: meaning-truth, (wisdom, faith); relatedness and communion with others, nature, the Divine, oneself; and purpose-life orientation. The claim that these three dimensions of spirituality—meaning, communion, and purpose—name fundamental experiences and expressions of our human spirit is based on consistent and converging confirmation stemming from various sources such as these: my clinical work and supervision, analysis of sacred texts, cultural anthropology, and comparative studies including literature in the fields of pastoral and spiritual care, and spiritual direction in particular. The reference to "searching for" connotes a process of deep longing, that is, a fundamental need as well as potential.

With these notions in mind, it is possible to identify a wide and rich variety of religious and non-religious spiritualities, including diverse streams within a given tradition. For example, in the case of the Christian tradition, a plurality of spiritualities can be identified, such as contemplative, evangelical, charismatic, prophetic, and others.[3] The construct of *spirit* is therefore inseparable from that of *psyche*, so the content of the former's "longing" or "searching for" must be viewed in continuity with ongoing psychological process and content.

It should be clear that this is assumed to be a transcultural model of the human spirit, that is, non-culturally specific in terms of both structure and dynamics. In other words, "transcultural" here means universal. The explicit anthropological claim is that, considered at their (spiritual) core, human beings demonstrate (contextually and particularly, to be sure) the need and potential for meaning, communion, and purpose. At the same time it is imperative to recognize that the human spirit expresses itself uniquely within specific socio-cultural contexts and (religious and nonreligious) faith traditions in particular. Further, we must also keep in mind that the spirit is always in process (as implied with the emphasis on "longing" and "searching for").

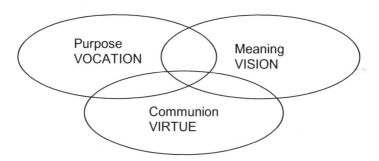

A transcultural model of the human spirit
(within family, social, global, cosmic contexts)

I have proposed that the *spiritual* self can be visualized analogously as having three interrelated expressions that I have chosen to name "Vision," "Virtue," and "Vocation." Thus, the following drawing may be viewed as a functional model of the wholesome human spirit.

3. Foster, *Streams of Living Water*.

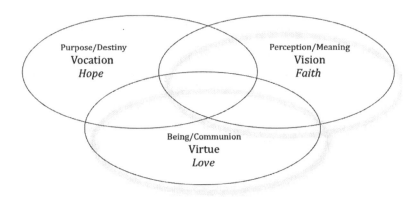

**Threefold expression of the wholesome spiritual self
(within family, social, global, cosmic contexts)**

"Vision" connotes ways of seeing and knowing reality, both self and world. Fundamentally, it names the need and potential for *deep perception* and *meaning*. Growth in Vision necessitates deepening dispositions and behaviors such as heightened awareness, attentiveness, admiration and contemplation, critical thinking, creative imagination, and discernment.

"Virtue" connotes ways of being and loving; fundamentally, it is *being in communion* grounded in love and community. Growth in Virtue may be viewed as requiring a process of formation and transformation shaping one's inmost affections and passions, dispositions and attitudes (i.e., "habits of the heart").

"Vocation" connotes a sense of life's *purpose* and existential orientation and *destiny*. It is about investing one's life, energies, time, and human potential in creative, life-giving, and community-building ways.

In the case of Christian theology this model can be understood in light of Trinitarian anthropological conceptions of the human self developed through the history of Christian thought. Further, from a theological perspective we can also posit a direct connection between these facets of the spiritual self and the gifts of Faith, Love, and Hope. I believe that caregivers from other traditions, including Humanism, can also broadly consider the categories of (religious and nonreligious) faith, love, and hope, as potentially helpful to name three main sets of existential experiences or conditions concerning spirituality and the spiritual self as such.

MENTAL AND SPIRITUAL HEALTH "CONNECTION": INTRA-SELF DYNAMICS

As asserted above, the psychological and spiritual dimensions of the self can be viewed as integrated and inseparable, but they are also distinguishable. The following claims are therefore in order.

The condition of mental health, emotional maturity, and wellness, makes it possible to experience spirituality more freely (for example, less fearfully, compulsively, or obsessively) and to express it verbally and otherwise more authentically than in the case of mental illness. Mental disorders and emotional immaturity always affect the subjective experience as well as the visible expressions of spirituality and spiritual health in some way and degree.[4]

However, mental health and emotional maturity are necessary but not sufficient conditions for spiritual health and maturity. Progress in treatment, or the restoration of mental health, does not automatically enhance people's spirituality and spiritual health; the spiritual self must be engaged intentionally. This claim is analogous to the one applicable to the possible connection between "natural" psycho-social development and spiritual (including moral) development in the course of our life cycle. The fact that psychological development occurs in the natural flow of our life does not ensure that spiritual (and moral) growth will take place as well. Nevertheless, such psychological development has the effect of opening broader and more complicated worlds to us, thus increasing the range and complexity of our spiritual self; hence, the range and complexity of our spirituality (e.g., in terms of deeper awareness of one's existential situation, sense of life orientation, connectedness with others, transcendence, etc.) and ways to nurture it (e.g., contemplation, meditation, prayer, compassionate service, etc.) tend to increase as well. Development can thus bring with it enhanced intentionality in, and responsibility for, both the personal ("inner") experience of spirituality as well as its visible expressions or manifestations.

Toxic spirituality, for instance in the form and content of sternly judgmental religiosity, can seriously undermine mental health. And the healing of the spiritual self—also known as *inner healing*—by the experience of grace and forgiveness, for example, always positively affects the psychological self. Therefore, even though spiritual caregivers are not mental health professionals strictly speaking, their work always engages the psychological self in ways that can contribute significantly to improved mental health and emotional maturity.

4 Pargament, *Spiritually Integrated Psychotherapy*, 179; Scazzero, *Emotionally Healthy Spirituality*.

ON THE UNIQUE CONTRIBUTION OF
PASTORAL AND SPIRITUAL CAREGIVERS

Two special core competencies—bilingual proficiency and a four-dimensional view—can be highlighted, as briefly discussed and illustrated below. The unique contribution of pastoral and spiritual caregivers within any health care team is that they need to view and work with the care receivers holistically while primarily engaging them psychologically as well as spiritually. Therefore, spiritual caregivers must develop the core competency of "bilingual proficiency" in terms of understanding the languages and resources of psychology and spirituality/theology (or non-theological worldviews) and employing such understandings and resources in spiritual assessment and all other verbal and nonverbal (e.g., rituals) caregiving practices.[5]

The pastoral and spiritual caregiver's main function is to connect persons in crisis to their spiritual resources and community. Given the plurality of sociocultural and religious variables at work, caregivers will be normally faced with situations that present either commonality, complementarity, or contrast and even conflict. Dagmar Grefe helpfully discusses this issue with the aid of three concentric circles of interreligious spiritual care. She discusses the following three categories of situations that can be addressed: (1) "common (universal) human experience," in which the caregiver functions primarily as *companion*; (2) "interconnected spiritual practice," in which the caregiver functions as *representative of the sacred*; and (3) "particular religious spiritual practice," in which the caregiver functions primarily as *resource agent* who relates (and often refers) care receivers and their families to their spiritual communities and resources.[6] In all cases, however, competent pastoral and spiritual caregivers will seek to engage in holistic care, as suggested in the following diagram.

5. Hunsinger, *Theology and Pastoral Counseling*.

6. Grefe, *Encounters*, 138–45.

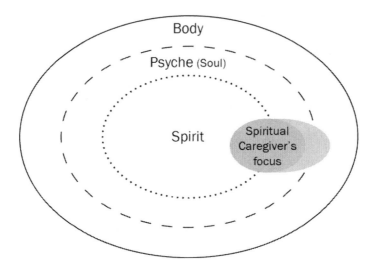

**Pastoral and spiritual care as holistic care
(within family, social, global, cosmic contexts)**

Spiritual care that is intentionally and consistently offered and reflected upon as a spiritual health discipline also calls for a four-dimensional view of reality. Psychotherapeutic and psychiatric approaches normally, however, assume a two-dimensional view involving the self (or selves, in the case of couples, family, or group therapy) and the lived world. The recent and ongoing "recovery" of spirituality in health care and, especially, counseling and psychotherapy includes emphasis on spiritual assessment,[7] engaging clients' spirituality (e.g., beliefs, sources of meaning and hope, etc.) during therapy,[8] and integration of spirituality into the therapeutic process[9] including issues and practices (e.g., meditation, prayer, sacred readings).[10] This is a welcome development. However, much is still missing in terms of clinical research and theoretical reflection, to say nothing of the arena of caregiving practice as such. A large majority of clinicians and theorists simply collapse the spiritual into the psychological and do not recognize the distinct place and function of the spiritual self and its inseparable connection to the psychological self. In any event, the relationship between the psychological and the spiritual self can be further understood in light of James E. Loder's contribution. In his words: "being human entails environment, selfhood, the possibility of

7. Richards and Bergin, *A Spiritual Strategy*, 219–49.

8. Miller, *Integrating Spirituality*; Pargament, *Spiritually Integrated Psychotherapy*.

9. Alten and Leach, *Spirituality*; Griffin and Griffith, *Encountering*; Hartz, *Spirituality*; Huguelet and Koenig, *Religion and Spirituality*.

10. Plante, *Spiritual Practice*.

non-being, and the possibility of new being. All four dimensions are essential, and none of them can be ignored without decisive loss to our understanding of what is essentially human."[11] For Loder, the four dimensions of human existence are the self, the lived world, the Void, and the Holy. The "Void" is the third of the fundamental four dimensions of human existence: human existence is destined to annihilation and the ultimate absence of being. The many faces of the Void include existential loneliness, despair, and death. The "Holy" constitutes the fourth dimension of human existence which has, by the power of the Spirit of God, the capacity to transform the other three dimensions.[12]

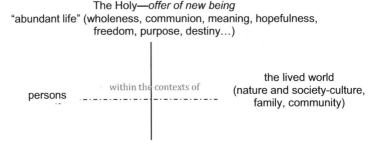

The Holy—*offer of new being*
"abundant life" (wholeness, communion, meaning, hopefulness, freedom, purpose, destiny…)

persons   · within the contexts of   the lived world (nature and society-culture, family, community)

The Void—*threat of non-being*
"languishing life" (emptiness, alienation, meaninglessness, despair, bondage, aimlessness, fate, condemnation…)

The four-dimensional framework of spiritual care

ON SPIRITUAL ASSESSMENT

One way of exploring the question of "healthy" and "toxic" spiritualities consists in studying them with an interdisciplinary approach that includes psychological and theological norms, as suggested in the diagrams that follow. Depending on the epistemological place given to theology in connection with psychology,[13] theological criteria and judgment may determine a priori that some spiritualities can never be "healthy" even if they are psychologically functional (integrating), as in the case of options [2] and [6] in the diagrams below. Conversely, theological norms may determine that certain spiritualities are "healthy" (faithful, from a certain theological

11. Loder, *The Transforming Moment*, 69.

12. Ibid., 80–91.

13. Hunsinger, *Theology and Pastoral Counseling.*

perspective) despite their possibly being psychologically dysfunctional, as in options [3] and [7] in the diagrams. Pastoral and spiritual care providers must always be able to assess spirituality and to help people access their spiritual resources in the direction of healthy integration (for instance, by moving beyond "negative religious coping").

1. Theologically adequate and Psychologically functional (e.g., life-giving, community-building spiritualities . . .)

2. Theologically inadequate and Psychologically functional (e.g., spirituality connected with "Prosperity Gospel")

3. Theologically adequate and Psychologically dysfunctional (e.g., prophetic spirituality confronted as antipatriotic)

4. Theologically inadequate and Psychologically dysfunctional (e.g., spirituality of "People's Temple" that led to mass suicide)

5. Theologically adequate and Psychologically functional (e.g., the [self-limiting] Divine as benevolent, partner in the suffering and in the healing process; God is closely present with compassion, in solidarity.)
   Positive religious coping: emotional-spiritual comfort; strength, peace

6. Theologically inadequate and Psychologically functional (e.g., "[micromanaging] God knows better . . . has a plan for my life . . . is testing me . . . I suffer here but will be compensated in heaven . . . I've been chosen for this test")
   Positive religious coping: meaning and purpose clarified; "blessings in disguise"

7. Theologically adequate and Psychologically dysfunctional (e.g., "God is just and wise, and has made us free. . . we face the consequences of that freedom [accident, illness]")
   Negative religious coping: increased sense of vulnerability, weakness; diminished hope

8. Theologically inadequate and Psychologically dysfunctional (e.g., "[micromanaging] God is punishing me. . . has abandoned me. . . I'm not worthy of God's love")
   Negative religious coping: increase angst, guilt, isolation, despair

INTERDISCIPLINARY UNDERSTANDING OF A SPIRITUAL CARE (OR "PASTORAL") PRACTICE

We can apply the same kind of analysis to our spiritual care (or "pastoral") practices. Let's consider, for instance, the case of praying during a hospital visit, and let us assume that the prayer was either requested by the patient or gladly welcomed when offered by the spiritual care provider. Of course, there are many different ways of praying wisely for a care receiver in a health care center. We might simply say that, in all instances, such prayer should be a source of blessing; it must communicate a deep spiritual-theological truth (e.g., the sustaining presence of Grace, however understood or defined, in all circumstances). At the same time, such prayer must be mentally and emotionally helpful (e.g., by fostering trust and hope in the face of anxiety and fear, by including the health care team and the family, etc.). Regretfully, there are also harmful ways of praying for those hospitalized, as suggested below with some simple examples in the chart with psychological and theological norms and criteria (cases # 2, 3, 4):

1. Theologically adequate and Psychologically functional
   (e.g., prayer that elicits sense of Grace, and activates emotional and spiritual resources of patient and family)

2. Theologically inadequate and Psychologically functional
   (e.g., prayer that momentarily alleviates anxiety and fear by persuading that quick healing is available)

3. Theologically adequate and Psychologically dysfunctional
   (e.g., prayer that focuses on human fragility or vulnerability, while failing to alleviate present anxiety)

4. Theologically inadequate and Psychologically dysfunctional
   (e.g., prayer that associates the medical condition with God's judgment and condemnation)

HOLISTIC FORMATION OF INTERFAITH CAREGIVERS

Competencies for Wise Interfaith Spiritual Care

The following paragraphs present a picture of excellence or *professional wisdom*. Wisdom in interfaith care involves not only what we know but also who we are and what we do. In other words, professional wisdom for quality interfaith care may be viewed as the integration of three interconnected domains: *knowing, being,* and *doing* as represented in the diagram below.

This is the case concerning both the clinical (i.e., attitudes, knowledge, and skills that define expertise) as well as ministerial (i.e., vocational identity, philosophy of care, and consistent practice) dimensions connoted in the adjective "professional."

We can draw a portrait by focusing on a number of core competencies within each of these domains. The resulting profile of wise spiritual care consists of three sets of core *competencies* which we can identify in the course of our spiritual care practice in teaching and supervision, in specialized research, and in extensive consultations and collaboration.

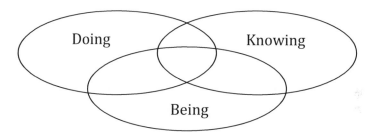

Three domains of core competencies

Three Domains of Core Competencies

Competencies are dispositions and capacities necessary to care well in interfaith situations. Core competencies correlate with professional standards normally articulated by organizations such as the Association for Clinical Pastoral Education, the Canadian Association for Spiritual Care, and the Association of Professional Chaplains. Governmental and faith-based organizations such as the National Association of Catholic Chaplains and the National Association of Jewish Chaplains also identify normative professional standards of certification and practice for their members.

Standards embody key values and vocational commitments; they also prescribe certain legally binding professional and ethical requirements for effective caregiving. In sum, competencies are personal and professional qualities or assets with which caregivers meet the standards of practice in a wide variety of caregiving settings. Before proceeding with a characterization of core competencies it will be useful to keep in mind some normative guidelines that support the view of necessary competencies for wise spiritual care.

Normative Guidelines

The following normative guidelines serve as a rationale for the way we identify, seek to embody, discuss, teach, and assess core competencies in spiritual care. Focusing on core competencies is not only a matter of *how* (i.e., functionality, how they "work" in actual caregiving practice) and *for what* (purpose, outcomes envisioned), but also a question of *why* (foundation, their reason for being). A threefold response to the *why* question follows.

First, core competencies are not only desirable *clinical-professional* features of excellence in spiritual care but also indicators of *personal, interpersonal, and institutional integrity*. Spiritual care is inherently partial (i.e., non-neutral) *in favor of* wellness; quality of life; meaningful suffering, healing, and dying; and compassion and justice, among other fundamental values. Spiritual care rightly viewed is also *against* meaningless and unnecessary suffering and dying, hopelessness, neglect, discrimination, and injustice. To be consistent with that realization calls for grounding core competencies explicitly in an *ethic of care*. Therefore, becoming holistically competent is a moral imperative first and foremost. In fact, it can be persuasively argued that the absence of such explicit ethical grounding and vocational commitment fosters a view of competence and competencies as merely a question of appropriate technique.

Second, *spiritual* care focuses primarily, although by no means exclusively, on *spirituality* and *spiritual experience*. For that reason I propose that it is necessary to work with an inclusive understanding of the *human spirit* that is not collapsed into either our psychological views of "mind" or our theologically specific conceptualizations about "spirit." Ironically, in spite of so much discussion about replacing "pastoral" with "spiritual," a systematic reflection on the human spirit is hard to find in the spiritual care literature! I have proposed that one way to conceptualize *human spirit* inclusively (that is, with language not primarily reflective of a given religious tradition or theological orientation) is to view it functionally as interrelated dimensions—*Vision, Virtue,* and *Vocation*—within a web or system. The practice of spiritual care always includes the possibility of visualizing how the relationship of caregiver-care receiver might contribute to the latter's ongoing process of human emergence, that is, personal growth understood as life-long "humanization," or becoming "more human," viewed contextually in the care receivers' terms. It follows that desired outcomes of a counseling session or a spiritual caregiver's visit, for instance, will include not only objectives such as neutralizing anxiety and evoking hope, but also supporting and resourcing the larger process of formation and transformation of the care receiver's *person as embodied psychological and spiritual self.* And that must be the case whether the care receiver contemplates emotional or physical recovery, or faces sickness and an uncertain diagnosis or treatment, or even death.

Third, as implied in the two previous paragraphs, core competencies should reflect the inherent normativeness of spiritual care and the need to focus on spirituality and the human spirit. Accordingly, we can then articulate guidelines that call for *good, true,* and *right* qualities that define wise or competent spiritual care. By using the Greek prefix "ortho," we might say that competencies must be identified in terms of the following: (a) *orthopathy* or *orthokardia* ("good heart": attitudes towards self and others, character strengths, etc., that make being genuinely present to care receivers and others, possible); (b) *orthodoxy* (true beliefs and knowledge, duly contextualized, that foster understanding); and (c) *orthopraxis* (right action for effective strategy, performance, and assessment of spiritual care as the art of companioning). This is precisely the reason for adopting the categories of *being, knowing,* and *doing,* in our work and reflection on core competencies in spiritual care.[14]

A PROFILE OF CORE COMPETENCIES
FOR WISE SPIRITUAL CARE

A number of practitioners and researchers in the wider field of care and counseling have also presented three sets of core competencies. This is the case, for example, with the well known contribution of Derald Wing Sue and David Sue concerning multicultural competence in counseling practice. These authors discuss fourteen competencies under the three categories of *awareness* (e.g., being aware of, and sensitive to one's own cultural heritage and to valuing and respecting differences); *knowledge* (e.g., becoming knowledgeable and informed on a number of culturally diverse groups, especially groups with which therapists work); and *skills* (e.g., being able to generate a wide variety of verbal and nonverbal helping responses).[15] Other writers have integrated the contribution of Sue and Sue and others in their own threefold characterization in terms of (a) caregivers' awareness of their own values and biases, (b) understanding of the clients' worldview, and (c) developing culturally appropriate intervention strategies and techniques. Government organizations also usually present a tripartite view of core competencies within categories such as knowledge, skills, and attitudes necessary for the practice of health care.

14. Schipani, *Multifaith Views,* 167–75.

15. Sue and Sue, *Counseling the Culturally Diverse,* 54–69.

Those considerations are very useful and, in principle, transferable with regard to interfaith caregiving. At the same time, we can see that the larger categories of *being, knowing,* and *doing,* help us to present a more complete view of professional wisdom. That is especially the case regarding the "being" dimension, because in it we can include competencies definable in terms of virtues (viewed as values embodied in the moral character of the caregiver) and faith development broadly viewed, which are not usually explicitly considered in current discussions and writings in the field. The following profile, which includes competencies highlighted by the contributors to this book, is comprehensive but certainly not assumed to be complete; it is meant as an ongoing collaborative work of reflection.

Competencies of Knowing (Understanding)

In order to grow in pastoral wisdom, spiritual caregivers participate in what we might call "circles of learning" that include four dimensions: 1) actual experience of being cared for and caring for others (learning by "feeling"); 2) observation and reflection on care provided by others (learning by actively "seeing" and "hearing"); 3) systematic analysis of those practices of care (learning by "thinking"); and, 4) active experimentation with new ways of caring well for others (learning by "doing"). The more intentionally and consistently we participate in the four dimensions of the "circle," the more likely that our knowledge about interfaith care will increase. Supervision, seminars, and consultation groups can be fertile settings for developing knowledge and understanding related to spiritual care in interfaith situations. A sample of indicators of professional wisdom directly connected with this domain (*knowing*) include:

- A philosophy of spiritual care, including a view of human wholeness, truth, the good life, and excellence in professional work (as seen especially in an ethic of care), grounded in one's faith tradition

- Theoretical integration of spirituality, behavioral and social science, and philosophical and theological perspectives that include a four-dimensional view of reality and knowing

- Understanding of the complexities, dynamics, and richness of interfaith situations, with appreciation for human and spiritual commonalities and due consideration to gender, culture, religious, family, and social and political contexts; *worldviewing* competence (with its hermeneutic, heuristic, and self-reflective dimensions)

- Philosophical and theological assessment that includes revisiting the validity of certain absolute, normative doctrinal claims; selective re-appropriation of theological and religious convictions; rediscovery of the simplicity and beauty of core spiritual clues for interfaith care, etc.

- Linguistic-conceptual and "multilingual" competency (knowing a variety of psychological, theological, and spiritual languages) born out of theological and human science perspectives and resources

- Clinical ways of knowing, such as interpretive frameworks (psychodynamic, systemic, etc.), that enhance understanding, communication, and ministerial practice of spiritual care.

Such comprehensive ways of *knowing* must always be closely related to the *being* and *doing* dimensions of professional wisdom, as briefly considered below.

Competencies of Being (Presence)

Professional wisdom is also a matter of "being" as well as "being with" that defines *presence*. Caregiving in interfaith situations involves special sensitivity and self-awareness regarding what one feels and experiences in the relationship. It also involves the sense that one represents not only a religious tradition and community but also, somehow, healing Grace. We deem such embodiment essential to remind care receivers that a caring Presence is available. Therefore, a sense of personal and professional (ministerial) identity is an essential component of being and presence. It is indispensable to engage the care receiver in a relationship characterized first of all by respectful attending and listening. Such a relationship allows the spiritual caregiver to be a witness, not primarily to "tell" care receivers how to cope with or fix their situation, but rather to "admire," to behold with love and hope the mystery that is the stranger. Among the traits related to the *being* dimension of professional wisdom, we find the following to be essential:

- Self-awareness, and other indicators of emotional and social intelligence, including acknowledgment of strengths and limitations; movement beyond preoccupation with one's "ministerial-therapeutic" self (while maintaining clarity regarding identity as spiritual caregiver); recognition of ways in which one's ministerial self influences the interfaith encounter; and *quietude*

- Moral character that integrates a plurality of attitudes and virtues such as a capacity for wonder and respect in the face of the stranger;

sensitivity and receptivity; courage to risk and to be surprised; freedom to be vulnerable and open to learning and growth; a disposition to recognize, accept, and honor those deemed to be different; hospitality grounded in compassion, humility, patience, and generosity; passion to care and creative energy to transform the inherent violence of separation, prejudice, and alienation into a way of being with (empathy) and for (sympathy) the other as neighbor and partner in care and healing; and living out the "seven sacred teachings" (love, respect, courage, humility, truth, honesty, wisdom)

- Spirituality defined in part in terms of a mature or "conjunctive faith" that informs ministry style[16] and denotes a desirable level of faith development: an ability to embrace ambiguity and paradox; a sense of truth that is multiform and complex; post-critical receptivity ("second naiveté") and readiness to participate in the reality expressed in symbols, myths, and rituals of one's own tradition; genuine and disciplined openness to the truths of communities and traditions other than one's own (not to be equated with relativism); and movement from the prevalence of certainty to the centrality of trust

- A sense of personal and spiritual wellbeing, integrity, and growth. (While being aware of their own woundedness, wise spiritual caregivers normally experience holistic wellness of body, soul, and spirit and an existentially fruitful and fulfilling life journey)

- A connection or a sense of partnership with a transcendent Source of wisdom and grace; dedication to one's own awakening; and appropriate devotion to one's mentors, or guru.

Competencies of Doing (companioning)

Accompaniment and *guidance* are words that name well what we actually do in spiritual care. On the one hand, spiritual caregivers are responsible for attending to and guiding the actual caregiving process as such. Guidance is a form of leading that includes, for example, setting appropriate boundaries of time, space, and contact, and remaining fully aware of what is going on in the caregiving process. Guidance may include gently probing questions, encouragement and support, instructing, confronting, and mediating. On the other hand, except in emergency or crisis situations, spiritual caregivers will not be directive and try to resolve the problems and struggles faced by

16. Fowler, *Stages of Faith*, 184 –98; *Faith Development*, 71–74, 92–98.

care receivers. Rather, especially in interfaith situations, wise caregivers will help patients and others use the specific spiritual resources that have been part of their lives or that may now be available for them.

In short, accompaniment and guidance will optimally be a practice of wisdom—knowing how to relate and act in order to care well in interfaith situations. There is actually an interesting etymological connection between *wisdom* and *guidance*. In English, the words *wisdom* and *wise* derive from the Indo-European root *weid-*, which means *to see* or *to know.* They are related to the Greek *eidos* (idea, form, seeing), to the Latin *videre* (to see), and to the modern German *wissen* (to know). The word *guide* comes from an ancient Romanic word, *widare*, which means to know. The words *wise, wisdom, wit,* and *guide* all share the same origin. Therefore, among other competencies and skills, effective caregivers will be able to:

- Relate to care-seekers, their relatives, and colleagues in ways that engage their spirituality and facilitate spiritual assessment, including the skill to articulate desired outcomes of spiritual care

- Empower care receivers by reflecting together on the power imbalance inherent in the therapeutic relationship

- Internally monitor ongoing caregiving practice so as to remain care receiver-centered, avoiding cultural and spiritual invasion or intrusiveness, and open to receiving manifold gifts from care receivers even while caring well for them

- Actively listen and discern the appropriateness and timeliness of specific caregiving gestures, use of language, and action. Fittingly provide opportune responses in a variety of caregiving modes (e.g., probing, supporting, encouraging, comforting, guiding, confronting, mediating, reconciling, evoking, advocating; praying, blessing, anointing and others)

- Reflect pastorally-theologically on ministerial practice on an ongoing basis and continually develop a practical theology of interfaith care, including assessment, consultation, and collaboration

- Actively emulate or partner with a transcendent Source of Wisdom and Grace or the Spirit of God while anticipating and participating in caregiving ministry (e.g., by privately praying for oneself and for care seekers, engaging in contemplation and meditation, and other spiritual disciplines)

- Maintain patterned practices of self-care with adequate attention to physical, emotional, and relational needs, and to spiritual nourishment;

consistently participate in a community that offers psycho-social and spiritual nurture, support, and accountability.

Finally, we must also keep in mind two additional key guidelines regarding core competencies. They have to do with timing and level of proficiency. First, concerning timing, some competencies relate especially, although not exclusively, to what is expected to happen before, during, or after actual spiritual caregiving practice. Second, in order to teach, practice, and assess core competencies, it is possible and, indeed, necessary to identify increasing levels of proficiency and guideposts to mark professional growth.

HOLISTIC PROFESSIONAL FORMATION

It has become more and more apparent that the education of interfaith spiritual caregivers in professional wisdom requires that theological education and clinical and ministerial formation be holistic and comprehensive. For example, as articulated in the standards of the Association of Theological Schools in the United States and Canada, such formation must include three equally important and interrelated aspects: academic, personal-spiritual, and professional. Further, such education must include specific pedagogies of interpretation and contextualization, formation and performance.

The *academic* formation of interfaith caregivers is indispensable because, among other things, it includes learning about one's own (religious or nonreligious) faith tradition or heritage, and as much as possible about other traditions. Philosophies, theoretical frameworks, and other resources stemming from the human sciences are also indispensable. Academic formation further includes learning about the social, cultural, and institutional contexts of caregiving work. Therefore, this dimension of education and ministerial formation must focus primarily, although by no means exclusively, on learning and developing competencies of *knowing* for wise caregiving as highlighted above.

Personal-spiritual formation focuses on the identity and integrity of interfaith spiritual caregivers, especially but not exclusively, as representatives of a given tradition. Personal-spiritual formation primarily involves attending to oneself as a human and spiritual being and nurturing one's moral character and particularly one's vocation. Hence, this dimension of education and ministerial formation is concerned primarily with fostering and nurturing the competencies of *being* for wise ministry practice. Indeed, those competencies will directly inform the content of specific curricular learning goals towards personal-spiritual formation.

The *vocational-professional* formation of wise spiritual caregivers centers on the development of clinical and other habits, skills, methods, and approaches necessary for caring effectively and faithfully. Therefore, the third aspect of theological education and ministerial formation of interfaith spiritual caregivers must focus primarily on the development and practice of competencies of performance—i.e., the *doing* dimension of the profile— as the main curricular goal.

COMPLEMENTARY PEDAGOGIES

These three resulting sets of goals of theological education and ministerial formation must be duly integrated and approached through appropriate, mutually complementary pedagogies. Recent reflection on pedagogies for educating clergy can be helpfully applied to the formation of wise spiritual caregivers as described below.[17]

Pedagogies of interpretation focus the attention of caregivers as interpreters on their interaction with their tradition and with other sources of knowledge, particularly their relationship with care seekers. These pedagogies cultivate the abilities to adequately "read" and analyze human situations, and to think and reflect critically and creatively. They are aimed at expanding and deepening *understanding* through interpretive practice. Pedagogies of contextualization are closely related, as they seek to develop a spiritual caregiver's consciousness of context, the ability to participate constructively in the encounter of diverse contexts, and the ability to engage in the transformation of contexts. From the students´ perspective, academic formation that is primarily fostered by pedagogies of interpretation and contextualization—including supervision in clinical education and advanced training in spiritual care—constitutes the curricular realm of "theory," theoretical learning, and knowing. It should be noted that I am intentionally using three categories—theory, experience, and practice—as fittingly holding the dimensions of theoretical, experiential, and practical wisdom normally described as complementary ways of learning and knowing in educational theory.

Pedagogies of formation aim at fostering personal integrity and professional identity. Specific strategies that contribute to the formation of ministering caregivers, especially those representing certain religious traditions, may include: awakening students to the presence of God; practicing

17. Foster et al., *Educating Clergy*, 67–186.

holiness, i.e., nurturing dispositions and habits that embody religious commitments integral to the identity of ministering persons; and practicing spiritual leadership whose very *presence* communicates Grace and Wisdom. Therefore, students' personal-spiritual formation will be supported primarily with pedagogies of formation within the curricular realm of "experience" and experiential learning and knowing in particular.

Finally, *pedagogies of performance* focus on the interaction of academic and religious expectations for effective leadership in ministerial practice. They seek to prepare caregivers to be proficient in meeting a wide variety of expectations for excellence in interfaith care in multifaith settings. In sum, they are learning strategies aimed at equipping caregivers for the ministerial art of *companioning*. Vocational-professional formation sustained with pedagogies of performance will therefore pertain in the curricular realm of "practice," practical learning, and knowing.

CONCLUSION

Pastoral and spiritual care fundamentally consists in connecting persons in crisis with their internal and external spiritual resources. Caregiving thus helps those who receive care to actualize and mobilize their potential to cope, heal, and even flourish.

In the face of increased deinstitutionalization and pluralization, as mentioned at the beginning of this chapter, there is a felt need for designing new training programs. They must aim at educating professional spiritual caregivers working in (late) modern and increasingly secular and multifaith social contexts. It is also a priority to care well for those persons who represent particular religious traditions. It is possible to witness a twofold movement in that direction, particularly in Europe, Canada, and the United States. On the one hand, in addition to programs associated with the Christian faith we now find others connected with different religious traditions, such as Jewish,[18] Islamic,[19] and Buddhist.[20] They can prepare caregivers primarily, although not exclusively, for intra-faith spiritual care. In many instances, those programs also seek to equip students for interfaith work carried out from the perspective of the tradition. On the other hand, new initiatives are also emerging, especially in university settings, which focus primarily on interfaith care; they can also offer the option for students to further their training within their own faith tradition, if any, including Hu-

18. Friedman, *Jewish Pastoral Care*.

19. Ahmed and Amer, *Counseling Muslims*.

20. Giles and Miller, *The Arts of Contemplative Care*.

manism. Given the need for balancing and mutually enriching intrafaith and interfaith care in the years ahead, it is expected that spiritual care as a discipline will be significantly enhanced as well.

BIBLIOGRAPHY

Alten, Jamie D., and Mark M. Leach, eds. *Spirituality and the Therapeutic Process: A Comprehensive Resource from Intake to Termination*. Washington, DC: American Psychological Association, 2009.

Benner, David G. *Soulful Spirituality: Becoming Fully Alive and Deeply Human*. Grand Rapids: Brazos, 2011.

Cobb, Mark, et al., eds. *Oxford Textbook of Spirituality in Healthcare*. New York: Oxford University Press, 2012.

Dunn, James D.G. *The Theology of Paul the Apostle*. Grand Rapids: Eerdmans, 1998.

Fitchett, George. *Assessing Spiritual Needs: A Guide for Caregivers,* Rev. ed. Lima: Academic Renewal, 2002.

Foster, Charles, et al.*Educating Clergy: Teaching Practices and Pastoral Imagination*. San Francisco: Jossey-Bass, 2006.

Foster, Richard J. *Streams of Living Water: Essential Practices from the Six Great Traditions of Christian Faith*. San Francisco: Harper & Row, 1998.

Fowler, James W. *Faith Development and Pastoral Care*. Philadelphia: Fortress, 1987.

———. *Stages of Faith: The Psychology of Human Development and the Quest for Meaning*. San Francisco: Harper & Row, 1981.

Friedman, Dayle A., ed. *Jewish Pastoral Care: A Practical Handbook from Traditional and Contemporary Sources*. 2nd ed. Woodstock, VT: Jewish Lights, 2005.

Giles, Cheryl A., and Willa B. Miller, eds. *The Arts of Contemplative Care: Pioneering Voices in Buddhist Chaplaincy and Pastoral Work*. Sommerville, MA: Wisdom, 2012.

Grefe, Dagmar. *Encounters for Change: Interreligious Cooperation in the Care of Individuals and Communities*. Eugene, OR: Wipf & Stock, 2011.

Griffin, James L. *Religion that Heals, Religion that Harms: A Guide for Clinical Practice*. New York: Guilford, 2010.

Griffin, James L. and Melissa Elliott Griffith. *Encountering the Sacred in Psychotherapy: How to Talk with People about their Spiritual Lives*. New York: Guilford, 2002.

Gritch, Eric W. *Toxic Spirituality: Four Enduring Temptations of Christian Faith,* Minneapolis: Fortress, 2009.

Hartz, Gary W. *Spirituality and Mental Health: Clinical Applications*. New York: Routledge, 2005.

Hodge, David R. *Spiritual Assessment in Social Work and Mental Health Practice*. New York: Columbia University Press, 2015.

Hunsinger, Deborah van Deusen. *Theology and Pastoral Counseling: A New Interdisciplinary Approach*. Grand Rapids, MI: Eerdmans, 1995.

Hodge, David R. "Assessing Spirituality and Religion in the Context of Counseling and Psychotherapy." In *APA Handbook of Psychology, Religion, and Spirituality.* Vol. 2, *An Applied Psychology of Religion and Spirituality,* edited by Kenneth I. Pargament et al., 93–123. Washington, DC: American Psychological Association, 2013.

Huguelet, Philippe and Harold G. Koenig, eds. *Religion and Spirituality in Psychiatry.* Cambridge: Cambridge University Press, 2009.

Koenig, Harold G. et al. *Handbook of Religion and Health.* 2nd ed. New York: Oxford University Press, 2012.

Loder, James E. *The Transforming Moment.* 2nd ed. Colorado Springs: Helmers & Howard, 1989.

Mabry, John R. *Noticing the Divine: An Introduction to Interfaith Spiritual Guidance.* New York: Morehouse, 2006.

———. *Spiritual Guidance across Religions: A Sourcebook for Spiritual Directors & Other Professionals Providing Counsel to People of Different Faith Traditions.* Woodstock, VT: Skylight Paths, 2014.

Norberg, Tilda. *Consenting to Grace: An Introduction to Gestalt Pastoral Care.* Staten Island, NY: Penn House, 2006.

Pargament, Kenneth I. *Spiritually Integrated Psychotherapy: Understanding and Addressing the Sacred.* New York: Guilford, 2007.

Pargament, Kenneth I., et al. *APA Handbook of Psychology, Religion, and Spirituality.* Vol. 1, *Context, Theory, and Research.* Vol. 2, *An Applied Psychology of Religion and Spirituality.* Washington, DC: American Psychological Association, 2013.

Plante, Thomas G. *Spiritual Practice in Psychotherapy: Thirteen Tools for Enhancing Psychological Health.* Washington, DC: American Psychological Association, 2009.

Richards, P. Scott, and Allen E. Bergin. *A Spiritual Strategy for Counseling and Psychotherapy.* 2nd ed. Washington, DC: American Psychological Association, 2005.

Sameera, Ahmed, and Mona M. Amer, eds. *Counseling Muslims: Handbook on Mental Health Issues and Interventions.* New York: Routledge, 2012.

Scazzero, Peter. *Emotionally Healthy Spirituality.* Nashville: Nelson, 2006.

Schipani, Daniel S., ed. *Multifaith Views in Spiritual Care.* Kitchener, ON: Pandora, 2013.

Schipani, Daniel S., and Leah Dawn Bueckert, eds. *Interfaith Spiritual Care: Understandings and Practices.* Kitchener, ON: Pandora, 2009.

Sperry, Len, and Edward P. Shafranske, eds. *Spiritually Oriented Psychotherapy.* Washington, DC: American Psychological Association, 2005.

Sue, Derald Wing, and David Sue. *Counseling the Culturally Diverse: Theory and Practice.* 7th ed. New York: Wiley, 2016.

Taylor, Elizabeth Johnston. *What Do I Say: Talking with Patients about Spirituality.* West Conshohocken, PA: Templeton Foundation, 2007.

Vest, Norvene, ed. *Tending the Holy: Spiritual Direction across Traditions.* New York: Morehouse, 2003.

9

Chaplaincy Education Meets Multireligious Literacy Development

Strategies for Teaching Models and Methods of Spiritual Caregiving in Multifaith Contexts

—Lucinda Mosher

"It's the best job in the world!" That is what the chaplain to a large metropolitan fire department always tells my students. They pay him rapt attention as he explains what his job entails: ministering to the First Responders to and victims of house fires, crane collapses, train wrecks, and more. And my students agree: he does have a wonderful job! They respect the grace with which he performs it. And they want what he has: a job as a professional spiritual-caregiver. They come from quite a variety of religious locations—some easily defined; others far less so, yet just as heartfelt. A few are looking for their first career. Others want to transition into this vocation from some other helping profession—social work, teaching, psychological counseling, nursing. Some are working as chaplains already. All of them are intrigued by the idea of (or are already committed to) being a chaplain; they want to know more about this calling, particularly about its multifaith aspects. That's why they are taking my course.

Chaplaincy Models and Methods was developed at Hartford Seminary—an institution that strives to equip spiritual caregivers, whatever their own religious convictions may be, with resources and skills for addressing the dynamics of multifaith contexts while remaining grounded in their own faith tradition. Hartford Seminary is home to a very successful Islamic Chaplaincy Program—the only such program in the U.S. that is fully accredited. Thus, the seminary's student body is now nearly 40 percent Muslim. Therefore, whenever I have taught this survey course on chaplaincy, at least half of the enrollees have been Muslim. Most of the others have been Christian—but some have been Jewish, Buddhist, Unitarian-Universalist, or Hindu. At least one defined herself as a Humanist; others might call themselves religiously eclectic. This, then, is the venue in which I have refined my thinking about the intersection of multifaith education and chaplain formation. What follows are the key points I seek to convey in a survey course on chaplaincy in multifaith contexts: an orientation to (or, in the case of advanced students, an opportunity for reflection on) the role of the chaplain and some of the methods suitable to the contexts in which chaplains characteristically serve. This course gives special attention to the importance of multi- and interfaith literacy for members of this profession, along with some of the methods and materials I have found useful. As I have implied, it has always attracted experienced chaplains as well as novices. Thus it is invariably the case that this course must do two things at once: provide an introduction for inquirers into the field, but also serve to expand the knowledge and skills of enrollees who are already working as chaplains (or in a similar capacity, but without that title). For simplicity's sake, in what follows I will, for the most part, speak as if the inquirers are our sole concern.

UNDERSTANDING THE BREADTH OF THE PROFESSION

Most simply, the term *chaplain* may be defined as a professional spiritual caregiver with particular responsibility to a person or community. In Christian practice, it has long meant "a clergyperson in charge of a *chapel* rather than a parish church"; or it may also connote *assistant* to the bishop, when the bishop is "on the road," calling on a parish or performing some other official task.[1] And there are other traditional uses of the term: each branch of the U.S. Congress has a chaplain, for example. In recent decades, *chaplain* has come to denote a religious leader (Christian or otherwise) who is assigned or attached to an institution other than a house of worship, providing it with ritual services and spiritual care. And while, because of its obviously Christian provenance, some religion-communities resist use of the term,

1. In the Episcopal Church, for example, the duty of "bishop's chaplain" is performed most often by a member of the bishop's senior staff, but a seminarian could be asked to perform this task.

the profession now nevertheless includes Jews, Muslims, Buddhists, Hindus, Unitarian-Universalists, Humanists, and others who wear the label *chaplain* proudly.

Inquirers may not understand just how broad an umbrella term "chaplaincy" is: just how diverse a large cluster of professions it covers; the sheer variety of venues in which chaplains are employed: hospitals, hospices, mental health facilities; in all branches of the U.S. military; in municipal police and fire departments; in the forest or game-warden service; at a number of major U.S. airports; with the Civil Air Patrol; at state or federal correctional facilities; at a great many universities, colleges, and independent schools; and even at some major corporations, as the notion of hiring a "workplace chaplain" has emerged in recent years. In a survey course such as *Chaplaincy Models and Methods,* simply providing the students with this list might suffice. However, I prefer that they have an opportunity to talk—in person or via Skype—with representatives of a variety of contexts and religious convictions: a Hindu hospital chaplain, a Muslim military chaplain, a Buddhist university chaplain, a chaplain whose own religious location is eclectic and who has particular experience in spiritual care for the extreme elderly. These conversations are frank, heartfelt, and eye-opening. As follow-up, I encourage students to read books and essays that provide windows into the chaplain's life. Kate Braestrup's *Here If You Need Me: A True Story* and Lucy Forster-Smith's *Crossing Thresholds: The Making and Re-making of a 21st-Century College Chaplain* are popular choices.

An aspect of introducing chaplaincy to a multireligious constituency, or in preparation for service in multifaith contexts, is exploration of the vocabulary of spiritual caregiving that is native to religions other than Christianity. The work of a chaplain is often described as "pastoral care." Again, because of its Christian roots, there exists some resistance to this descriptor's use multireligiously. We therefore consider how the work might otherwise be named, and the extent to which it is helpful to speak of "spiritual" or "contemplative" care—or to house the work in an Office of Spiritual Life or Department of Religious Life.

This matter of nomenclature extends to talk about the chaplain's milieu—and inquirers into this profession may be confused by this. Novices to the field need to understand that, in some contexts, "interfaith" and "multifaith" are synonymous. By "interfaith chaplain," some institutions mean "someone ready and willing—and perhaps explicitly prepared—to deal with anyone—regardless of their own religious persuasion." But in the hospital served by one of my colleagues, "interfaith chaplain" means "the non-Roman-Catholic spiritual caregiver." There exist "interfaith chaplaincy" programs that "commission" their graduates as chaplains. Inquirers need to understand that, different from such institutions, schools like Hartford Seminary offer educational experiences that should be useful to chaplains of whatever religious affiliation who are serving in (or preparing to serve in) *multifaith contexts*,[2] but the matter of "being commissioned" as a chaplain must be taken up with the relevant office of the chaplain-endorsing body for a student's particular faith tradition.

Furthermore, I find it necessary to be clear with inquirers that contexts in which chaplains work may often be appropriately labeled "multifaith" or "multireligious"—but the work itself might not be "interfaith." That is, in some multireligious venues, a particular chaplain's specific job is to minister to persons of the chaplain's own religious affiliation. Even so, such a chaplain would benefit from better understanding of religious diversity. For example, at a university with a multireligious student body, the responsibility of the Jewish chaplain is to the Jewish students; but she or he might still benefit from better understanding of the Muslim or Hindu students on campus—and may even make common cause with *their* chaplains. This is the lesson of the documentary *Of Many*[3]—a short film I have my students view and discuss—which tells the story of the friendship between the Muslim and the Orthodox Jewish chaplains at New York University, and the Jewish-Muslim collaborative community service they have facilitated.

UNDERSTANDING ENTRY REQUIREMENTS

Given our glance at the diversity of settings in which chaplains can be found, it is perhaps not surprising that there is no uniform training or credential that *must* be obtained in order to wear the title *chaplain*. Yet, at the same time, there are indeed standards; there is indeed a need for adequate training of people who plan to make a career of dealing with vulnerable populations! Inquirers of the chaplaincy field need to be aware of the ensuing paradoxes. In this regard, I might recount to my students a recent conversation in which a hospital chaplain—a Protestant—asserted her strenuous

2. Currently, Hartford Seminary offers a number of courses useful to chaplains. It also offers a Master of Arts in Religious Studies (forty-eight credits); a Master of Transformative Leadership and Spirituality degree (thirty-six credits); and a Cooperative Master of Divinity program through which forty-eight of the requisite seventy-two credits can be earned at Hartford Seminary, then transferred to a partner institution. All three can provide good foundational education for a profession in chaplaincy. For Muslims seeking to become professional chaplains, Hartford Seminary offers a Graduate Certificate in Islamic Studies (twenty-four credits) to be earned after completion of the seminary's Master of Arts degree.

3. Mills and Clinton, *Of Many*.

conviction that ordination should be mandatory. But exceptions are plenti-ful—and necessary. For female Roman Catholics, to mention but one obvi-ous example, ordination is not an option; yet Roman Catholic women can nevertheless become excellent chaplains.

One emphasis of my survey course on chaplaincy is cultivation of awareness of the progress made toward professionalizing it. Indeed, many—perhaps most—Christian and Jewish chaplains have completed the same training and have been ordained through the same processes and proce-dures as congregational clergy. Membership of the Association of Profes-sional Chaplains (APC) remains mostly Protestant, but in recent years has become significantly more multifaith—with its rolls of credentialed chap-lains now including Jews, Muslims, and Buddhists, and at least one Hindu. Applicants for certification by the Board of Chaplaincy Certification, Inc. (BCCI)—a widely recognized credential—must have earned a seventy-two-hour graduate theological degree (the Master of Divinity or its equivalent). In addition, the applicant must have completed four units of Clinical Pas-toral Education (CPE)—a program of 1600 hours of training, most often conducted in a healthcare setting; and then, must have logged an additional 2000 hours of on-the-job experience as a chaplain.[4] One goal of *Chaplaincy Models and Methods* is to clarify for inquirers what CPE is, how to apply, and why it is important even for people whose goal is spiritual caregiving in some venue other than a healthcare facility.

As chaplaincy has become an appealing profession to adherents of religions other than Christianity and Judaism, a major question has arisen: Where can Muslims, Buddhists, Hindus (the list goes on) receive educa-tion that is both authentic to their religious tradition and recognized by the BCCI as academically sound? Naropa University and the University of the West have developed rigorous chaplaincy-training programs for Bud-dhists. In 2006, the APC received a white paper on *Equivalency Issues for Buddhist Candidates for Board Certification Through the Board of Chap-laincy Certification Inc.*[5] During one of the chaplaincy sessions at the 2014 Annual Meeting of the American Academy of Religion, a point was made about the need for a similar way forward for Humanists and the religiously eclectic who believe themselves to be competent spiritual caregivers and wish to be credentialed as chaplains. America's Hindu community has long

4. "Associate" and "Provisional" certifications are also possible. For the full list of application requirements, see: http://bcci.professionalchaplains.org/content.asp?admi n=Y&pl=16&sl=16&contentid-30. Click on the link labeled "Application Procedures (Word doc)."

5. Available as a Word doc at http://bcci.professionalchaplains.org/content.asp?pl= 19&contentid=19.

been asking how best to translate the 2006 Buddhist guidelines into Hindu terms. Unwilling to wait, some Hindus have entered the chaplaincy field by earning a Master of Divinity in a Christian seminary in a program with no Hindu content. Some have combined study at a Christian seminary with online courses in Hindu Studies.[6] Still others have found work as the Hindu chaplain on a university campus on the basis of their master's degree in some other field, such as social work or counseling. After many years of discussion, 2015 saw the launch of a program through which American Hindus can become "Certified Volunteer Chaplains of the Hindu Faith."[7] However, it is unclear whether this new credential will be recognized by the BCCI or by potential employers of chaplains.

Indeed, although they may well require evidence of any number of qualifications, including good standing with an endorsing body, universities and schools rarely specify chaplaincy-board certification as a prerequisite for serving in campus ministry. Christians, Jews, Muslims, Hindus, Buddhists, Humanists, and others can and do find work as chaplains or similar sorts of spiritual caregivers without passing a review by a chaplaincy certification board. To say otherwise to my students would not be truthful. But one can hope that these uncertified spiritual caregivers are still well prepared for the work they do. I want my students to want that for themselves: to be competent spiritual caregivers in our multifaith world—which brings us to the matter of what specific competencies are desirable.

COMPETENCIES FOR SPIRITUAL CAREGIVING IN MULTIFAITH CONTEXTS

My point to students is that, while there is no single process nor hard-and-fast set of requirements for securing employment as a chaplain, chaplaincy standards have nevertheless been established. The *Chaplaincy Models and Methods* syllabus is informed by a list of twenty-nine competencies endorsed in 2004 by six professional pastoral care provider, counselor, or educator organizations representing more than 10,000 chaplains, pastoral counselors, and clinical pastoral educators in healthcare, counseling centers, prisons, and the military—and published as *Common Standards for Professional Chaplaincy*.[8] These agreed-upon chaplaincy standards fall into four

---

6. The Oxford Center for Hindu Studies has been helpful to one of my mentees. http://www.ochs.org.uk/.

7. http://www.hua.edu/doc/HUA-Chaplaincy.pdf

8 http://www.professionalchaplains.org/Files/professional_standards/ common_standards/common

categories: theology of pastoral care; identity and conduct; applied pastoral skills; and professional skills. Because I teach a multireligious student body and have special concern for ministry in multireligious contexts, I teach about these competencies from a range of religious viewpoints. By means of a workbook I have created for their use, I invite my students to assess their own progress toward each competency from "benchmark" (basic understanding of what a given competency entails) to "milestone" (evidence of adequate command) to "capstone" (readiness to appear before evaluators).[9]

In an effort to complement Common Standards with a competency matrix specific to spiritual caregiving in multifaith contexts, this self-assessment workbook also contains checklists I have collected and adapted from several sources. This includes a *multireligious* literacy inventory—a means for assessing the breadth and depth of one's knowledge of the beliefs and practices of a number of religions. Another is an *interfaith* literacy inventory—by which one may track one's cultivation of specific skills my colleagues and I deem useful for the actual work of religious leadership and interfaith collaboration. The *Pluralism and Worldview Engagement Rubric* developed by Elon University, Interfaith Youth Core, and Wofford College (2013) is useful in this regard.[10]

Yet another matrix is based on the assertion made in Daniel Schipani's *Multifaith Views in Spiritual Care* that "wise spiritual caregiving" requires three sets of core competencies: competencies of *knowing*, of *being*, and of *doing* (or "companioning"). As explained therein, Competencies of Knowing comprise (1) ability to articulate a philosophy of spiritual care; (2) an "understanding of the complexities, dynamics, and richness of interfaith situations"; (3) ability to conduct a theological assessment of oneself; (4) evidence of one's own psychological, theological, and spiritual "multilingualism"; and (5) awareness of and ability to make use of "interpretive frameworks" adapted from various social sciences. Competencies of Being have to do with one's own emotional intelligence—thus one's own sense of wellbeing, openness to difference, openness to the possibility that truth is "multiform"—and the implications of that notion, and one's own connection with "transcendence." Competencies of doing/companioning include markers of professionalism demanded by the Common Standards, but also include the ability to monitor one's "own ongoing caregiving practice," facility with "a variety of caregiving modes," continued refinement of one's

_standards_professional_chaplaincy.pdf.

9. Omitted from this workbook are those standards that have to do with professional association or religious membership and certification maintenance.

10. https://www.ifyc.org/sites/default/files/u4/PluralismWorldviewEngagementRubric2.pdf.

own theology of interfaith care, and maintenance of one's own spiritual discipline and self-care. My students work collaboratively to articulate what would constitute a benchmark, a milestone, and a capstone for each indicator of competence, then locate themselves in this matrix.[11]

Integration of Theology and Theory

The Common Standards call for the ability to "articulate a theology of spiritual care that is integrated with a theory of pastoral practice."[12] In my *Chaplaincy Models and Methods* course, I ask my students to discern such integration of theology and theory in memoirs and reflection pieces (some of which may be in video rather than written form) featuring chaplains representing a range of religious affiliations. I encourage my students to practice stating their own religion-location clearly and succinctly—that is, to develop and rehearse their own "religion-location elevator speech." I expect them to glean their claimed tradition(s) for models and methods for spiritual caregiving. By way of example, we read Storm Swain's explicitly Trinitarian *Trauma and Transformation at Ground Zero: A Pastoral Theology* and selections from the Giles and Miller anthology, *The Arts of Contemplative Care: Pioneering Voices in Buddhist Chaplaincy and Pastoral Work*; then we ask, given our own sacred texts and traditions, how might our own spiritual caregiving be framed? In terms of presence and incarnation? Of being the Prophet Muhammad in action? Of walking in the footsteps of the Buddha? Something else?

Closely related is cognizance of "the complexities, dynamics, [and] richness of interfaith situations" and development of "conjunctive faith" (defined as "ability to embrace ambiguity and paradox"—thus a sense of truth as multiform and complex; "readiness to participate in symbols, myths and rituals of one's own tradition"; "genuine and disciplined openness to the truths of communities and traditions other than one's own"; "movement from the prevalence of certainty to the centrality of trust")—some of the "core competencies of wise interfaith spiritual caregivers" delineated in the Epilogue to Daniel Schipani's *Multifaith Views in Spiritual Care*.[13] We make use of Robert Anderson's "five-step process of [spiritual/cultural] competency assessment" in chaplaincy practice,[14] and consider the seven topics of concern raised by Fukuyama and Sevig regarding "cultural diversity in

11. Schipani, *Multifaith Views*, particularly 167–77.
12. See Common Standards, TPC 1.
13. Schipani, *Multifaith Views in Spiritual Care*, 167–77.
14. Anderson, "The Search for Spiritual/Cultural Competency," 1–24.

pastoral care."[15] In response, I ask my students to explore theologies of religious manyness in their claimed tradition(s). I stress that, in jobs (such as in healthcare) that require chaplains to attend to people whose religious commitments differ from theirs, such caregiving must be construable as an act of faithfulness. I ask them, therefore, to search for resources from within their claimed religious location that will enable them, not only to *be* openheartedness to religious difference, but to explain such openheartedness to their own community. They are then expected to write up their own integration of theology and theory—if only in preliminary form.

Identity and Conduct

The Common Standards of identity and conduct have to do primarily with both respect for physical, emotional, and spiritual boundaries, and recognition of the strengths, limits, and assumptions affecting pastoral care. I assume that development of identity-and-conduct competencies is the domain of Clinical Pastoral Education (CPE); my job is to introduce them (or to reinforce what has been taught about them elsewhere). Therefore, we take time for close reading of the *Common Code of Ethics for Chaplains, Pastoral Counselors, Pastoral Educators and Students,* fifty-two "ethical principles" affirmed in 2004 by the same six professional associations that developed the Common Standards.[16] We share what in our own religion's texts and traditions enables us to abide by these principles. We discuss how accountability to one's faith community (the focus of the third of the seven sets of principles) would be monitored in each of our cases—given our particular religious locations.

Interestingly, the competencies under the "Identity and Conduct" header of the Common Standards for Professional Chaplaincy include attendance to one's "own physical, emotional, and spiritual well-being."[17] Thus "chaplain self-care" is a recurring theme in my approach to chaplain education. Class time is dedicated to a visit from a spiritual director with a multi-religious clientele of directees and student-directors. She brings one of her colleagues in order to model a spiritual direction session for my students. Through her, my students learn the differences and overlaps between spiritual direction and chaplaining. Her instruction is reinforced by our reading

15. Fukuyama and Sevig, "Cultural Diversity," 25–42.
16. http://www.professionalchaplains.org/files/professional_standards/common_standards/common_code_ethics.pdf.
17. Common Standards, IDC7.

of essays by Jewish, Buddhist, and Muslim spiritual directors.[18] With new appreciation for the value of this approach to self-care, we interview chaplains about their own methods.

Pastoral Skills

The "Pastoral" category of the Common Standards is the domain of hands-on skills. It almost goes without saying that one skill in this section would be the ability to conduct a "spiritual assessment." Acknowledging that Clinical Pastoral Education will provide the opportunity for honing this skill, *Chaplaincy Models and Methods* nevertheless introduces spiritual assessment techniques. We draw upon Christine Puchalski's categories of screening-questions.[19] I acknowledge George Fitchett's popular method, laid out in his *Assessing Spiritual Needs: A Guide for Caregivers*; but I feel that these methods can be applied more effectively when the chaplain has some breadth of knowledge of the beliefs, rituals and practices, and community life of religion-communities whose members s/he may encounter on the job.

With this in mind, I point out that, in fact, in the Common Standards' "Pastoral" category, actual reference to the need for multireligious literacy appears in the competency descriptions to a degree not found in other sections of the list. In an introductory course like *Chaplaincy Models and Methods,* we can only begin the process of improving basic knowledge of other people's beliefs and practices. I encourage my students to continue their learning by enrolling in an experiential introduction to America's religious diversity—or, if that be not possible, by availing themselves of audio-visual resources from Harvard's Pluralism Project.[20] I urge them to include in their libraries a compendium such as John Mabry's edited volume, *Spiritual Guidance across Religions*, or a fine world-religions textbook such as Mary Pat Fisher's *Living Religions*. Some find my own *Faith in the Neighborhood* series useful in that it takes an anecdotal, conversational approach to explaining a wide range of religious beliefs and practices.

Basic familiarity with what Diana Eck has long been calling "America's changing religious landscape" and with the internal diversity of America's

18. For example, Weiss, "Jewish Spiritual Direction"; Taylor, "What to Expect in Buddhist Spiritual Direction"; and Rahman, "What to Expect in Islamic Spiritual Direction."

19. Puchalski's method is known by the acronym FICA, which stands for Faith, Importance/Influence (of beliefs), (religious or spiritual) Community, and (what the patient would like the caregiver to) Address. See Puchalski and Romer, "Taking a Spiritual History."

20. www.pluralism.org.

many religions is a first step.[21] The Common Standards call for more than this. In several ways, they demand openness to religious difference and real skill in ministering to people—especially for those who are experiencing loss—whose religious commitments and practices differ significantly from those of the spiritual care provider. Other desirable practical skills include the ability to plan and facilitate public worship "appropriate to diverse settings and needs."[22] In addressing these standards, we revisit our theologies of religious difference. We draw upon cultural competency textbooks such as the Jossey-Bass publication, *Honoring Patient Preferences: A Guide to Complying With Multicultural Patient Requirements*, edited by Anne Rundle and others, is encyclopedic; Geri-Ann Galanti's *Caring for Patients from Different Cultures* may be an easier place to start. We also make extensive use of interfaith pastoral care case studies as a means of practicing what we are learning about how to offer appropriate spiritual care in a multireligious context.

Closely related is the Common Standards' expectation of ability to respond appropriately in crisis situations—some of which will be inherently multireligious. I feel strongly that specialized training in spiritual caregiving in mass casualty situations is valuable for all religious leaders; it provides information and skills applicable to any trauma situation. Thus, through a partnership with National Disaster Interfaiths Network (NDIN), I make disaster spiritual care available to my students—either as a unit within my chaplaincy course or as a freestanding workshop.[23] In addition to its daylong training on disaster spiritual care best practices and its two-day disaster chaplaincy training, NDIN now also offers a rigorous three-day training in multireligious literacy for disaster responders, plus many "tip sheets" (downloadable handouts) on this and related topics. My *Faith in the Neighborhood: Loss* includes a section on responses to disasters by a range of religion-communities.[24] It is worthwhile for chaplains and chaplains-in-training to study or review such materials as a reminder, not only with regard to how to offer spiritual care sensitively to a multireligious constituency, but

---

21. "A New Religious Landscape" was a chapter of the multimedia resource *On Common Ground: World Religions in America*, developed under Eck's leadership by Harvard University's *Pluralism Project* and first released in 1997 as a CD-ROM. Therein, when narrating one of this resource's many slideshows, Eck is heard to say, "The religious landscape of America is changing." Versions of this idiom continue to be used by Eck in her lectures and by the *Pluralism Project*. See, for example, http://pluralism. org/landscape/.

22. Common Standards, PAS8.

23. http://www.n-din.org/.

24. Mosher, *Loss*, 136–46.

also to be aware of how individuals and communities will be drawing on the beliefs and practices of their own religions to sustain them under such duress.

Professional Skills

A chaplain, as Joel Curtis Graves put it, is "a person (clergy or lay) who represents a religious and/or spiritual perspective in an institution or organization, and who ministers to people in need."[25] Thus, according to the "Professional" section of the Common Standards, chaplains must be competent in discerning the culture of the institution or organization in which they serve, in integrating spiritual care into that system, and in supporting its efforts to function ethically—to name but three necessary competencies. To develop such skills, chaplains-in-training need courses in institutional dynamics, dialogue, and conflict transformation. But they also need an understanding of how chaplains may be perceived in institutions they may serve eventually. Books such as sociologist Wendy Cadge's *Paging God*—a study of how chaplains function and are perceived by the medical staff in a sampling of non-affiliated U.S. hospitals—are useful in this regard. So are chaplain memoirs that are honest enough to show the rough edges of professional life.

Typically, Graves continues, chaplain responses to problems or crises are characterized by a synergy of leadership, management, and ministry.[26] As I see it, the task of programs or courses seeking to form chaplains for multifaith contexts is to equip people with skills and information that will make them lead, manage, and minister in the midst of religious manyness. In recent years, parallel to *Chaplaincy Models and Methods*, I have offered courses that combine lessons to bolster students' religious multilingualism with teaching of concrete leadership techniques useful in multifaith contexts. Chaplains or chaplains-in-training have been encouraged to enroll.

In writing about Buddhist chaplains, Jennifer Block defines chaplaincy as "a modern-day discipline and profession at the intersection between [a faith tradition] and suffering."[27] No matter the environment in which they serve, chaplains do spend a lot of time in that intersection; but chaplaining may also involve officiating at a wedding; offering the invocation at a holiday gathering; facilitating a study-circle; or organizing a work-party for a community service project. In *Chaplaincy Models and Methods*, we make use

25. Graves, *Leadership Paradigms in Chaplaincy*, 4.

26. Ibid., 1.

27. Block, "Toward a Definition," 3–8.

of case studies presenting not only challenging but also joyous scenarios. I suggest that coursework in "Life's Transitions"—preferably taught from a multireligious point of view—would provide excellent follow-up.

Variants of case study method are useful in providing opportunities to apply and sharpen chaplaincy students' interreligious literacy. Sharon Grant and Paul McKenna, of Scarboro Missions—a Canadian Roman Catholic organization that specializes in addressing the challenges of multireligious environments—have made available online an outline for a workshop for chaplains and spiritual caregivers wishing to improve their sensitivity to multifaith issues.[28] The heart of this resource is a set of twenty-four on-the-job scenarios—each a short description of a situation posing an interfaith dilemma. These make excellent discussion prompts. In *Multifaith Views in Spiritual Care,* editor Daniel Schipani provides a more in-depth resource for coursework on chaplaincy. This volume brings together essays by Aboriginal, Hindu, Buddhist, Jewish, Christian, Islamic, and Humanist caregivers—each one discussing that tradition's sources and foundational concepts for spiritual caregiving generally and in multifaith situations specifically; offering a case study as a practical example that may raise questions about the challenges and efficacy of interfaith caregiving; and identifying core interfaith spiritual care competencies.

CONCLUSION

We are fortunate that, to the vast library of books from a Christian point of view on chaplaincy, volumes are being added from other religious perspectives: for example, the aforementioned *The Arts of Contemplative Care: Pioneering Voices in Buddhist Chaplaincy and Pastoral Work,* edited by Cheryl A Giles and Willa B. Miller; *Jewish Pastoral Care: A Practical Handbook from Traditional and Contemporary Sources,* by Dayle A. Friedman; and *Islamic Approaches to Patient Care: Muslim Beliefs and Healthcare Practices for Caregivers* by Ra'ufa Sherry Tuell. I am aware that a broader and deeper handbook on Islamic chaplaincy is in the planning stages, as is one from a Hindu perspective. Surely other such religion-specific resources will follow.

Literature on spiritual care in multifaith contexts is likewise expanding: *Disaster Spiritual Care: Practical Clergy Responses to Community, Regional and National Tragedy,* co-edited by Stephen. B. Roberts (a Jewish chaplain) and Willard Ashley (a Christian); Roberts' more recent *Professional Spiritual & Pastoral Care: A Practical Clergy and Chaplain's Handbook*; Robert

28. http://www.scarboromissions.ca/interfaith-dialogue/curriculum-resources/workshop-outline-for-chaplains-and-spiritual-caregivers.

G. Anderson and Mary A. Fukuyama's *Ministry in the Spiritual and Cultural Diversity of Healthcare: Increasing the Competency of Chaplains*; and Dagmar Grefe's *Encounters for Change: Interreligious Cooperation in the Care of Individuals and Communities* are a few such titles, along with the works by Schipani and Mabry to which I have referred. Healthcare Chaplaincy Network offers a plethora of educational materials online.[29]

In short, resources abound for an engaging and effective survey course on chaplaincy in multifaith contexts. My own *Chaplaincy Models and Methods* course is taught as a five-day intensive seminar, now augmented by asynchronous online learning, with a series of assignments to be completed during the weeks following the face-to-face instruction. It would work as well, however, to configure the instruction in some other way: as five daylong face-to-face meetings, scheduled at intervals throughout a term, with reading and writing to be done between sessions, for example; or in a traditional mode involving twelve to fourteen weekly meetings for a semester. Whatever the way in which the instruction is configured, such a course provides excellent preparation for Clinical Pastoral Education. For students who come to it later in their formation process, it can reinforce and contextualize much of what they learned in CPE. For working chaplains, it can provide a useful continuing education experience. In every case, it has as much potential to dispel misconceptions about the field as it does to promote the desire for competence within it. In recent years, several U.S. theological schools have piloted multifaith chaplaincy certificate or degree programs. In almost every case this has proven not to be cost effective. Yet interest in the field abounds—which suggests that a survey course on chaplaincy in multifaith contexts is, therefore, a practical addition to any seminary's catalogue.

BIBLIOGRAPHY

Anderson, Robert G., and Mary A. Fukuyama. *Ministry in the Spiritual and Cultural Diversity of Healthcare: Increasing the Competency of Chaplains*. Binghamton, NY: Haworth Pastoral, 2004.
Braestrup, Kate. *Here If You Need Me: A True Story*. Boston: Little, Brown, 2007.
Cadge, Wendy. *Paging God: Religion in the Halls of Medicine*. Chicago: University of Chicago Press, 2013.
Cooper-White, Pamela. *Shared Wisdom: Use of the Self in Pastoral Care and Counseling*. Minneapolis: Fortress, 2004.
Cutter, William, ed. *Healing and the Jewish Imagination: Spiritual and Practical Perspectives on Judaism and Health*. Woodstock, VT: Jewish Lights, 2007.

29. http://www.healthcarechaplaincy.org/.

Eck, Diana L. *On Common Ground: World Religions in America.* CD-ROM. New York: Columbia University Press, 1997.

Equivalency Issues for Buddhist Candidates for Board Certification through the Board of Chaplaincy Certification Inc. http://bcci.professionalchaplains.org/content.asp?pl=19&contentid=19.

Fisher, Mary Pat. *Living Religions.* 9th ed. New York: Pearson, 2013.

Fitchett, George. *Assessing Spiritual Needs: A Guide for Caregivers.* Lima, OH: Academic Renewal, 2002.

Fitchett, George, and Steve Nolan, eds. *Spiritual Care in Practice: Case Studies in Healthcare Chaplaincy.* London: Kingsley, 2015.

Forster-Smith, Lucy A. *Crossing Thresholds: The Making and Remaking of a 21st-Century College Chaplain.* Eugene, OR: Cascade Books, 2015.

———, ed. *College & University Chaplaincy in the 21st Century: A Multifaith Look at the Practice of Ministry on Campuses across America.* Woodstock, VT: Skylight Paths, 2013.

Friedman, Dayle A. *Jewish Pastoral Care: A Practical Handbook from Traditional and Contemporary Sources,* 2nd ed. Woodstock, VT: Jewish Lights, 2005.

———. *Jewish Visions for Aging: A Professional Guide for Fostering Wholeness.* Woodstock, VT: Jewish Lights, 2008.

Galanti, Geri-Ann. *Caring for Patients from Different Cultures.* Philadelphia: University of Pennsylvania Press, 2004.

Giles, Cheryl A., and Willa B. Miller, eds. *The Arts of Contemplative Care: Pioneering Voices in Buddhist Chaplaincy and Pastoral Work.* Somerville, MA: Wisdom, 2012.

Grefe, Dagmar. *Encounters for Change: Interreligious Cooperation in the Care of Individuals and Communities.* Eugene, OR: Wipf & Stock, 2011.

Gubi, Peter Madsen. *Spiritual Accompaniment and Counseling: Journey with Psyche and Soul.* London: Kingsley, 2015.

Gunderson, Gary. *Deeply Woven Roots: Improving the Quality of Life in Your Community.* Minneapolis: Fortress, 1997.

Jacobs, Martha R. *Clergy Guide to End-of-Life Issues.* Cleveland, OH: Pilgrim, 2010.

Lee, Jonathan. *Memento Mori: Funerals for the Unaffiliated.* Saarbrücken, Germany: Lap Lambert, 2014.

Mabry, John R., ed. *Spiritual Guidance across Religions: A Sourcebook for Spiritual Directors and Other Professionals Providing Counsel to People of Differing Faith Traditions.* Woodstock, VT: Skylight Paths, 2014.

Matlins, Stuart M., ed. *The Perfect Stranger's Guide to Funerals and Grieving Practices: A Guide to Etiquette in Other People's Religious Ceremonies.* Woodstock, VT: Skylight Paths, 2000.

Moore, S. K. *Military Chaplains as Agents of Peace: Religious Leader Engagement in Conflict and Post-Conflict Environments.* Lanham, MD: Lexington, 2012.

Mosher, Lucinda. *Faith in the Neighborhood: Belonging.* New York: Seabury, 2005.

———. *Faith in the Neighborhood: Loss.* New York: Seabury, 2007.

———. *Faith in the Neighborhood: Praying: Rituals of Faith.* New York: Seabury, 2006.

Nash, Paul, et al. *Spiritual Care with Sick Children and Young People: A Handbook for Chaplains, Paediatric Health Professionals, Arts Therapists and Youth Workers.* London: Kingsley, 2015.

Of Many. DVD. Directed by Linda Mills, produced by Chelsea Clinton. New York: The of Many Institute for Multifaith Leadership, 2015.

Patton, John H. *From Ministry to Theology: Pastoral Action and Reflection.* 1997. Reprint, Eugene, OR: Wipf & Stock, 2009.

Puchalski, Christine, and Anna L. Romer. "Taking a Spiritual History Allows Clinicians to Understand Patients More Fully." *Journal of Palliative Medicine* 3/1 (2000) 129–37.

Rahman, Jamal. "What to Expect in Islamic Spiritual Direction." *Presence* 13/3 (2007) 36–41.

Roberts, Stephen B., ed. *Professional Spiritual & Pastoral Care: A Practical Clergy and Chaplain's Handbook.* Woodstock, VT: Skylight Paths, 2012.

Roberts, Stephen. B., and Willard Ashley. *Disaster Spiritual Care: Practical Clergy Responses to Community, Regional and National Tragedy.* Woodstock, VT: Skylight Paths, 2008.

Rundle, Anne Knights, et al., eds. *Honoring Patient Preferences: A Guide to Complying with Multicultural Patient Requirements.* San Francisco: Jossey-Bass, 1999.

Scaper, Donna. *Approaching the End of Life: A Practical and Spiritual Guide.* Lanham, MD: Rowman & Littlefield, 2015.

Schipani, Daniel S., ed. *Multifaith Views in Spiritual Care.* Kitchener, ON: Pandora, 2013.

Swain, Storm. "The T. Mort. Chaplaincy at Ground Zero: Presence and Privilege on Holy Ground." *Journal of Religion and Health* 50 (2011) 481–98.

———. *Trauma and Transformation at Ground Zero: A Pastoral Theology.* Minneapolis: Fortress, 2011.

Taylor, Sally. "What to Expect in Buddhist Spiritual Direction." *Presence* 13/3 (2007) 46–52.

Tuell, Ra'ufa Sherry. *Islamic Approaches to Patient Care: Muslim Beliefs and Healthcare Practices for Caregivers.* Beltsville, MD: Amana, 2010.

Waggoner, Ed. "Taking Religion Seriously in the U.S. Military: The Chaplaincy as a National Strategic Asset." *Journal of the American Academy of Religion* 82 (September 2014) 702–35.

Weiss, Zari. "Jewish Spiritual Direction." *Presence: An International Journal of Spiritual Direction* 5/2 (1999) 29–34.

Wimberly, Edward P. *Recalling Our Own Stories: Spiritual Renewal for Religious Caregivers.* San Francisco: Jossey-Bass, 1997.

10

Public Ministry in a World of Many Faiths[1]

—SHANTA PREMAWARDHANA

"LISTENING TO, LEARNING FROM and living in deep solidarity with those in the margins" is a slogan that my organization, Seminary Consortium for Urban Pastoral Education (SCUPE), recently adopted. We agreed with Gayatri Chakravorty Spivak that the margin "is not a place of weakness or self- deprecation, rather, it is a place pulsating with critical activity, it is alive with argument, controversy and creative discourse,"[2] and with Homi Bhabha (and Martin Heidegger before him) that the margin is where "something new begins its presencing."[3] We also agreed with Paul Tillich, that the calling of Christians is "to hold out at the boundary and to resist the temptation to flee this condition of pressure by settling down on one side of the boundary or the other."[4]

At its best, public theology is done by people in the margins. They are the ones most in need of, and they are the ones most eager to challenge and change the *status quo,* from the structures that oppress to those that liberate. Therefore with the Brazilian educator, Paulo Freire—of *Pedagogy of the*

1. This paper is based on a lecture offered at the United Theological Seminary of the Twin Cities (New Brighton, Minnesota) on May 15, 2015, titled "Faithful Discipleship: A Public Theologian Takes On the Multireligious World."

2. Spivak, *Critic*, 156.

3. Bhabha, *Culture*, 1.

4. Tillich, *Religiöse Verwirklichung,* 12.

Oppressed fame—we focus deeply on contextual learning as our method of theological reflection. When students come to our classes one of the first things they do is to go out into the streets and neighborhoods of the city and listen to people's questions and stories: stories of their struggle and pain, as well as their joy and laughter. They also go to its institutions, including religious houses of worship, to discover if and how they respond to those questions and stories. They will come back and subject those questions to critical analysis to examine the deeper causes of the questions that have been raised. It is only then that they will go to scripture and tradition. At the end, the students build a theological framework that is inductive, innovative, experiential, and relevant, and that engages the students in creating effective practical solutions to the real questions people are asking. They also receive skills in organizing people and money in order to build powerful movements to address the most pressing questions of our time.

For forty years, SCUPE has specialized in such an Urban Contextual Theology. A pivotal moment in my own ministry as an urban pastor occurred when Dr. Yvonne Delk spoke at one of SCUPE's Congresses on Urban Ministry. "You are not just a pastor to your congregation, you are a pastor to your community," she said, and added, "Your church pays you to be a pastor to the community. They don't know it yet, so you have to teach that to them!" Such pastors are powerful leaders. They recognize their privilege but identify with the margins and view social, political, and economic institutions from that perspective. They understand that the church has fallen prey to the values of the dominant culture and is willing to both challenge and use the church for the sake of the Gospel. When they preach, speak, or write, their voice is public. Courageous in speaking truth to power, they are skilled in engaging in public dialogue and debate with public officials, business and civic leaders about how institutions can come into compliance with the values and ethics of the Gospel. They are trained in the methods of organizing people and organizing money in order to build a powerful base out of which they can challenge institutions and create change.

Rev. Osagyefo Uhuru Sekou, an African American minister who since August 2014—since Michael Brown's murder—has been in Ferguson, at the forefront of the protest movement organizing and training the young people in methods and disciplines of nonviolent civil disobedience. In a presentation to our students, this former SCUPE faculty member spoke about how to think theologically about what is going on in Ferguson, and gave them an unforgettable hands-on training in nonviolent civil disobedience. These young people, he said over and over again. These queer, black, young women, and these saggy-panted young men are the very ones leading the movement toward justice. Those who are most marginalized in society is leading where the church is failing to go. This is where God is speaking, and the church is not listening. Its fifty years since Martin Luther King, he said, fifty years since the Voting Rights Act, fifty years since Bloody Sunday in Selma, but it is as if nothing has changed—it's open season on black men and women. So, he asks: "What is wrong with our *theology* that fifty years later we are still struggling with this?"

This framing, "What's wrong with our theology?" puts the onus on theologians, theological educators, and preachers for not privileging the contextuality of the streets of Ferguson, Baltimore, and Chicago. Sekou's criticism is also this: had the discipline of theology taken seriously the racial revolution of fifty years ago, and allowed a theological revolution that questioned some of its fundamental theological premises, would the churches allow the atrocity of police brutality to happen today? This requires a paradigm shift for theologians, who are used to holding the "received" tradition sacrosanct. The best we know to do with the questions and struggles that arise from the context is to tinker at the edges of our received theological traditions.

Rev. Martina Severin-Kaiser, a Lutheran church executive from Hamburg, Germany, following Rev. Sekou's presentation, reminded us that about seventy-five years ago Germany experienced the horror of the extermination of six and a half million Jews. She reminded us that it was baptized Christians who were the perpetrators of this terrible evil. Christian theology had to ask some hard questions of itself, she said, and as a result it has not been the same. We have struggled to find what in our scripture and theological tradition led Christians, not in spite of our theology, but *because* of our theology, to do such a horrible thing. Did the contextual horror of the Holocaust actually penetrate into the center of German theology? This, we noted, is being put to the test today, as Germany struggles with a massive influx of refugees. How they will be integrated into German society will say a great deal about whether German theologies, in fact, adequately shifted following the horror of the Holocaust.

The theological work that is still before us is not only within Christianity, but other religions as well. This came into stark relief for me while serving as the director for interreligious dialogue and cooperation at the World Council of Churches (WCC). I was invited to an interreligious conference convened by the late King Abdullah of Saudi Arabia. As it invariably happens when religious leaders are invited, most were older men. Less than 10 percent of some 250 participants were women or people under thirty. In response to a strong objection raised from the floor, the organizers quickly found a young Muslim scholar, Dr. Mekia Nedjar from the University of Madrid. In her speech challenging Islamic theology, she recalled that Christian theology is not the same since the Holocaust, and indeed Muslim theology is not the same since 9/11. There have been theological movements in both religions to think about how and why these happened, and how we can think differently, she said. But both these were atrocities perpetrated by men. How is it possible, she asked, that male dominated theology still remains the same?

"What is wrong with our theology that fifty years after the civil rights movement we still struggle with blatant and brutal racism?" is a good question to ask. James Cone in his *The Cross and the Lynching Tree* points to this "blindness" with a strong critique of one of America's foremost theologians, and his own predecessor at Union Theological Seminary, Reinhold Niebuhr. Despite his astute explications of a public theology, Niebuhr did not see the utter horror of lynching as a theological metaphor applicable uniquely to the U.S. context. Similarly, many churches today don't see the killing of young African Americans or the Black Lives Matter movement as having an impact on our theological constructs, and constructive theologies that are written on that matter still don't address the central notions of our received theologies.

The public theologian who has her ear to the ground must ask some hard questions of received theologies. The deeper questions are systemic: what's wrong with our theology, she might ask, that in most of our cities, there are areas of concentrated poverty, and other areas of concentrated wealth? Myron Orfield, who has given a well-researched answer to this question, is not a theologian, but professor of law at the University of Minnesota and former Minnesota state senator. In his two books *Metropolitics* and *American Metropolitics*, he pointed out that the problem is not the local economies, but is located within economic policies and tax bases determined by lawmakers in state governments. It is likely that many, perhaps most, lawmakers who created these policies were faithful members of their (predominantly Protestant) churches. Either the preaching and teaching in those churches had no effect on their policymaking, or the preaching and teaching tacitly supported those unjust policies. Privileging the context requires us to ask what is wrong with our theology that we allowed this to happen. Orfield also tells us how we can break that cycle. We need to build alliances he says, between the inner core of the city and the inner ring suburbs, across racial/ethnic and economic barriers to create a power block in the state legislature that will stand against the power of those who represent concentrated wealth. Had he been more aware of the power of religious communities to mobilize for the work of justice, he may have added that we need to build alliances across religious communities; that Baha'is and Buddhists, Christians, Jews, and Muslims, Hindus, Jains, and Sikhs and those of traditional religions must work together. And the public theologian must ask, what is wrong with our theology that we can't do that?

The widening wealth gap is another such question for the public theologian. SCUPE's Congress on Urban Ministry (June 2014) addressed this question. We noted that the world's richest sixty-seven people control the same amount of wealth as half the world's population, over 3.5 billion people. Here's another way to look at it: Each of the wealthiest sixty-seven has access to the same resources as about forty-two million people. These are incredible numbers. They lead to a serious problem, in the U.S. particularly, but also globally—the rise of a plutocracy, where the super-rich controls the political and economic processes that leave everyone else out.

We invited South African theologian Dr. Allan Boesak to address this question. In the forefront of the anti-apartheid struggle in South Africa, Boesak worked closely with Nelson Mandela and Desmond Tutu. At the time, apartheid was a theologically approved doctrine of the church. The most powerful church in the country, the South African Reformed Church found scriptural backing for keeping races separate, just as much as in the U.S. and Europe we found enough scriptural justification for slavery and racism, and many still find for homophobia. Boesak's singular contribution to the struggle happened in 1982. He spearheaded a theological movement that led the World Alliance of Reformed Churches (WARC) to declare apartheid a heresy. Having done that, they excommunicated the South African Reformed Church and elected Boesak as its president. And with that, the back of apartheid was broken.

We said to Boesak that we need another theological movement. We used to believe in an important idea called the Common Good. It was a biblical idea that has its origins in the early Christian community, which shared all that they had with each other so that there was no one in need among them.[5] The idea of wealth held in common was so normal and accepted, that many of the early American colonies and states called themselves Commonwealths. We have lost that in favor of our pursuit of individual wealth such that we are living in a time of soaring wealth disparity in the U.S. and around the world. We need a theological movement, we said to Boesak, which, in ways similar to 1982, will break the back of theologies that say that those who are rich are favored by God and, its corollary, those who are poor have lost God's favor. These are not just the so-called prosperity theologies. They are also in the mainstream traditions reinforced weekly in liturgies, hymnody, and preaching. Following challenging presentations and agitations by Dr. Allan Boesak, Rev. Otis Moss III, Bishop Sally Dyck, and

5. Acts 4:34.

Dr. Saskia Sassen, the Congress approved the document, "Together Building a Just Economy."[6]

In its preamble, this document acknowledges that it is written by Christians, and that effective action on this matter requires partners of other religions. Therefore, it encourages other religious communities to engage in similar processes and offer similar contributions. Taking that cue, the Parliament of the World's Religions, gathering in October 2015 in Salt Lake City, affirmed a similar statement from a multireligious perspective.[7]

If my first point is the need for Public Theologians to ask hard questions of received theologies, my second point is to acknowledge that sometimes Christians don't have all, or the best answers; sometimes the other religious traditions to which our colleagues and neighbors belong have a better answer than we do. I will stay with the economic disparity theme.

In March 2009, about six months after the global financial crisis hit, the Churches' Commission on International Affairs (CCIA)—an advisory body of the WCC—met in Matanzas, Cuba, to reflect on this crisis, and they made three important affirmations.[8] First, they identified the cause of the crisis as unbridled greed, and declared it a form of violence. "[T]he accumulation of wealth and the presence of poverty are not simply accidents but are often part of a strategy for some people to accumulate power and wealth at the expense of others. As such, greed is a form of violence which on personal, community, national, regional and international levels isolates and injures us." In offering the provocative comment "greed is a form of violence," the CCIA is connecting a word—violence—which evokes strong condemnation, with a word that it believes is equally condemnable—greed; and they are advocating a robust theological reflection on greed, as there has been on violence. Second, the CCIA recognizes that religions over centuries have deeply reflected on the question of greed and have significant wisdom to offer. It acknowledges that Christianity alone does not have the resources to resolve these problems but that it must seek the ethical wisdom of other traditions both in its analysis and action. It specifically identifies Buddhism as having long tradition of reflection on greed. Third, the CCIA identifies the need to listen to the voices of the poor. "We acknowledge that in our various positions of leadership we are not always well-placed to hear the voice of the oppressed, of indigenous people, of women, of the disabled, of refugees and displaced people, of the poor and of the most silenced among us."

6. SCUPE Congress on Urban Ministry, *Together Building.*

7. Parliament of the World's Religions, *Declaration.*

8. CCIA, *Report.*

On the CCIA's first point: The WCC has engaged in theological reflections on Poverty, Wealth, and Ecology for many years. These discussions that included theologians, economists, and sociologists yielded a groundbreaking proposal for a new financial architecture, issued in October 2012.[9] It calls for the replacement of GDP growth as the primary indicator of economic progress and advocates the use of other indicators such as the growth of decent work, quality and quantity of health and education, social inclusion, gender justice, and measures of environmental sustainability. It names over-consumption and greed as key factors to be addressed in seeking a more just distribution of the world's resources.

An interesting idea that arose out of these conversations is the establishment of a "Greed Line." A study group established to study this idea published its report recently.[10] Countries use various indicators and measurements to establish a poverty line, below which a person can be said to be in poverty, and therefore requiring public assistance. For example, in the U.S. the Census Bureau determines poverty status by comparing pre-tax cash income against a threshold that is set at three times the cost of a minimum food diet in 1963, updated annually for inflation, and adjusted for family size, composition, and age of householder. In 2014, the poverty threshold for a family of four was $24,230. The official national poverty rate was 14.8 percent, and 46.7 million people lived in poverty in the United States.[11]

The question is, by using a similar criteria and measurements, can economists establish a greed line, above which a person can be said to be greedy? In one such assessment, Clement Kwayu attempts to calculate a national wealth line for Tanzania proposing that any income beyond the level of "ten times the gross domestic product (GDP) per capita" would constitute greed.[12] This is a rather uncomplicated measurement. A real greed line, however, requires multidimensional indicators such as wealth accumulation and resulting increase in the levels of poverty, levels of wealth disparity, and the increase of an ecological footprint due to increased consumption. The indicators are also not merely economic or sociological, they are also ethical and political. The Greed Line Study Group points out two key functions of a greed line. First to "expose the collective and structural manifestations of greed and their economic, social and ecological consequences; and second, to serve as alarms or 'red lights' signaling to the general public and policy-

9. WCC, São Paolo.

10. Peralta and Mshana, The Greed Line.

11. Institute for Research on Poverty, How is Poverty Measured.

12. Peralta and Mshana, The Greed Line, 26.

makers that critical limits are being overstepped with potentially disastrous effects."[13]

Despite the good work done by the Greed Line Study Group, many questions remain. I wish to raise three that pertain to the scope of this chapter. First, greed, at bottom, is not an economic question, but a spiritual one, requiring spiritual answers. Therefore, the only institutions with competency to address that question are the religious communities. However, as long as religious communities are themselves caught up in an economic system based on greed, do not have adequate theological resources, or do not have the courage to address it, they will not be a part of such a movement. How do we prepare the preachers and teachers within religious communities to address this difficult spiritual question? Second, religious communities have usually used such theological reflections to help individual adherents to free themselves from power of greed in their lives. The WCC study group's stance, however, has been to offer a bold theological critique and an alternative proposal based on its theological values to the public square. How should other religious communities follow this lead to address the public square? The third question arises from the second. The only way policymakers will even consider reading such radical proposals is if their hand is forced through organized movements that call for such an overhaul of the economic system. How can religious communities come together and collaborate to form such an organized movement for effective action?

CCIA's second affirmation was that religions over centuries have deeply reflected on the question of greed and have significant wisdom to offer. It acknowledged that Christianity alone does not have the resources to resolve these problems but that it must seek the ethical wisdom of other traditions in both its analysis and action.

Chicago lawyer Thomas Geoghegan, addressed this question of the religious roots of greed in his article in the April 2009 *Harper's Magazine*. He points out that although many people think that the financial crisis of 2008 was simply a failure to regulate financial instruments such as derivatives or hedge funds, the deregulation was of a much older, even ancient, set of laws. Since the time of the ancient Babylonian Empire, every civilization had some form of legal or religious sanction against usury. Until President Jimmy Carter's term, there was a ceiling on the interest rates banks could charge from their customers. In the 1970s, deregulation began with a Supreme Court decision that effectively removed all interest rate caps. As a result, today it does not seem unusual if banks charge up to 35 percent. It has also led to the springing up of companies that do predatory lending such as

---

13. Ibid., 36.

Payday Loans. Locating themselves near the poorest areas in U.S. cities, they prey upon low income people, and charge them up to 400 percent for a loan against their next salary.

This is not likely to happen in the world of sharia-compliant banking. In fact, through the financial crisis Islamic banks have been resilient. Muslims are not allowed to benefit from lending money. Earning interest is therefore, *haram*—whether you are an individual or a bank—and therefore interest is not paid on Islamic checking or savings accounts or charged on Islamic mortgages. The prohibition dissuades Islamic banks from engaging in contracts considered excessively risky. And because they are not particularly motivated by producing a high volume, they are known to be much more engaged with the customer and with the assets in which they are investing. Islamic banks therefore will not engage in the kinds of products that got U.S. financial institutions into trouble—subprime mortgages, collateralized debt obligations, or credit default swaps, etc. This has made some U.S. companies consider these practices as good for business.

As a result of rising demand for Islamic-friendly investments, multinational corporations are considering what the Qur'an has to say about their business practices. In the financial sector, big banks such as Citigroup, HSBC, and Deutsche Bank have products that are sharia-compliant. An estimated 300 Islamic financial institutions hold at least $500 billion in assets, and issue sharia-compliant loans, bonds, credit cards, and even derivatives. In Islamic banking, financiers are required to share borrowers' risks, and depositors are treated more like shareholders, earning a portion of profits.

Theologically, the question boils down to the affirmation of common good for the community, the *ummah*. Islam recognizes that greed is a human condition and that if left unchecked it will lead to the exploitation of those who are poor. It will get them into debts that are impossible to pay off, and thereby force them in to slavery for generations. This does not serve the common good. Muslims do not adhere to that prohibition out of their goodwill. Sharia-compliance is enforceable by law.

In its acknowledgement that Christianity does not have all the answers, the CCIA specifically cited Buddhism as having a long tradition of teaching on the question of greed. This teaching includes greed's disastrous consequences, the value of simplicity for the lay community of disciples, and renunciation and voluntary poverty for the monastic community.

At the most basic level, the Four Noble Truths affirm that all existence is *dukkha* or unsatisfactoriness, and the cause for this is *tanhā*, which is craving or greed. Finding release, or *nirvana* from craving is the goal of Buddhism. And the fourth noble truth outlines an eightfold path to achieve that end. *Tanhā* is also known as one of three poisons—greed, hatred, and delusion—that affect a human being's ability to be enlightened, or achieve wisdom. The wisdom here is nothing less than the ability to both comprehend and appropriate to one's being the truth that *everything* is impermanent (*aniccā*). This is the philosophical basis for asserting that there is nothing—not one's own body, which decays, and not even a permanent soul—that will exist eternally (*anattā*). Additionally, the sophisticated analysis on the concept of *śūnyatā* (inadequately translated as "emptiness") founds impermanence on an even deeper philosophical bedrock. When one deeply comprehends and appropriates this worldview into his or her life, renouncing worldly possessions, embracing voluntary poverty, and living a life dedicated to the well-being of all become not what the occasional ascetic does, but everyone's normal practice. Many other religious traditions, too, have sophisticated understandings about greed and ways to overcome it.

Following the encouragement of the CCIA, the WCC and the Lutheran World Federation organized together a Buddhist-Christian consultation in Chiang Mai, Thailand in 2010. Buddhists from several countries and a variety of traditions engaged with Christians from a variety of traditions in a consultation entitled "Buddhists and Christians engaging structural greed."[14] The organizers acknowledged that the question was not simply a matter of individual greed, but that greed permeated our social and political life and, in that sense, greed was structural.

Very quickly, an interesting challenge was observed. Some Buddhists were very clear that the issue is not structural but has to do with individuals who need to find their emancipation by following the eightfold path. They were similar to some Christians, particularly from the Evangelical traditions, who asserted that individual sin is the cause. But Buddhists in the tradition of Engaged Buddhism and Christians in the more ecumenical traditions strongly argued for the position that greed today must be dealt with structurally. We finally agreed that not only all human beings, but all sentient beings, are deeply connected to each other. "Inter-being," a construct proposed by Thich Nhat Hanh, one of the main proponents of Engaged Buddhism, became an important point of departure. He paints this picture for us:

> In one sheet of paper, we see everything, the cloud, the forest, the logger. I am, therefore you are. You are, therefore I am. We inter-are. I know that in our previous lives we were trees, and even in this life we continue to be trees. Without trees we cannot have people; therefore trees and people inter-are. We are trees

14. Sinaga, *A Common Word*.

and air, bushes and clouds. If trees cannot survive, humankind
is not going to survive either.[15]

If we were to assert, "I am, therefore you are; you are, therefore I am,"
it suggests that there is no autonomous, independent, absolute, and sovereign subject. The Buddhist subject is relational, interdependent, socially
constituted, and vulnerable. Our mutual vulnerability–not only in the sense
that we could injure or kill one another, but also in the sense that we are sus-
ceptible to one another's touch, care, etc.—makes us human. This condition
is one that must be cultivated for we would be losing an important human
condition if we were to overcome vulnerability, which is constitutive of the
being human.

Sulak Sivaraksa, a leading voice in Engaged Buddhism speaking at that
consultation said: "Since we inter-are, your loss would greatly impact my
very being as if a part of me had gone or were missing as well. As human beings our existence only comes in the form of being-with or being-together.
Engaged Buddhists thus seek to maximize the livability of all sentient beings; that is, seek to foster conditions that would help guarantee that all
sentient beings have livable lives. This implies that violent structures have to
be dismantled. Being a good Buddhist involves rupturing the unjust status
quo and stirring trouble!"

The CCIA's third observation was about who's at the table. When we
gather with colleagues from other religions at conferences, read each other's
papers, and engage in dialogues and debates, we rarely ask this question
or, more importantly, the question: who's not at the table? The CCIA in its
incisive critique, made this observation about how we must listen to the
voices of those who are poor.

The religious leaders who comprise the CCIA are well-educated, in-
fluential, and elite leaders in their societies. This is true of the theological
establishment as well. Most theologians, almost by definition, are members
of the intellectual elite. Harvey Cox, back in 1980, wrote in an essay[16] that
this elitism is understandable, given that the minimal conditions for doing
theology include the ability to read and write, familiarity with the received
tradition of concepts and categories, sufficient leisure to reflect on these, and
the power to get one's ideas published or otherwise heard. Are theologians
prepared to take the next step, he asks, beyond the self-critical awareness
we now have—for example, of how the rhetorical conventions and cultural
symbols of any period shape even its most original theology—to a recognition of how the pervasive ideology of the dominant class influences the

15. Sivaraksa, "Challenge," 35.

16. Cox, "Theology," 874–78.

theology it produces? Indeed, because of the class position of those who write it, most theology is freighted with an overload of the dominant class ideology. For Cox, this is why theology could not be reasonably expected to struggle with serious ethical problems such as greed.

Cox's 1980 article, as are some of his other writings, was clearly influenced by the burgeoning Liberation Theology movement. A formative event of that movement, the 1968 Latin American Roman Catholic Bishops (CELAM) meeting in Medellín, Colombia, changed the methodological paradigm.

Three items about that shift are worth noting. First, while previous ecclesiastical meetings had canonical representation (delegates from each ecclesiastical region), the Medellín table included pastoral representatives, who for the most part lived among those who were poor and marginalized. In addition, rather than beginning with pronouncements from Rome, this event began with an analysis of the issues that came up from the grassroots. The change represented a shift from a perspective that was dogmatic, deductive, and top-to-bottom to one that was bottom-to-top, inductive, and exploratory. Second, they brought to the discipline of ideologically-based Western theology an alternative critique from Marxist analysis. That alternative analysis yielded a theological premise which has had an enormous impact on present theological thinking: "God's preferential option for the poor." Third, we learned, quite definitively, that there is no such thing as theology in the abstract. All theologies, including the classical theologies that were once considered normative by those who held power, are contextual. What we have learned as theology is properly called "North Atlantic Theology." This remarkable shift has led to a recognition of the alternative traditions of theology, such that today we cannot speak of "theology" without an adjective: feminist theologies, black theologies, Dalit theologies, and so on. It has enfranchised many whose voices had not been previously heard and have given legitimacy to significant movements of human liberation.

While what the CELAM theologians did is utterly commendable, it still fell short. The concerns of the poor were brought to the conference by pastoral representatives. They did their utmost to express the real concerns of poor people, but it was still inadequate. The poor themselves were not present. Their concerns were presented through the sieves of the pastoral representatives whose education and social location prompted them to sift and analyze those concerns through the frame of Marxist ideology. In the 1960s, several countries in Latin America were buzzing with Marxist-influenced revolutionary fervor. Yet, Marxist ideology was not indigenous to the people of those countries. We must therefore raise this question: had the poor people themselves been engaged in the analysis, would they not have sought paradigms more authentic to their Mesoamerican and native religious traditions?

Paul Knitter, in a 2002 volume he edited with Chandra Muzzafer entitled *Subverting Greed,* makes a similar proposal. He claims that as religions seek to respond to the economic plight of the poor, they are realizing "that the poor are aiding them [religious people] to better understand themselves and to better understand one another."[17] Not middle class religious leaders or scholars but those who are poor themselves are in a position to become mediators of dialogue.

How do you dialogue with the poor? When we ask that question, we are immediately confronted with the problem of defining "the poor." Those who talk about "the poor" rarely identify themselves with that designation. An interesting case in point is Liberation Theology's use of the theological principle, "God's preferential option for the poor." While acknowledging the importance of that claim for contemporary theological discourse, it is necessary to notice that it uses a binary identity designation, setting the theologians apart from "the poor." The Medellín theologians, themselves a part of an elite social class, did not necessarily consider themselves "the poor." The theologians who proclaim the theological principle of God's preference for the poor were themselves excluded from that preference!

Jesuit theologian Aloysius Pieris offers us an insight from his Sri Lankan context. In his *Asian Theology of Liberation* he insists that an authentic Sri Lankan theology must undergo a double baptism, in the Jordan of its religious diversity, and the cross of its grinding poverty. These two axes of religious diversity and poverty are basic facts of the Sri Lankan context. Dialogue, he says—and we might add, theology—is more than an academic exercise done in religious seminars organized and financed by Western agencies, by people who do not have their feet on the ground. It is not an abstract concern, but a daily existential experience; never merely an intellectual exercise, it is a moral commitment. Pieris' analysis suggests that if we want to engage in dialogue we need to incarnate ourselves in the context. It requires a double baptism of immersion in the world of religious diversity and in the context of grinding poverty.

The question, however, is even more complex. There is plenty of dialogue that goes on in poor communities. Poor Christians, Buddhists, Hindus, Muslims, and those of other religions often live in the same communities, share each other's concerns and needs, and reflect with each other about their fortunes and misfortunes and the ultimate meanings of day to day events. The difficulty for us middle class theologians is that we have no

17. Knitter and Muzzafer, eds., *Subverting Greed,* 2.

access to that conversation. Many difficulties, including those of communication and building trust, become serious obstacles when we try to come from outside and listen to their dialogue.

So, is there any hope for theology or interreligious dialogue? According to Pieris, there is no alternative but to engage in voluntary poverty, which, for religious people, he reminds us, is a positive value. We must struggle against forced poverty, but voluntary poverty is a spiritual calling we must embrace. Some of the greatest saints and revered gurus in religious traditions were people who renounced worldly comforts and pleasures. Some entered the monastic life, others such as Gandhi, became engaged in social justice. Pieris asserts that it is simply not possible for people with a middle class mindset to really understand and appreciate those who are poor. Those who engage in the disciplines of theology and of interreligious dialogue must therefore undergo a conversion, and undertake the baptism of voluntary poverty themselves.

Many, perhaps most Christians, have a great deal of difficulty engaging in this way, I think, because we have an exclusivistic theological orientation, and a missional mindset. We have been taught to look upon people who are poor as objects for our charity—since they are deprived of God's favor, and people of other religions as objects for conversion—since we know that truth and they don't. It is with this mindset that the colonial missionary movement for 500 years went out to the rest of the world. Those who still have that mindset find it difficult to engage in dialogue with others.

This is what SCUPE does. We put our students into the streets of the city, to its local communities, to areas of concentrated poverty, where we expect the students to listen to the questions, struggles, and stories of pain and laughter. We bring those questions together, subject them to deeper analysis, and then ask what does scripture and tradition have to say about these questions. Indeed, in the margins our students have seen dialogue burst into argument, controversy, and creativity. There, it never stays a mere dialogue, but moves quickly to action. At the margins people are conscientized: they strategize, organize, and move in to agitate their religious and political leaders. When religious leaders do not have the courage to do the right thing, it is the organized religious people at the grassroots who are able to hold their religious leaders as well as their political leaders accountable, so that rather than compromise on the ethical principles, they are able to courageously advance the cause of justice, such that it leads to peace.

An important hermeneutical key was offered at the 2013 WCC General Assembly in Busan by the Commission on World Mission and Evangelism, in its new statement on mission entitled *Together Towards Life*.[18] Mission is from the margins, it states, and invites the church to reimagine mission as a vocation from God's Spirit who works for a world where fullness of life is available to all. In other words, mission is not to those who are a poor, or to those who are the religious other, as we always thought; rather, mission is from those who are poor and marginalized to the privileged center.

This is a profound statement. It stands on its head all our previous understandings of mission. Those of us at the privileged center, the theologians, the religious leaders, the pastors and teachers, the middle class elite, are the very ones that need to be missionized. It says to us powerfully that those who are hungry today have something important to teach us about life and its meaning, and about the importance of sharing and community. Those who are working two or three jobs at minimum wage and have kids to take care of at home have something important to teach us about economic justice. Those who are still struggling in places where climate change wreaks havoc have something important to teach us about life's fragility and resilience. Those who are Buddhists, Hindus, Jews, and Muslims have something to teach us not only about greed, but also about God and Jesus and the Holy Spirit. When we get that, we will discover that our questions are different, our answers are different, and more than anything else our attitude toward life, and our lifestyle will be different.

What happened in 2008, what is happening in cities around our nation, and what is happening with religious extremism and theological justifications of injustice and violence must cause us to stop and ask what is wrong with our theology. We need to deconstruct those theologies that create barriers to our engagement with each other, and reconstruct theologies that enable us to learn from other religious traditions the wisdom they have to offer, and about how we can work together. We must ask how we can engage with those in the margins of our communities by locating ourselves in the margins. I hope I have rekindled some hope that the religious communities have the theological or philosophical basis for such engagement, and the capacity to be organized to act on these questions. But in order for that to be so, we must allow those in the margins to teach us, missionize us, and, indeed, convert us.

BIBLIOGRAPHY

Bhabha, Homi J. *The Location of Culture*. London: Routledge, 1994.

18. CWME, *Together.*

Churches' Commission on International Affairs (CCIA). "Report of the March 2009 CCIA Meeting." World Council of Churches (2009). http://www.oikoumene.org/ gr/resources/documents/wcc-commissions/international-affairs/commission-oninternational-affairs-policy/report-of-the-march-2009-ccia-meeting.html.

Commission on World Mission and Evangelism (CWME). *Together Towards Life: Mission and Evangelism in Changing Landscapes* (2013). http://www.oikoumene. org/en/resources/documents/wcc-commissions/mission-and-evangelism/ together-towards-life-mission-and-evangelism-in-changing-landscapes#_edn28.

Cone, James. *The Cross and the Lynching Tree.* Maryknoll, NY: Orbis, 2011.

Cox, Harvey. "Theology: What Is It? Who Does It? How Is It Done?" *Christian Century* (Sept 24, 1980). http://www.religion-online.org/showarticle.asp?title=1730.

Freire, Paulo. *Pedagogy of the Oppressed.* New York: Bloomsbury Academic, 2000.

Geoghegan, Thomas. "Infinite Debt: How Unlimited Interest Rates Destroyed the Economy." *Harper's Magazine* (April 2009) 31–39.

Institute for Research on Poverty. *How is Poverty Measured in the United States?* http:// www.irp.wisc.edu/faqs/faq2.htm.

Knitter, Paul F., and Chandra Muzaffer, eds. *Subverting Greed: Religious Perspectives on the Global Economy.* Maryknoll, NY: Orbis, 2002.

Orfield, Myron. *Metropolitics: A Regional Agenda for Community and Stability.* Washington, DC: Brookings Institution, 1998.

———. *American Metropolitics: The New Suburban Reality.* Washington, DC: Brookings Institution, 2002.

Parliament of World Religions. *Declaration on Income Inequality and the Widening Wealth Gap.* (2015). https://parliamentofreligions.org/civicrm/petition/ sign?sid=3&reset=1.

Peralta, Athena, and Rogate Mshana, eds. *The Greed Line: Tool for a Just Economy.* Geneva: World Council of Churches, 2016.

Pieris, Aloysius. *An Asian Theology of Liberation* Maryknoll, NY: Orbis, 1988.

SCUPE Congress on Urban Ministry. *Together Building a Just Economy.* (2014). https:// scupe.org/wp-content/uploads/2014/07/ManifestoForPeopleOfFaith1.pdf.

Sinaga, Martin, ed. *A Common Word: Buddhists and Christians Engage Structural Greed.* Minneapolis: Lutheran University Press, 2012.

Spivak, Gayatri Chakravorty. *The Post-Colonial Critic: Interviews, Strategies, Dialogues.* London: Routledge, 1990.

Tillich, Paul. *Religiöse Verwirklichung.* Berlin: Furche, 1930.

World Council of Churches. *São Paulo Statement: International Financial Transformation for the Economy of Life.* (Oct 2012). https://www.oikoumene.org/ en/resources/documents/wcc-programmes/public-witness-addressing-power-affirming-peace/poverty-wealth-and-ecology/finance-speculation-debt/sao-paulo-statement-international-financial-transformation-for-the-economy-of-life.

11

Letting the Arts Lead
The Role of the Arts in Interfaith Dialogue

—CINDI BETH JOHNSON, with JANN CATHER WEAVER

IN AN ADDRESS DELIVERED at Spring Convocation at United Theological Seminary of the Twin Cites (United), Professor Eleazar Fernandez described the relationship between the arts and constructive theology:

> What could be more fitting a partner for constructive theology than the arts in the enterprise of discipleship and imaginative reconstruction of new ways of thinking and dwelling. To be sure, philosophy, social, and natural sciences are vital disciplines for constructive theology to relate with and integrate. But the arts offer something essential and distinctive, so much so that constructive theology would be an orphan without it. Moreover, constructive theology would not really be true to its calling if it were not in itself a form of art or an artistic enterprise.[1]

In this chapter I will propose in a similar way that the arts are also a fitting partner for interfaith dialogue; that they too help us as we reconstruct new ways of thinking and dwelling amid our diversity. I will argue that their ability to do this comes from their power to tap into our ways of knowing (epistemological)—and unknowing—in a deep and often mysterious way. They have the power to offer multiple perspectives, to change us—to be transformative. Finally, I will offer examples of how the arts might inform

1. Fernandez, "Constructive Theology."

interfaith work at the seminary level by offering potential ideas for creative collaboration and imaginative possibilities for this work going forward.

Fernandez's use of the word "enterprise" is no doubt intentional. The word can be defined as "a project or understanding, typically one that is difficult or requires effort."[2] There are multiple ways to apply this, yet it is important to note that the writing and reflection on the intersections between art and interfaith dialogue is relatively new. There are not many guiding methods that have been developed. While a great deal of work is happening within both the arts and interfaith work, there has not been a systematic effort to investigate their intersectional relationship. In time, with further study and exploration, the power of what we can learn and then do with this dynamic collaboration will be increased. Hence, it is important to begin to explore what might be possible in this new and developing partnership.

A note about what I mean when I talk about the arts "leading the way": Our first experience with art is often in reading children's books, where images are used to "illustrate" a story being told in words. The "art" does not "lead the way," but rather plays a supplementary role to the written text. As is common in our culture, we are conditioned to see the arts as a secondary supporter of the primacy of words or concepts, diminishing the power of art to "lead the way." As a consequence, subtly or not so subtly, we are often more comfortable with words or concepts rather than an artistic experience: at the theater, we devour the playbill notes before the curtain goes up; in a gallery, we read the associated label to know what to see before even glancing at the work of art.

The arts, however, have the power to go ahead of us—to "lead"—and take us into places we might not otherwise access. If we start with art, our experience will inevitably be different, avoiding any preconditioning or predisposition to interpret the art from a particular angle or lens. Thus, saying the arts "lead the way" acknowledges they have, in and of themselves, an inherent power—a power with which to be reckoned and heeded.

ARTISTIC CHARACTERISTICS: MYSTERY, POLYVALENCY, AND TRANSFORMATION

How is it that the arts have this ability to move us to transcend and see another? Why should the arts at times have a primordial role? Let us explore three characteristics of the arts (and artists) that will be helpful as we

---

2. *Webster's Dictionary*, s.v. "Enterprise."

consider the intersection of the arts with interfaith dialogue: arts as mystery, polyvalent, and transformative.[3]

Mystery

In a review written for the Harvard Divinity Journal, Sarah Sentilles confesses that she "think[s] artists might be better at theology than many theologians are."[4] She calls upon her experience as an art teacher, describing her students, unlike theologians, as "comfortable in the gap, with mystery, with the unfinished—because that's where art lives."[5] This "gap, with mystery, with the unfinished" is one of the characteristics of the arts.

Theologian Paul Tillich describes mystery as more than what we currently do not understand or what in the future could "be discovered by a methodical cognitive approach." Mystery is a profound unknowing. "'Mystery'. . . is derived from *muein* [Greek], 'closing the eyes' or 'closing the mouth.' In gaining ordinary knowledge it is necessary to open one's eyes in order to grasp the object and to open one's mouth in order to communicate with other people and to have one's insights tested. A genuine mystery, however, is experienced in an attitude that contradicts the attitude of ordinary cognition."[6] It lives beyond known language. Tillich asserts, mystery "cannot lose its mysteriousness even when it is revealed."[7] Mystery remains "unfinished." That is, mystery can never be a phenomenon—or perception—that is resolved or grasped, only ineffably experienced. Mystery contains a tension between "ordinary knowledge" and ineffable experience. Mystery, then, as a characteristic of the arts, is experienced through practice and process; artists "live in" mystery, in a tension between cognition and inexpressible experience.

Like the arts, mystery is key in most faith traditions and practices, an ineffable experience beyond what Tillich names as "ordinary knowledge."[8] This experience of mystery increases every time an interfaith dialogue invites another faith partner into the conversation. So how can the work of artists help us understand this experience of mystery, especially as we engage in interfaith dialogue?

---

3. These are only three characteristics; others could and should be considered.

4. Sentilles, "Artists Make Good Theologians."

5. Ibid.

6. Tillich, *Systematic Theology*, vol. 1, 108–9.

7. Ibid.

8. Ibid.

Think for a moment about artists' regular creative processes. For example, fabric artists tie rubber bands around pieces of cloth and drop them into vats of dye to create a batik print. While they might have an intention for the pattern or an outcome, they know what is revealed in the end will be a mystery. A jazz trio will improvise a song, knowingly playing in the key of G, yet—through their improvisation and listening to each other and their audience—they do not know how the notes will come together until all the extemporized elements have emerged and merged when the sound of their instruments meet. In these few examples, we see how art and artists experience mystery in their creative work.

Let us draw upon this practice of artists as we bring the ability to "live in" and experience the unknowing—the mystery—into interfaith dialogue. Even though it is not clear or resolved, let us enter into this conversation and explore new relationships. For living with mystery calls for living with the tension of unknowing, with inexpressible experiences we hold side by side, yet which will not be resolved or finished.

Since a mystery remains unresolved, we have to find a way to live with the tension mystery creates. Artists are skilled at holding things in tension, between the known and unknown. It might be the pause before the crescendo in an orchestral piece or the final line from center stage; it might be the suspended moments a dancer holds a pose; it might be putting contrasting colors next to each other in a new way so that they vibrate with mysterious difference, yet still choosing to let the colors live next to each other; it might be pausing while listening before speaking; it might be knowing you are entering an experience that holds an anxious unknown "result."

As an example of this tension within mystery, let us talk about a moment at United when the arts informed our interfaith understanding by helping us see the tension, see the unresolved mystery. United has a significant program in the arts, integrated throughout the curriculum, including rotating art exhibitions. The main gallery space is located intentionally in the classroom wing. In this location, the gallery becomes an extension of the classroom, a space where concepts and ideas discussed in courses are often reflected in the artwork in the gallery.

One of the more poignant experiences happened when, by coincidence, we had a Muslim artist Fawzia Reda on campus as an artist-in-residence during the 2003 American invasion of Iraq. Reda had installed an exhibition of Islamic Calligraphy in the gallery, featuring three internationally renowned Muslim calligraphers and planned related educational events. Conversations in classrooms about theology, ethics, or just war theory became transformed when students had to first walk through a visual depiction of sacred Islamic texts on their way to preaching, Older Testament, or church history classes. The dissonance between the reports in the media and the beautifully shaped calligraphy—documenting love as understood in the Islamic tradition—had a significant impact; the art demanded we hold these conflicting experiences in the tension of mystery.

During the run of the exhibition, we had several related events including a workshop on calligraphy at United. Our students had the opportunity to work side-by-side with young people from the Islamic Center of Minnesota, located only two miles from the seminary. Having to "live in" mystery—unresolved tension—was immediately obvious. During break time, the male Muslim students went through the line for refreshments before the Muslim women, something that was not usual at United. Instead of letting this difference in custom become an awkward, acrimonious or even threatening situation, we all chose to live with the mystery and remain with the objective that brought us together in the first place—to be informed by the calligraphy texts on the walls and by the new pieces we made together. While academic reflection is important in interfaith dialogue, so also is this way of engaging the arts to help us build bridges instead of walls. Through the arts we "lived in" and experienced the tension of mystery, rather than needing a resolution between our differences.

Polyvalency

The concept of polyvalency is another characteristic of the arts, explored by the late Doug Adams, a leading theologian of the arts. The arts offer multiple perspectives and interpretations, that is, they are "polyvalent." Polyvalent stems from the Greek prefix *poly-* meaning "many, much, multi-," and the Latin verb *valentem*, meaning, "be worth." In its etymological roots, polyvalent means, "many or multiple worths."[9]

In a presentation to the faculty at United, Adams described his notion of polyvalency in the arts when he told of a typical class assignment in which he would ask students to work with five other classmates and spend an hour at a museum looking at the same work of art. During the course of a term, the process was repeated six different times. After each session, students were instructed to write a paper and present their observations to members of their small group.[10]

In the presentations, students quickly realized that while looking at the same artwork as their classmates, they all had distinctly different

9. *Online Etymology Dictionary*, s.v. "Poly-"

10. Faculty in-service at United Theological Seminary of the Twin Cities, Spring, 1998.

perceptions; the same work was seen in five distinctive ways. The students' reality of these multiple interpretations quickly moves to an appreciation of the artwork as polyvalent or indeterminate. The additional value of this process is that in the conversational give-and-take of "I see this" with "Yet, I see this," the point of discussion moved to a subject outside of themselves, that is, the polyvalency of artwork. A model emerged for how to be in dialogue about art and faith with this underlying, *a priori* assumption: we will have polyvalent "unresolved" perspectives and interpretations on the same subject matter.

Another example of the additive value of the arts through the concept of polyvalency for interfaith dialogue can be found in the work of Minneapolis photo documentarian, Wing Young Huie. Huie, who spent a year at United as an artist-in-residence, engages the medium of photography to tell stories. His photographs, almost exclusively in black and white, show contrasts amongst people, encourage questions, and invite multiple perspectives. Huie says of his art, "My goal is to move people beyond a sense of 'other' to a place where there is a connection or a sense of understanding."[11] Huie describes himself as a "tour guide," helping people move beyond the cultural bubbles and islands within which we often work and live.[12] Huie wants us to see what lies in-between our "cultural bubbles." As with Adams' classroom perspective-taking, Huie doesn't expect we will all perceive the same thing.[13] In viewing his photography, he assumes we will bring our own lens, our own perspective, while remaining open to the polyvalency discovered through his story-telling photographic art.[14]

A regular presenter in schools, corporations, and other settings, Huie invites audiences to look at an image that comes from the often 'unseen' parts of a community, such as photographs of a diversity of people often including different faith traditions.[15] His photographs have a polyvalency of meaning, some meanings particularly provocative. He does not seek, however, to be confrontational with his photographs. Rather, he seeks to

11. Conversation with the artist, October, 2014.

12. Combs, "Art Hero." In 2012, Marianne Combs, an arts reporter for Minnesota Public Radio, named Wing Young Huie an "Art Hero" for his photographic work. An Art Hero is someone who, "chooses to use his or her artistic talents to make the world a better place . . . [A] person who commits themselves day in and day out to transforming their communities through their art." Combs states that Huie's photographic work challenges us to move beyond "those people" and acknowledge "the other in us" and the "we" in all.

13. Boyd, "Minneapolis Photographer."

14. Ibid.

15. Regan, "Visual Arts | Wing."

help people further understand that their particular point of view—their lens—is framed by their life experience. Using a similar model to Doug Adams, when Huie asks a group to respond to the same photographic image, viewers quickly realize that multiple interpretations of the same image exist—and multiple experiences within the same community. Through this model incorporating art, viewers' lenses expand beyond the limited frame of their life experiences, opening them to perceive people (and other faith traditions) in polyvalent ways.[16]

Transformation

Finally, let us consider the third characteristic of the arts—transformation. Intermedia Arts, an arts organization in Minneapolis, has as its tag line, "Art Changes Everything."[17] While the claim is bold, it is not far off. The arts have the power to transform; they are agents of change. Art historian and theologian, Robin Jensen, in her book, *The Substance of Things Seen: Art, Faith, and the Christian Community*, illuminates this idea:

> When we consciously attend to an object, especially an art object, we will have some kind of reaction to it. The response may be subtle or it may be strong. It may be positive or negative. We may be turned off, aroused, repulsed, delighted, or disappointed. We may be moved to tears, frightened, bored, or baffled. Our responses may be different from those of the person next to us. But no matter how we respond, we are slightly or significantly different for having had the viewing, or the hearing—for having paid attention. Maybe only a single atom of our consciousness has shifted; maybe a landslide has taken place in our souls. Indelible memories may be fixed or recovered. We may not be aware of much impact, or we may recognize that this was a significant moment. Still, something happens. The experience and our response often resist explanation in words, reminding us that we can know or learn things without the benefit of language. Our memories, even our ideas, are essentially constructed out of images and colors, spatial relationships, smells, sensations, and sounds, more than they are made of words ordered into sentences—even when we record and transmit them this way.[18]

16. Huie, "Changing Lenses."
17. Intermedia Arts Mission Statement.
18. Jensen, *The Substance of Things Seen*, 3.

While Jensen refers to a visual art object, the same can be said when experiencing a piece of music, poetry, or any other art form: "something has happened." In ways beyond language, we are transformed as we "live in" the mystery of the arts experience: during a theater performance, it is that moment when the audience transforms to become part of the story the cast is telling; during a dance recital or spoken-word performance, it is that second when everyone transforms into a collective breath taken amid a deeply moving scene; during a poetry reading or a movie, it is that instant when we transform to a collective body, leaning forward for the pinnacle plot twist or leaning back in utter stillness. These are moments where "something has happened," where transformation has shifted our souls, when we "live in" the arts.

Similarly, as we let the arts "lead the way," in our engagement in interfaith dialogue, we have to be open to change—and to being changed. We have to begin with the faith and belief that if we are fully present and involved in dialogue, something will happen—*transformation.* Like the experience of the arts, interfaith dialogue leads us into the profound unknown, expanding our lens, leaving us forever changed as human beings and people of faith.

Let us further engage the concept of transformation by calling upon the writing of Maureen H. O'Connell in her book, *If These Walls Could Talk: Community Muralism and the Beauty of Justice.* O'Connell describes how the City of Philadelphia Mural Arts Program (Mural Arts), the nation's largest public art program, is a model for community development, healing, and restorative justice across the country and around the world.[19]

Founded by Jane Golden, Mural Arts began in 1984 as part of an effort to address the city's graffiti problems. In time, the program shifted its focus from anti-graffiti to a mural arts collective. Through the collaborative partnerships of organizations in the community—nonprofit and community groups, the private sector, schools, philanthropic organizations, and city agencies—community members have created more than 3,800 public murals.[20]

Much like Intermedia Arts in Minneapolis, the Mural Arts program has as its mission statement, "We believe art ignites change.[21]" Their work involves a wide range of restorative-justice initiatives centered on the arts for youth and people struggling with mental illness, trauma, or addiction. The process, "empowers artists to be change agents, stimulates dialogue

19. O'Connell, *If These Walls Could Talk,* xi–xiv.
20. City of Philadelphia Mural Arts, "City of Philadelphia Mural."
21. Ibid.

about critical issues, and builds bridges of connection and understanding."[22] The community-wide Mural Arts builds indispensable bridges for interfaith understanding.

O'Connell suggests that the scenes from the murals create and project a "visible religion." Says O'Connell: "[The murals] make it possible for urban faith communities to take up these questions and risk engaging religious difference with intentionality and integrity."[23] O'Connell notes that the Mural Arts Program has brought together community activists, neighborhoods, educators, religious leaders, artists, and persons interested in the transformative power of the arts.[24] It is not, however, just the act of gathering that brings about transformation—several components must be in place for transformation to happen. First, the process must be intentional—an intentional model for interaction and dialogue. This process must generate new and multiple perspectives for people in an environment that invites true listening and an openness to change. Second, the process must include sharing experiences with people never before met, for this creates new and multiple perspectives. These new and multiple perspectives, in turn, bring about a transformation, the shifting, the new understanding in our souls. Finally, the change, the transformation, must be fueled by the unique power of the arts to be dynamic and expansive beyond one particular community or tradition.[25]

Gayle Lacks, a participant in Mural Arts and member of the Mount Airy Synagogue P'Nai Or in Philadelphia, says she discovered painting murals with those of other faiths and traditions is critical to understanding and building community.[26] O'Connell describes it this way: "Effective interreligious dialogue begins with embodied contact among believers. . .[Even] the process of mural making begins not with a focus on the final product, but rather with attention on the people who come together to create it."[27] O'Connell goes on to write, "[I]nterfaith muralists do not begin with

22. Ibid.

23. O'Connell, *If These Walls Could Talk*, 253–54.

24. Salisbury, "Interfaith Effort." Sculptor Joe Brenman, a member of Mishkan Shalom synagogue in Philadelphia and a planner of the mural process, states, "The whole project is about interfaith and people from different cultures getting along." Current Philadelphia city mayor, James Kenney, participated in a mural project in the basement of Al-Aqsa Islamic Society. He recounts, "joining in with dozens of children and adults who were Muslims, Jews, Christians, and probably some unbelievers, all busy using paint brushes, rolling clay, and decorating unfired tiles."

25. O'Connell, *If These Walls Could Talk*, 254.

26. Salisbury, "Interfaith Effort."

27. O'Connell, *If These Walls Could Talk*, 255.

what Islam, Judaism, or Buddhism might have to say about poverty, violence, or religion in public life. Rather, they begin by listening to what their Muslim, Jewish, or Buddhist neighbors have to say about these issues in light of the way they influence through mural art a particular space in the community. In many ways, the final product—the visual culmination of this engagement—is secondary, even from the perspective of the lead muralist."[28]

Two factors are at work here: the embodied knowing and listening, and the ability to see something outside of ourselves. As Adams points out in his work on polyvalency, anytime we take something that we revere and attempt to see it outside of our singular perspective, the possibility of being more objective and less protective becomes actualized. O'Connell writes that the creation of "visible religion" out of mural-making allows people not only to work together (embodied knowing and listening), but also to see the things about which they might disagree, literally outside of themselves, on a wall, as part of a mural artwork.[29] This unique ability happens, in part, because the arts work as symbols, like mystery (according to Tillich), pointing beyond language. Since language can be misinterpreted or divisive, leading with the arts on one hand, helps us avoid the brokenness of being stymied by our canopied theological constructions, which by their grammar of faith generally fail to offer a starting point for shared viewpoints and symbols; and on the other hand, using the arts, whether by doing, performing, or viewing them, we move beyond our constructive language to discover a starting point with our neighbor, regardless of their tradition or tribe, to see, to imagine, to understand one another and ourselves in these traditions, and as neighbors in faith. We can actualize interfaith dialogue, advancing a deeper knowing of each other.

Even with the best intentions, interfaith dialogue that begins only with words can quickly fall captive to a practice of comparing doctrines looking for places of resonance or dissimilarity.[30] In contrast, in the practice of art "images in the faith-based community murals—angels, crucifixes, geometric shapes, doves, lotus flowers, families, trees, streams, bridges, doorways—transcend the limits of word-driven or word-bound interreligious dialogue and invoke the imagination as a viable method of communication across religious difference."[31] As "visible religion," they invite a conversation between people that does not depend on language, but rather on art images that speak

28. Ibid.

29. Ibid., 253–62.

30. Ibid., 252–63.

31. Ibid., 254.

to commonly held and shared values.[32] O'Connell writes: "A visible religion identifies shared visions of the common good and identifies practices—not simply verbal statements—that bring that vision into being. It is not wary of emotions that often drive wedges between religious communities but welcomes them as a common denominator of the human experience and a means of motivating shared commitment to certain values."[33]

The community mural project perhaps represents all three artistic characteristics—mystery, polyvalency, and transformation. In the act of gathering and living in mystery, the muralists experience the profound unknowing amongst themselves; in creating "visible religion" they multiply perspectives; in experiencing the arts together they discover the transcendent truths held in each religion, their souls shift, and they are transformed.

IMPLICATIONS AND POSSIBILITIES
FOR SEMINARIES AND FAITH COMMUNITIES

Let us turn now to what this might mean for seminaries and the interfaith communities they serve. How might we live into the expectation of educating leaders who can function with imagination and faithfulness to their tradition, and unconditionally dwell with hospitality in the pluralism of our time? In this section, I will suggest options for teaching, resources, and the possibilities that exist for community partnerships.

Not every seminary will have the same resources or an arts focus in their curriculum, yet most schools can lead with the arts to serve as a partner in teaching and learning. We do not have to be artists or art historians to draw upon the arts in teaching. We *do* need to engage the arts with thoughtfulness and integrity. And if we are willing to take the risk of engaging with faithfulness with our interfaith partners (and if we heed the cautions listed later), we will be rewarded.

Seminaries can and should look to the community for collaborative partners in teaching and learning. In reflecting on the ways in which the arts can lead, we might begin by noticing that artists and arts organizations—galleries, museums, theaters, city tours of sacred spaces, etc.—are already leading the way in interfaith conversation. While artists might not create their work with an explicit theological lens, we can engage them in teaching and dialogue concerning how their art intersects with the interfaith traditions found in the communities in which they live. For instance, the art collections of museums offer a possibility for inviting students to experience

32. Ibid., 253–62.
33. Ibid., 254.

mystery, multiple perspectives (polyvalency), and transformation. We will explore more explicitly some existing collaborations later in this chapter.

In creating syllabi or class assignments, faculty should invite students to be involved in arts experiences, including the creation of artwork, which exposes them to the characteristics of mystery, polyvalency, and transformation. Faculty also need to participate in these experiences. That means, in addition to traditional forms of learning, there need to be opportunities to teach and learn that engage the wider community's artists and arts organizations beyond the classroom.

One can invite the arts to lead the way in interfaith dialogue at one's doorstep. It does not require traveling to an international context. An interchange between the arts and interfaith dialogue can be found in a local setting or an online platform. For example, world religion classes could assign visits to places of worship outside the faith traditions of the students, attendance of religious services, and engagement with religious symbols, ritual objects, statuary, and other religious artworks. Leaders of the community who are fluent in the arts and various religious traditions can be utilized as guest instructors or one-time presenters. Faculty should strive to develop fluency and understand the arts, as well as acknowledging the value of others as experts in their respective traditions and roles. Guest instructors leading a class can also relieve the resident faculty of teaching responsibilities, allowing them to experience more fully the power of the arts and architecture in the same context as the students.

Faculty members might find in some geographic locations that architectural tours of religious structures are readily available. Chicago has a significant series entitled, "Beautiful Spaces, Sacred Spaces: Sacred Space International Tour Series." This tour series, founded in 2002 by Suzanne Morgan, aims to promote interfaith education and dialogue through the understanding of religious architecture. Morgan, a retired architect with expertise in liturgical design, started the organization in response to the events of 9/11 and the subsequent climate of fear and misunderstanding of Islam. Morgan believes religious architecture can serve as a catalyst for interfaith dialogue and education. Without promoting any single faith or tradition, the tour series seeks to use the common language of architecture as an educational means to foster reciprocal respect, new perspectives, and mutual appreciation of the multiple faith traditions comprising our pluralistic society.[34] Deidre Colgan, the executive director of this Chicago-based

---

34. Colgan, "Sacred Spaces."

Sacred Space International tour series, says, "Architecture is the most visual and accessible way to understand a faith and its practices."[35]

The PBS production, *God in America*, a co-production of *American Experience* and *Frontline*, incorporates the Chicago-based Sacred Space International tour series, making it accessible on the Internet.[36] The tour series also provides a guide for planning a tour in one's local area, and is available as a downloadable PDF.[37] This guide, written by Colgan, includes information for faculty to pre-plan tours, as well as providing material for students on appropriate dress, "Dos and Don'ts," and questions to consider for dialogue about the experience. Similar sacred-spaces tour download-able guides are also available for other cities including Atlanta, Boston, New Orleans, the New York City area, Portland (Oregon), San Francisco, and Santa Fe.[38] These guides can be used as case studies or as models for how to engage the transformative experience of the interfaith sacred spaces in your own area.

Let us briefly consider now two other examples of community collabo-ration with arts organizations and interfaith conversation. I offer them as examples of what could be done and what partnerships might be available.

In 2014, the Cincinnati Art Museum offered a series entitled, "Spiritu-al Pilgrimage in Art." The five-part series explored "how Jewish, Christian, Islamic and Hindu pilgrimage traditions are manifested through artistic expression."[39] The event drew upon not only the works in the museums, but again invited viewers into houses of worship. The list of community partners included The Center for Interfaith Community Engagement at Xavier University, the Islamic Center of Greater Cincinnati, places of wor-ship, educational partners, and three museums. In addition to the explicit invitation of welcome and hospitality into houses of worship, the program included self-guided tours and plenary sessions.

A second example of community collaboration with the arts and inter-faith dialogue is the British Museum exhibition, "Hajj: Journey to the Heart of Islam." Premiering in 2012, and now available as an online exhibition, it includes objects (both historical and contemporary) that brought to life the Hajj, the fifth pillar of Islam.[40] The exhibition offered visitors (Muslim and non-Muslim) insight into the Hajj, an obligatory historical and spiritual

35. Bracheaer, *Seeker*.
36. Colgan, "Sacred Spaces."
37. Sacred Spaces International, "Visiting Sacred Spaces."
38. Colgan, "Sacred Spaces."
39. ÆQUI, "Collaborative Partnership."
40. Baker, "Mysteries of the Hajj."

journey (Qur'an, Surah 3:97). In addition to the exhibition catalogue (which could be used as a class resource), the website offers images, and personal "Hajj stories."[41] A notable work, "Magnetism," offers a tangible representation of the movement around the Ka'ba (Kaaba) that happens during the Hajj. Iron fillings, attracted by magnets, give us a visual glimpse of the mystery and power of the experience. One of the largest spiritual pilgrimages in the world comes alive in new ways through art objects and stories that convey the transformative power of the Hajj ritual. These are not solitary examples; they are two of many such possibilities that can be accessed by faculty.

In some cases the invitation to engage in these transformative experiences becomes easier when the participant can enter through what some might call a more "neutral" space. Peter Morrin writes, "It is not always easy for a Catholic to visit a synagogue. . . but under the museum auspices, people of different faiths feel welcome. The whole idea is to promote mutual understanding among the congregations through art," to create, Morrin says, "a common language, a language based on art and architecture."[42] In addition to the transformative experiences that museums present, the other important benefit of working with a museum is that they almost always provide educational materials to help visitors learn and reflect. While their mission is to provide a greater understanding of art, they can also serve as a helpful partner in interfaith understanding and experience by leading with the arts.

The importance of these interactions, in person or online, is not only for current students within a course; these types of assignments also model the ways in which future graduates can engage their confirmation students and adults in their congregations in learning about other faith traditions. The experiential model can lead others in learning how to live thoughtfully and at ease in a multifaith world.

EXPANDING THE FRAME: A CASE STUDY

Finally, let me offer an example that again lifts up the work of an artist as leading us into interfaith dialogue. Another avenue for creative engagement comes from becoming immersed—being present—to the work of performing artists. In the spring of 2015, United held a conference entitled, "Faithful Leaders in a Multifaith World."[43] The event, designed to assist participants

41. The British Museum, "Hajj."
42. Mason, "Museum Hosts Interfaith Exchange."
43. United Theological Seminary, "Faithful Leadership."

in expanding their literacy in multifaith settings, included plenary sessions, workshops, and the arts. In this latter case, we invited three performance artists to share their moving personal narratives about their experiences navigating Minnesota's primarily Christian landscape. Within moments during each performance, we were pulled into their first-person narratives; vivid and often painful descriptions of what it meant for them to live in a place where they were not part of the dominant religious or ethnic culture.

Each story was poignant and meaningful; yet let me reflect particularly on a four-minute scene performed by Aamera Siddiqu, a Minneapolis artist. Siddiqu identifies as a non-practicing Muslim, born in India. The scene Siddiqu narrated, entitled, "Communion," comes from her play "American as Curry Pie." Siddiqu begins by sitting in a chair, taking on the posture of an eleven-year-old dressed in the required uniform for Holy Cross Catholic School and Church.

Siddiqu, re-enacting a moment from her Catholic school, suddenly jolts the audience as the shrill voice of Sister Mary Frances hissing out a command, "Psst, you—don't take communion." Siddiqu looks up at Sister Mary Frances, aware that these sharp words are repeated to her each Friday morning when the class receives communion. Sister Mary Frances whispers again, "Psst, you—don't take communion." Each week the same words, an act of exclusion, were offered even as others were welcome. With those words, a meal meant to be a radical act of hospitality became again and again a radical experience of exclusion.

By giving us the flavor of the language and voice she heard from Sister Mary Francis, along with the other obstacles she encountered, Siddiqu brought us into her story, offering us her perspective. In that moment, her first-person narrative drew us in, not to judge, but to participate in her experience. We were there with her, sitting in a school desk, dressed in a school uniform, looking over her shoulder—we were in that moment, hearing the harsh words of Sister Mary Francis.

In Siddiqui's flawless performance, it was obvious she had not only performed but also *re-lived* the experience. She asked us to stand in her shoes, to sit in her desk, to see it in a new way. She allowed us into that grade-school class to hear the disrespect of her sacred tradition, the dismissal of what she knew to be holy. The transformative power of the arts meant we shifted in soul from being ourselves to being her; our ground of being shook.

The arts invite us to "see" from different perspectives, to suspend for a moment what we know, to enter into another's dance or verse or song or storied symbol, to "see" from their perspective. As is true with interfaith dialogue, we arrive at that place with our own brokenness, our own inability to "see" other people. Even in our attempt to love the other, we fail to truly "live in" the mystery. Yet, these artistic moments grant us bold invitations, momentary opportunities for change, for "ah ha!" moments. Siddiqui could have shared a whole litany of statistics about the number of mosques in Minnesota that day, or lectured about the experience of being a Muslim, but in that four-minute story we learned much more. And we were changed.

The gathered audience (alums, clergy, religious leaders, and students) sat motionless, drawn in by Siddiqu's words, equally moved by the stories others shared. After the last spoken-word performer, time had been built in to pause and silently reflect, after which the facilitator asked, "How did it make you feel?" The words came quickly—embarrassed, ashamed, sorry—judging our way of being, our inability to "see." The power of the stories permeated our hearts and drew us in. We were firsthand witnesses to the pain and struggle of living in a place where the dominant culture was so ignorant. We could see the ways in which we were all complicit in adding to those hurtful experiences. This shared realization led us into the possibility of profound transformation.

The performers offered multiple perspectives, inviting us into the experience of mystery; we entered into a new dialogue that, while not resolved, had changed us in significant ways. In our hospitality to invite another into our school, our world, our story, we also were the visitors welcomed into the hospitality of the artist who shared her storytelling, her lived experience, and her symbols with us.

WORDS OF CAUTION

Let us consider some words of caution as we lead with the arts in interfaith dialogue. A conversation with Gail Anderson, founder of EmpathyWorks, Minneapolis and former director of Interfaith and Intercultural Initiatives at United, offers the following insights:

> We must realize that in interfaith dialogue, encountering art from another faith tradition can open the door to dialogue but when we look at or experience art we must realize that a superficial look will not bring greater understanding *prima facie*. We must understand that our viewpoint will always be limited by our distance from the context of what it (the art) means both from a different religious perspective and from an arts perspective. For instance, are we to appreciate the art in an interfaith context as art or as religious symbol? In either case we must acknowledge and appreciate that we have a built-in limitation

when engaging art that does not come out of our own faith tradition.[44]

We would be wise to approach a work of Muslim Calligraphy as an inquirer. In addition to attending to the artistic aesthetics, we might invite a learned companion to join us to help us engage with the work's religious meaning. In this way we can embody the hospitality of seeing art in community and have the ability to look at a work over the shoulder of someone who comes from the tradition, someone from the Muslim faith who understands what it means to create, observe and understand it not only from an arts perspective but also from a faith perspective.

The words of caution by Wilson Yates are similarly helpful here. Yates, president emeritus and distinguished professor emeritus of Religion, Society and the Arts at United, talks about the difference between being a tourist and a pilgrim when it comes to the arts. In talking about the theological treatment of art, Yates makes the case that to approach a work of art we must come with an intention to participate in a dialogue and not a monologue. A dialogue, Yates says, will necessarily involve three actors—the artist, the work of art, and the viewer. As a viewer, we must always acknowledge that each work of art has its own identity, its own autonomous presence. Each work of art has a history, a cultural context, and a style. The same is true for the artist. As a viewer, we bring all of these pieces with us as well—our context, our background, and our own biased understanding.[45]

Yates asserts that, as theologians, we must take the artist seriously in the dialogue. We must figuratively make room for the artist at the table and invite them to sit down, not stand at a distance, but participate. We must provide the artist and the artwork with hospitality and welcome, that is, to "live in" their mystery. Thus begins a dialogue in which all three actors—the artist, the work of art, and the theologian/viewer—are on equal footing, a place where hospitality can truly take place.[46] The arts, with this model of caution, dialogue, and hospitality, can lead interfaith dialogue by example into a richer knowing across traditions.

CONCLUDING THOUGHTS

Sarah Sentilles recalls the words of the late Harvard professor and theologian, Gordon Kaufman, who taught her "theologians are artists. Their

44. Conversation with Gail Anderson, March 2016.
45. Yates, "Theology and the Arts, 39–41."
46. Ibid.

creations are not works of art to be hung on the wall; . . . rather they are worlds to be lived in."[47] Likewise, the arts are not merely hung objects to beautify our walls at home or in a seminary setting. Rather, arts of all forms draw us into "worlds to be lived in," worlds that hold mystery, polyvalency, and the possibility of change. By inviting the arts and artists to lead the way into interfaith dialogue, the worlds in which we live will surge with uncommon, ineffable experiences and rich perspectives, along with subtle as well as profound transformations.

In the end, what does this all mean? It means it will not be easy; it will be an enterprise—yet one worthy of our efforts. It means hospitality must be offered, and interfaith dialogue needs to make a place at the table for poets and writers, dancers and actors, musicians and painters. It means we must be "comfortable in the gap . . . with the unfinished"[48] answers, yet knowing we will have created a sacred space in which we will "live in" the mystery. It means living with the unknowing—the unresolved—in the way artists teach us to live.

This chapter only begins to address some of the existing possibilities. We need a more ongoing and thorough investigation in order to expand on this partnership. While I have not covered all of the possible opportunities, I believe I have offered suggestions and insights to inform our settings, challenging us to consider fresh options in advancing interfaith dialogue with the arts leading the way. I know, as we end here, we will find our way—yet only if we willingly labor together to build artistic bridges, desiring and seeking greater understanding.

BIBLIOGRAPHY

Adams, Doug. *Transcendence with the Human Body in Art: George Segal, Stephen de Staebler, Jasper Johns, and Christo.* New York: Crossroad, 1991.

ÆQUI. "Collaborative Partnership of Museums and Houses of Worship Explore Spiritual Pilgrimage in Art." February 8, 2014. http://aeqai.com/main/2014/02/collaborative-partnership-of-museums-and-houses-of-worship-explore-spiritual-pilgrimage-in-art/.

Baker, David R. "Mysteries of the Hajj Revealed as British Museum Opens Exhibition On Muslim Pilgrimage to Mecca." *Daily Mail* (January, 2012). http://www.dailymail.co.uk/news/article-2092056/British-Museum-Hajj-Exhibition-Mysteries-Muslim-pilgrimage-Mecca-revealed.html.

Bednarowski, Mary. "Theological Creativity and the Powerful Persistence of Traditional Religious Symbols." *ARTS (Arts in Religious and Theological Studies)* 12/2 (2000) 27–32.

47. Sentilles, "Artists Make Good Theologians."
48. Ibid.

Boyd, Cynthia Boyd. "Minneapolis Photographer Uses His Camera to Bring Diverse Community Together." https://www.minnpost.com/community-sketchbook/2013/05/minneapolis-photographer-uses-his-camera-bring-diverse-community-togeth.

Brachaer, Manya. "The Seeker." http://newsblogs.chicagotribune.com/religion_theseeker/2009/07/architecture-interfaith.html.

The British Museum. "An exhibition of profound cultural importance." 2012. http://www.britishmuseum.org/whats_on/Past_exhibitions/2012/hajj.aspx.

———. "Hajj: Journey to the Heart of Islam." 2012. http://www.britishmuseum.org/whats_on/past_exhibitions/2012/hajj/hajj_stories.aspx.

City of Philadelphia Mural Arts Program. "City of Philadelphia Mural." http://www.muralarts.org/about.

Colgan, Deirdre. "Sacred Spaces: Chicago." 2010. http://www.pbs.org/godinamerica/outreach/sacred-spaces-chicago.html.

Combs, Marianne. "Art Hero Wing Young Huie." November 19, 2012. http://www.mprnews.org/story/2012/11/19/arts/art-hero-wing-young-huie.

Fernandez, Eleazar. "Constructive Theology, Art, and Prophetic Moral Imagination." Lecture, Spring Convocation on "The Church and the Arts," United Theological Seminary of the Twin Cities, New Brighton, MN, April 27, 2005.

Henson, David R. "Be a Poet, Not a Preacher During Holy Week: Why #WorldPoetryDay Matters to the Church." May, 2016. http://www.patheos.com/blogs/davidhenson/2016/03/be-a-poet-not-a-preacher-during-holy-week-why-worldpoetryday-matters-to-the-church/.

Huie, Wing Young. "Changing Lenses." In *From the Archive—Roosevelt High School Students, Minneapolis, MN Lake Street USA (1997–2000)* (blog). *(k)now: A Blog by Wing Young Huie,* n.d. http://know.wingyounghuie.com/page/3.

Iraqi+American Reconciliation Project. "The Interfaith Bridging Initiative." September, 2009. http://reconciliationproject.org/2012/arts-and-bridges-exhibit/.

Jensen, Robin M. *The Substance of Things Seen: Art, Faith, and the Christian Community.* Grand Rapids: Eerdmans, 2004.

Mason, M.S. "Museum Hosts Interfaith Exchange through Art." *The Christian Science Monitor,* May 7, 1997. http://www.csmonitor.com/1997/0507/050797.feat.arts.1.html.

Nightingale, Eithne. "Religion and Material Culture at the Victoria." *Material Religion* 6/3 (2010) 218–35.

O'Connell, Maureen. *If These Walls Could Talk: Community Muralism and the Beauty of Justice.* Collegeville, MN: Liturgical, 2012.

Patel, Eboo. "New Rooms in the Interfaith Movement." *Harvard Divinity Bulletin* 43 (Winter/Spring 2015) n.p. http://bulletin.hds.harvard.edu/articles/winterspring2015/new-rooms-interfaith-movement.

Rosen, Aaron. *Art + Religion in the 21st Century.* London: Thames & Hudson, 2015.

Sacred Space International. "Visiting Sacred Spaces: 'How To' Guide." 2010. www-tc.pbs.org/godinamerica/art/VisitingSacredSpaces.pdf.

Salisbury, Stephan. "Interfaith Effort Works to Beautify Philadelphia Mosque." *Philly.Com* (January 11, 2016). http://articles.philly.com/2016-01-11/news/69656572_1_islamic-state-mural-arts-program-west-philadelphia.

Sentilles, Sarah. "Artists Make Good Theologians." *Harvard Divinity Bulletin* 43/1–2 (2015) n.p. http://bulletin.hds.harvard.edu/articles/winterspring2015/artists-make-good-theologians.

Steckel, Clyde. "The Role of the Arts in Theological Education." Lecture, United Theological Seminary of the Twin Cities, New Brighton, MN, May 29, 2014.

Tillich, Paul. *Systematic Theology.* Vol. 1. Chicago: University of Chicago Press, 1973.

United Theological Seminary of the Twin Cities. "Faithful Leadership in a Multifaith World" (video). May 15, 2015. https://www.youtube.com/watch?v=f4oM1_rh71A.

The University of St. Thomas. "Interfaith Art pARTners: A Twin Cities Festival." 2011. http://www.stthomas.edu/interfaithart/.

Yates, Wilson. "The Arts as Companions on the Spiritual Journey." Lecture, ATS Biennial pre-conference, Guthrie Theatre, Minneapolis, June 19, 2011.

———. "The Intersections of Art and Religion: Reflections on Works from the Minneapolis Institute of Arts." *ARTS (Arts in Religious and Theological Studies)* 10/1 (1998) 17–27.

———. "Theology and the Arts after Seventy Years: Toward a Dialogical Approach." *ARTS (Arts in Religious and Theological Studies)* 26/3 (2015) 35–41.

12

"The Sacrament of Human Life"
Cultivating Intentional Interreligious Learning in Congregations[1]

—SHERYL A. KUJAWA-HOLBROOK

The sacrament of human life is the sacrament
that supersedes our religions.
We live before we believe,
and we are human before we are religious.
Our life together is a temple where we all meet.[2]

—SAMIR SELMANOVIC

INTERRELIGIOUS LEARNING EMANATES FROM the collective belief that we are all, despite our religious differences, part of one human community; if life is improved for just one person due to our efforts, all benefit. Samir Selmanovic, a Christian minister, and the founder of Faith House Manhattan, an intentionally interreligious community, refers to "the sacrament of human life" as the lived experience in which women and men

---

1. This article is based in research from my ten-year study of interreligious learning in congregations. See Kujawa-Holbrook, *God beyond Borders*.

2. Selmanovic, *It's Really All about God*, 58.

of all religious and philosophies share, and develop deeper relationships where mutual understanding is possible. Selmanovic said that he founded Faith House out of an interest to "build a church where Christians are not in charge. . . . We wanted to include all the people who have a right to belong and be partners in the discussion, not as outsiders that need to be converted, but as insiders that we need to be interdependent with."[3] Selmanovic believes that communities like Faith House are urgently needed in this world, and that, through shared study and spiritual practices, people from different religious traditions will *actually learn to need one another.*"[4] This compelling vision of interreligious learning also serves to challenge our faith communities. How might congregations more effectively cultivate interreligious learning?

Many of the religious leaders of the world support the notion that while there are many differences between religions, we also share in the common work of peace and reconciliation for the sake of a better world and for the preservation of our planet. "My humanity is bound up in yours," said Desmond Tutu, Archbishop emeritus of Cape Town, "for we can only be human together."[5] "There is so much work yet to be done," says Juliet Hollister, founder of The Temple of Understanding, a group dedicated to interreligious education and dialogue. "It is so clear to me that all we have to do is awaken to the fact that we are all ONE, or as my friend Father Thomas Merton has so rightly said, 'We are already ONE . . . what we have to become is what we already are.' It seems so simple, doesn't it? Yet there is so much more work to do. So much more work."[6] Betty Williams of The Peace People movement of Northern Ireland believes that building a sense of our common humanity has a direct connection to the reality of peace for all people. "We believe in taking down the barriers, but we also believe in the most energetic reconciliation among people by getting them to know each other, talk each other's languages, understand each other's fears and beliefs, getting to know each other physically, philosophically and spirituality. It is much harder to kill your neighbor than the thousands of unknown and hostile aliens at the end of a missile."[7]

The Jewish tradition refers to the practice of *tikkun olam,* or the healing and the repair of the world. People of goodwill, people of faith, are knit together in a global and interdependent world, and have the opportunity

3. Ibid.
4. Ibid.
5. Tutu, Tutu Foundation.
6. Hollister, The Temple of Understanding.
7. Williams, The Peace People, Northern Ireland.

through interreligious learning to be transformed for the sake of one another and for the world. Each generation is called to respond to the promises and the challenges of their day, and while the promises and the challenges of the early twenty-first century are numerous indeed, the demographics alone suggest that how we are to live with and respect religious differences is a prevailing question. Of course, we can choose to ignore the realities of people of other religious traditions living in our midst.

Kate Galloway, leader of the Iona Community in Scotland, an ecumenical group that has been praying for peace since 1938, wonders if the priorities of faith communities are self-obsessed, rather than engaged in ways to do something better for people in their local communities, and elsewhere in the world. "Were our beautiful church buildings, our wonderful liturgies, our plainsong and musical Passions, our magnificent artwork, our gilded cities worth one single child's life, one African, one indigenous, one Jewish child's life?" she asks.[8]

Eboo Patel, the founder and executive director of the Interfaith Youth Core, and a Muslim, works with young people and many groups across the country to encourage them to actively and positively engage with religious diversity. He delineates seven responses made by religious communities in response to religious pluralism. The first is to build a "bubble" in the belief that the particular tradition is to be followed so closely that adherents need to be closed off from others. There are traditions that have succeeded in doing this in ways that are respectful of others, such as Amish communities. But for those communities that have neither the commitment nor the resources to exist in a bubble, Patel explores other options, including "the barrier," or those who accentuate the differences between their religious tradition and others. The third is "the bomb," for those who seek to kill those of other religious traditions. "Bigotry," the fourth option, goes beyond the option of the barrier in that it not only opposes other religious traditions, but it also denigrates them. The fifth option is "bifurcation," or those who live two different lives, a faith life and a church life. The sixth option, "blasé," is for those so confused by religious diversity that they opt out completely altogether.[9]

The last option, the *bridge*, embraces Patel's image for faith communities interested in cultivating interreligious learning. "I think the theology of the bridge, the practice of the bridge, the faith formation of the bridge is going to be key not only to civil life in the 21st century but to maintaining faith

---

8. Galloway, "From the Holy City," 3–4.
9. Patel, "Acts of Faith," 37–39.

identity," he says.[10] Further, Patel extends the image of the bridge to his own faith community: "My highest hope is that Muslims in America can situate themselves as a stone in this bridge, just one stone. We are next to a Jewish stone and a Christian stone, each of us together forming an arch for humanity to cross this bridge from a time of crisis to a time of cooperation."[11]

Patel believes that faith communities interested in building bridges need to break out of the "clash of civilizations" mentality, prevalent in many media approaches to religious pluralism. Instead of starting with the assumption that different traditions are locked in adversarial relationships, a position that in actuality gives honor to extremists of all religious groups, Patel proposes that we begin with the assumption of interreligious cooperation. "We live in a world of Jews, Muslims, Christians, Hindus, Secularists, Buddhists, Baha'is, who want to live in equal dignity and mutual loyalty with the other in a world in which extremists want to dominate all of us," he says. "We do not honor extremists by giving them the title 'Muslim,' 'Jewish,' 'Christian,' 'Secularist,' or 'Hindu.' We call them what they are: the extremists of all traditions belong to one tradition, the tradition of extremism."[12]

The challenges of cultivating interreligious learning are not with Christianity, Islam, Judaism, Buddhism, Hunduism, or other religious traditions *per se*, but rather with the conflicts which arise between adherents—Christians, Jews, Muslims, etc. In other words, the knowledge of other religious traditions, as important as it is, cannot build bridges alone. Patel emphasizes both the need for knowledge, including teaching our children about their own tradition and their religious neighbors, along with the skills needed to fully appreciate religious diversity and creatively engage those of traditions and cultures different from our own. "It's the way we put these stones together that create a bridge that people can walk over," he says.[13]

Sociologist of religion Robert Wuthnow believes that one of the impacts of globalization is that American Christianity, as well as other religions, are involved in increasing global engagement. The greater ease of transportation, communication, migration, and integration with other parts of the world is inextricably linked with the various cultures we are a part of, including religious culture. While there is no single world culture, local communities find themselves more connected with people in other parts of the world now more than ever. The overall global shift in world Christianities to the Southern Hemisphere has also brought Christians into

10. Ibid., 40.

11. Ibid.

12. Ibid., 40.

13. Ibid.

close encounter with other religions. One positive result of globalization is the growth in religious and humanitarian aid and relief organizations, many of which are interreligious in character. These organizations have created new alliances for the betterment of all humanity and the planet. On a local level in faith communities, preaching and teaching about the common bond between peoples, and the responsibility to be engaged with neighbors of other religious traditions, is a recurring theme. "The challenge for congregations large or small will nevertheless be one of striking an appropriate balance between the needs of the congregation itself and people of other countries [and other religious groups]," claims Wuthnow. "Because of the tendency to emphasize local concerns, effort will be required to motivate involvement in global activities."[14]

Wuthnow's research on congregational engagement finds that projects in local congregations that are based in the encounter of people from different religions, cultures, or locations are best organized in ways which bridge local to local, in other words where the focus is from one congregation to another congregation, faith community, or region. With a more manageable focus the connection between partners is more personal, visits are more possible, and projects can have more easily defined starts and endings. Wuthnow also affirms the need to start with the needs and interests of those involved as a way to begin a longer-term partnership, always utilizing existing networks and resources when available.[15]

Faith communities are rooted in their local contexts, and thus it is not possible to suggest one "recipe" for enhancing interreligious learning in a community. Faith communities of all sizes, locations, and economic levels are capable of cultivating interreligious learning; what is integral is that a faith community see interreligious learning as central to its mission and to its own self-interest, rather than as a special program or an "add-on." Though all congregations are likely to experience growth due to cultivating interreligious learning, some will experience losses as a result of the changes and conflicts that ensue. Growth here means more than increased membership, although some congregations do grow numerically due to their interreligious relationships. Some congregations experienced growth beyond numbers—profound spiritual growth, growth in the knowledge of their own tradition, growth in community involvement, growth in hospitality, and growth in relationships between members due to interreligious partnerships. It is a basic assumption of this article that all congregations, no

14. Wuthnow, *Boundless Faith*, 140.
15. Ibid., 141.

matter the location or the resources available, have the capacity to embrace interreligious learning in some way, and will be enriched for their efforts.

PRACTICES FOR INTERRELIGIOUS LEARNING

Without minimizing the distinctiveness of each congregation, it is possible to point to some characteristics of interreligious learning that are applicable in a variety of contexts. There is no one way to undertake interreligious learning, and yet there are values held and experiences shared by many different congregations along the way. These characteristics offer faith communities, religious organizations, and other groups interested in interreligious community some guidance and opportunities for further reflection.[16]

Build on Health

Congregations or religious organizations that are self-involved, riddled with unresolved internal conflicts, lacking skilled leadership, without coherent management, failing to provide spiritual care to members, or avoidant and hostile to the surrounding community are not in a good position to begin to build healthy relationships across religious differences. On a very basic level, congregations interested in interreligious learning need to practice sustained relationships based in mutuality, and to commit to affirming the dignity of every human person. Although the term "health" is a relative one, and while all congregations and organizations experience transitions, building relationships across religious differences requires those involved have the capacity to trust, and have some positive experience of community for support and nurture. Healthy communities are those where people interact with each other in respectful and appropriate ways, where feelings and ideas are expressed directly and openly, where the gifts of all are welcomed and leadership is exercised for the common good, where there is an openness to ongoing education and to issues in the community, and where people feel their pastoral needs are addressed. It is important to begin building relationships with people of other religious traditions *before* a crisis occurs locally, nationally, or internationally. Bonds of friendship are integral for interreligious relationships to withstand the bigotry, threats, natural disasters, and international incidents that undermine them. In short, interreligious

16. Because of the dynamic relationship between race and religion, these characteristics are also related to my earlier work in anti-racism in congregations. See, Kujawa-Holbrook, *A House of Prayer for All Peoples*, 180–85.

relationships will not be any deeper or more respectful than the relationships felt within the home congregation.

Practice Hospitality

One of the key characteristics and skills of congregations committed to interreligious learning is their practice of hospitality that extends beyond members into the wider community and the world. Many religious leaders committed to cultivating interreligious learning attest to the belief that their congregations are there for all people, adherents to their own faith or not, and they make this belief a cornerstone of their mission. Many interreligious encounters are enhanced through simple acts of hospitality, such as good food that all can eat, sensitive scheduling, and the appropriateness of the site. Besides a commitment to hospitality as an aspect of mission, these congregations also intentionally work on members' skills in welcome. For a congregation to say that its members support hospitality, and to *practice* hospitality are not necessarily identical. How does your congregation welcome its neighbors? How does your congregation open itself to people perceived as "strangers" or those unlike members? Lavish hospitality need not be expensive, but it must come from open hearts. Tenzin Gyatso, the Fourteenth Dalai Lama, once said, "My religion is kindness."[17] Most of the religions of the world urge adherents to practice hospitality, and some promise followers rewards in the afterlife for showing kindness to a neighbor.[18]

Support Multifaith Families

Increasingly, congregations interested in cultivating interreligious learning are finding ways to be more inclusive of multifaith families in their communal life. A 2008 survey by the Pew Forum on Religion and Public Life found that more than one quarter of married Americans have a spouse of a different faith.[19] Extended family occasions such as religious holidays, marriages, and funerals in particular, may be challenging for multifaith families, potentially as they can unearth issues that lay beneath the surface during other times of the year. Congregations interested in outreach to multifaith families respond with a range of strategies, including courses of instruction specifically geared for the partners of intermarried members, special groups

17 Gyatso, "First of Five Quotes."

18. For instance, see Amin, "Kindness to a Non-Muslim Neighbor."

19. Pew Research Center, "Religiously Mixed Couples."

for multifaith families, women and men, specific interreligious celebrations, and pre-marriage counseling. Perhaps most of all, multifaith families appreciate respectful welcome and open learning environments when seeking congregational homes. Typically, congregations sensitive to multifaith families actively encourage full participation in family and adult activities, and, when possible, integrate family members in committees and service organizations.

Commit to Lifelong Learning

Congregations and religious organizations destined to be more than museums most often have a deep commitment to lifelong learning for all ages. This type of education and formation reveals (and at times challenges) both the heritage and traditions of a given religious group, and leads to further investigation of other religions. The members of congregations that are deeply grounded in their own faith, are more willing to critically examine their religious beliefs from the perspective of other religious groups. The study of a spiritual path is a means toward transforming the members' sense of where they are and where they wish to go in the future. Certainly, in terms of participating in open and honest interreligious dialogue, it is imperative that people feel "religiously literate" or informed in their own religious tradition. Open and honest interreligious dialogue also requires knowledge of and openness to exploring the ways in which one's own religious tradition has been oppressive to others. Denial of negative history will not only prevent the formation of authentic interreligious community, it will also serve to maintain divisions between religious groups.

Moreover, just as it is crucial for individuals involved in interreligious learning to continue to maintain their own spiritual practice, it is critical for congregations and religious organizations to undergo a similar process of investigation, interpretation, and ultimately renewal. Transformational learning is always reciprocal; that is, just as we learn from our own religious community, we learn equally from those whom we have engaged from other religious traditions. Through compassionate listening and critical reflection, and through the challenge of presenting one's own faith to others, interreligious relationships offer opportunities to gain fresh insights about our own faith, and to learn new things about God from each other.

Foster Multicultural Competency

Faith communities interested in cultivating interreligious learning often have a high degree of comfort with navigating diverse expressions of religion, ethnicity, race, language, and culture as they are manifest in human communities. They are also aware of the dynamics of cross-cultural encounters and strive to more deeply welcome "the other." The experience of interreligious encounters, whether in public forums or in family homes, presents a range of varying cultural customs and practices for participants to navigate, including food-related practices, domestic customs, sacred rituals, gender roles, linguistic differences, communication differences, the use of space, etc. Some of these differences emanate from particular religious traditions, some may be attributable to a group within a religious tradition, while some may be due to the part of the world the group comes from, or historic or environmental factors.

For example, we know that persons from many of the religions of the world do not perceive the separation between the "sacred" and the "secular" in the same way as many North Americans and Europeans do. Multicultural competency stresses the need to differentiate between what is religious tradition or religious teaching, what is cultural and/or ethnic custom, and the importance of not comparing religious groups without understanding these distinctions. Cultural differences are often magnified in *intra-religious* dialogue where groups share a particular religious tradition, but express that tradition across a variety of cultural contexts. For instance, there is not just one Christian church or group that expresses the totality of world Christianity. Rather, each local congregation is one expression of the rich cultural mosaic we call the Christian church. Sometimes our divisions can be traced to theological differences or the different ways we interpret the Bible, at other times our differences are based in cultural conflicts between different racial or ethnic groups of Christians. In much the same way other religious communities throughout the world, such as Buddhists, Jews, Muslims, and others, live out their beliefs within the context of a variety of cultures. For instance, North American Buddhists and Asian Buddhists share similar beliefs and values, and at the same time there are cultural differences between the various groups. Interestingly, different branches of the same religious traditions often meet within interreligious contexts, when otherwise they might not. Multicultural competency not only helps congregations recognize cultural differences between groups, but also equips members with skills to appreciate differences and form relationships across differences.

Support Visionary Leaders

Leadership is a key variable among congregations and other religious organizations concerned with cultivating interreligious learning over the long haul. Stories from the congregations indicate that leaders of interreligious learning come from many different religious traditions, and that they are clergy and laity, women and men, some employed by religious organizations and some not. Yet a characteristic many share is their capacity to see interreligious learning in terms of a long-term *process* rather than a *program* or *product*. Many of those leaders committed to interreligious learning have an abiding belief in the importance of interreligious dialogue, and a vision of people from all religious traditions united for the common good. Christians devoted to interreligious learning often express this vision as a sense of vocation, or a "call" to work in the world in ways that build healthy relationships among people of faith. Leaders committed to interreligious learning tend to share a sacrificial commitment. Many have received criticism from their own faith communities for their interreligious commitments.

Interreligious leaders come from many different backgrounds, yet many share common experience in that they often express some "turning point" or "conversion" resulting from a direct and personal encounter across the boundaries of religious difference that dramatically shifted the way they viewed the world. Grounded and nourished through spiritual practice, these leaders tend to envision their work as a "partnership" and hence, tend to be non-dominant, preferring to lead through example, support, encouragement, and participation. Interreligious leaders have a tested yet optimistic view of humanity, and fundamentally believe that much can happen through the agency of people of good will. Moreover, they tend to view interreligious learning as an integral part of all they do in the world, rather than a distinct or segmented activity. On the skill level, committed interreligious leaders tend to be compassionate leaders, reflective teachers and/or preachers, risk takers open to failure, knowledgeable in group process and institutional change, multiculturally competent, active in the wider community, skilled with media, and, perhaps most importantly, *persistent*. Because interreligious learning is characterized by dynamic relationships, it is important that such leaders are able to withstand periods of frustration and disillusionment.

Many interreligious leaders report that they are criticized for their involvement in interreligious efforts, and that it is sometimes perceived in their home communities that they are not prioritizing members of their own religious traditions. Interreligious learning signals change and people in congregations will often experience those changes as painful losses, rather than opportunities for hope. Interreligious leaders need to be prepared for resistance and conflict, and should cultivate support systems for their work. At the same time, many interreligious leaders find joy in their work, and are supported and nurtured through the process of working for positive change in their local communities and the wider world.

Emphasize Prayer

While there are differences of opinion about the extent of shared worship, it is also the case that interreligious leaders recognize the power of shared prayer in the myriad forms that it takes place. One of the characteristics of interreligious learning is its rich symbolic life, and its attention to the ritual and aesthetic needs of a wide variety of religious cultures. One of the common "entry points" for many congregations is the sharing of sacred spaces. The promises and challenges of space sharing partnerships often lead to increasing interreligious relationships and other joint learning and initiatives between those involved. For many, the task of including symbols, texts, language, images, and rituals of other traditions into an experience of shared prayer is challenging, but also an opportunity for deep learning. For some, the desire to include elements of other traditions without insensitive misappropriation is a challenge, while for others the critical reflection on one's own tradition from the perspective of another religious group is enlightening, or even disturbing.

How does the prayer life of the congregation depict other religious traditions? Those congregations and religious organizations committed to interreligious learning stress the importance of prayer to this work, and share a commitment to cultivate and expand their spiritual lives on an ongoing basis. Many of the congregational leaders interviewed for this essay adapted to the challenge of making the symbolic lives of their congregations, as well as their sacred spaces, more hospitable for interreligious participation. Congregations interested in interreligious learning need to go through the process of reexamining their worship, music, education, and all other aspects of congregational life from an interreligious perspective.

Develop Networks and Democratic Partnerships

Most interreligious leaders attest to the importance of building and participating in networks from a variety of sources: local communities, denominations, official interreligious groups, global organizations, ecumenical partnerships, etc. Congregations that engage interreligious learning come from diverse theological perspectives, yet they share a vibrant faith and commitment to work for the good of all people of God. Though all are grounded in their own faith tradition and many have a denominational home, these congregations do not limit their role in the world solely to their membership, and all provide leadership in their local communities and beyond. These congregations have developed skills in community advocacy and in building alliances and partnerships. When working in their local communities or globally, these congregations demonstrate a commitment to democratic partnerships. They know how to listen to the needs of their partners, they know the difference between "acting for" and "working with" other individuals and groups, and they know how to shape a shared agenda. Not only are these congregations knowledgeable about the interreligious work and resources of their own tradition, as they provide leadership for these efforts, they seek connections and resources on an ongoing basis, remaining open to new partnerships and ways of growing interreligiously.

Invest in the Wider Community

There are rich connections between interreligious learning and practical action for the common good, most notably through local faith communities and interreligious organizations. One of the opportunities resulting from interreligious learning is that faith communities come together to care for the wider community. Religious communities that discover the power of the values and visions they hold in common and that work together for the good of all humanity and the planet are themselves transformed. The Fourteenth Dalai Lama, Tenzin Gyatso, says that compassion and love are two aspects of the same thing and give rise to such qualities as hope, courage, determination, and inner strength. Compassion is the wish for another to be free of suffering, while love is the desire for them to have happiness. "Genuine compassion is based not on our own projections and expectations, but rather on the needs of the other; irrespective of whether another person is a close friend or an enemy, as long as that person wishes for peace and happiness and wishes to overcome suffering, then on that basis we develop genuine compassion for their problem," he writes.[20]

The Parliament of the World's Religions believes that now "sustained encounters between people of different religious, spiritual, and cultural traditions have created heightened momentum toward actualizing our many visions of a better world, as well as stronger possibilities for establishing

---

20. Gyatso, *An Open Heart*, 26.

ethical common ground."[21] Faith communities can accomplish what economic plans and political programs cannot attain: That is, an inner change, a change of heart, a conversion to a new vision of humanity in relationship with others. The hope of the Parliament of the World's Religions is that local religious institutions and communities will creatively engage each other and cooperate on behalf of the peoples of the world to address disintegrating community, the unrelenting demands on the earth's resources, growing injustices and divisions, and spiritual indirection. According to the Parliament, the common critical issues for local faith communities to address today include "building community in diversity, and thus restoring respect and mutuality in place of tension, hostility, and violence; finding sustainable and peaceful ways to meet the needs of people while preserving the integrity of all life on the planet; alleviating the suffering of the majority of the human community through economic, political, and social reform; identifying compassionately with others and building solidarity among peoples; and seeking spiritual grounding from the wisdom of the religious traditions of the world to move beyond self-interest, building community in the spirit of hospitality, and expressing compassion through service."[22]

Practice Reconciliation

God calls all of humanity to a life of rich diversity. Our capacity and the capacity of our congregations to build relationships with God, each other, our neighbors, and the larger world are consistent with the vision of many of the religions of the world across cultures and national boundaries. Throughout the New Testament, Jesus is frequently found reaching out to and in communication with people from religions and cultures different than his own. Congregations practice reconciliation when they seek to heal the divisions and enmity between people within the congregation and beyond. Interreligious conversations are a vehicle for groups to relate positively to each other and heal negative prejudices and historic divisions. The process of living out interreligious community impacts our hearts, our minds, and our lives and brings about new understandings of God and our own religious community. These realizations come with the understanding that as people of faith we are called to respond to a world filled with suffering and broken relationships. To practice reconciliation means, in part, to perceive that our differences and our interdependence are a divine gift. It means that peace will not be built on separatism or political arguments, but on the transformation of

21. Parliament of the World's Religions, "A Call to our Guiding Institutions."
22. Council for the Parliament of the World's Religions, 1999; 5, 7–9.

hearts. Congregations that practice reconciliation know the importance of relationships, have the ability to remain in relationship through conflict, and recognize that every interreligious encounter in some way contributes to the relationship between the world's religions. Compassionate listening skills, mediation skills, and knowledge of conflict resolution are all integral to the practice of reconciliation, as is the creation of a community where the ability to speak the truth in love is a reality.

Plan, Monitor, and Evaluate

Regardless of size or resources, congregations committed to interreligious learning need to develop a formal plan to build and maintain interreligious community, as they continue to monitor their interreligious relationships and evaluate their experiences. In many cases, the most successful interreligious action plans in congregations are those with clarity of purpose, and with enough flexibility to allow for needed changes and the surprises that occur in the course of all human relationships. As congregations discern their needs and capacities for interreligious community, and discover what has worked for others in similar situations, specific strategies best emerge from the specific context. Without ongoing evaluation that includes discernment, reflection, adjustments, and modifications, any plan will eventually lose its energy or purpose. Given that building interreligious community is a long-term commitment, planning, monitoring, and evaluation not only clarify goals, but also help congregations deepen interreligious relationships. Planning processes that begin with bringing all parties together for joint projects is optimal for building interreligious community, as is openness to learning and the ability to adapt as opportunities emerge. Team-building skills, including clear communications, and a spirit of mutual respect are critical for cooperative interreligious projects. The importance of people from different religious traditions planning collaboratively is integral to the building of interreligious relationships.

THE PENTECOST PARADIGM

In the Christian tradition, the account of the event during Pentecost (Acts 2:1–12) is one example of the consequences of a genuine encounter with the Spirit of God, and how people who do not understand each other can change the way they see themselves, each other, and the world.

Christian theologian Christopher Duraisingh uses the Pentecost story as a way to illustrate both the power and the potential of religious pluralism.

He argues out that the Pentecost narrative in the Acts of the Apostles carefully holds in creative tension the terms "all" and "each." *All* cultures and
languages are affirmed by the Spirit, and yet *each* hears in their own language—Jews, Arabs, Libyans, Romans, and Iranians, a microcosm of the
plurality found in the known world at the time. "This story suggests that it
is in the midst of the promise and the pain that immigration entails in our
postcolonial times that we discern the Spirit," writes Duraisingh. "The inter-
wovenness, the intermingling of the plurality of peoples is not something of
which to be afraid. For the Spirit breaks forth in the midst of this diversity
and is made known as the transforming power of God."[23] The relationships
across differences formed through the Pentecost paradigm are deeper than
just celebrating our diversity. Rather, the story suggests that the disciples are
drawn to the Spirit and into communion for mutual enrichment *through*
their differences. "It is as they mutually share their differences that they
come to know and witness to what the author of Ephesians calls 'the multi-
colored wisdom of God.'"[24]

The story of Pentecost illustrates an authentic way of dealing with pluralism, one that "de-centers" individual and collective identities believed to
be autonomous and self-sufficient. None of us is ever really self-sufficient.
Whether we recognize it or not, we are bound together through a common humanity that is shared, despite our differences. The Pentecost story is
told in the context of the disciples' questions to Jesus about whether or not
the kingdom of Israel will be restored. Jesus' response is to tell the disciples
that they will in fact be dispersed, and find their identities with the diverse
peoples among whom they go to witness. There is no longer a single language or central place. Later on, the disciples learn that baptism is in itself
a new identity, one that points to a new and radically inclusive humanity.
"Pentecost points to a de-centering of centers and identities that exclude, a
courageous crossing of borders and a promotion of multi-vocal, polyphonic
community."[25]

Key to this vision of Pentecost for individuals and congregations
interested in cultivating interreligious learning is the concept of "courageous border crossings." For instance, in the Acts of the Apostles we are
first introduced to Peter and his reluctance to cross the borders of race and
religion, notably in terms of his attitudes toward the gentile, Cornelius, and
Peter's fears about allowing those like Cornelius in the community. Yet the
Spirit of Pentecost had an impact on Peter and changed the way he judged

23. Duraisingh, "The Multi-Colored Wisdom of God," 13–14.

24. Ibid., 14.

25. Ibid.

what he originally held as impermeable cultural and religious boundaries. He was confronted with the possibility that God does not have favorites, and he was given the strength and the wisdom to negotiate the borders of his religious culture and welcome those from another religious background into the community.

Many cultural and religious conflicts are based in the inability of people to move beyond the boundaries of their own groups, and hence the need for faith communities to work conscientiously at broadening people's sense of the larger human community. Further, "courageous border-crossing" not only requires "passing over" or going over to the standpoint of another religion, or another way of life: it also requires a "coming back" process. That is, coming back to one's own religion or one's own way of life and integrating new insights, new appreciations, new experiences. "Here there is no fusion of borders so that our individual or group [religious] identities are lost. Nor is it a border diffusion or dissolution," says Duraisingh. "But it is a crossing over and a returning so that the coordinates of one's identities may now be redrawn in a much richer way due to the gift from the other."[26]

Living within the Pentecost paradigm has its risks. In order to do so, it means giving up exclusivist claims. It means risking criticism from members of one's own religious tradition. In some cases, congregations that have crossed borders and built interreligious community with their neighbors have lost some members for doing so. But the Pentecost paradigm teaches that it is only through crossing borders and coming back that the creativity of the Spirit is unleashed, faith is deepened, relationships formed, and new insights are gained.

There is yet another vision of border crossing in Isaiah 19:23–24. In the passage, three former enemies, Egypt, Assyria, and Israel, walk back and forth to each other on a highway built by God. Although the decision to join the alliance was costly for Israel—they had to give up a privileged identity as God's people—the prophet envisioned the broader purpose as God's dream for all of humanity: "Blessed be Egypt my people, and Assyria the work of my hands, and Israel my heritage."[27] Duraisingh writes, "The mission of the church today, I submit, is building such a highway over which people of diverse cultures, religions, and races can cross borders for both integration as well as enrichment of their particular identities."[28]

The lessons of Pentecost point to a need for the creation of intentional communities where people can be affirmed in their own religious, social,

26. Ibid., 15.

27. NRSV, Isa 19:25b.

28. Ibid., 15.

and cultural identities, and at the same time be creatively transformed through authentic engagement with others. Congregations that cultivate interreligious learning are these types of communities, as they create spaces for dialogues to take place and for relationships to be transformed. They are places where we can relate to the wider world, and where we can claim our own voices, as well as hear and speak to others. They are places where we can begin to cross the borders of our limited understandings about God and meet companions along the way. Congregations that actually encourage a plurality of voices also tend to be places where power-sharing is critical in the way decisions are made and common life organized. "Today the call comes afresh to Christians everywhere, to cross boundaries and traditions that divide us in the pattern and power of the One who crossed every human boundary and broke every middle wall of division in order that the one new humanity where there is no longer Jew or Greek, slave or free, male or female may be brought about," writes Duraisingh. "Each a border-crossing in the power of the Spirit of the Risen Christ for the glory of the Triune God is our vocation, and our reward."[29]

All congregations have the capacity to cultivate interreligious learning in meaningful ways. In an effort to end on a practical note, here are ten concrete and achievable strategies for congregations interested in cultivating interreligious learning:

TEN THINGS CONGREGATIONS CAN DO TO CULTIVATE INTERRELIGIOUS LEARNING

1. Investigate the "religious landscape" of your home community. What religious groups are present? Do you have a contact list for the various groups?

2. Reflect on the religious pluralism *within* your congregation. Are there any interreligious families? Staff members or volunteers from other religious groups? How might your congregation better serve those from other religious groups in your midst?

3. Ask people from other religious traditions to tell you about their communities, as regards religious education, worship, etc. If your congregation already has formed some interreligious relationships, are there ways they might be deepened or expanded?

29. Ibid., 17.

4. Visit another religious group in your community when they hold an open day or offer a community program. Hold a visiting day at your own congregation and invite the wider community for hospitality.

5. Find ways, when working on common issues such as poverty, homelessness, education, etc., to work with other religious groups in your local community.

6. Study. In your own congregation or with another religious group, design an educational experience or share in a book group.

7. In order to build relationships, do business intentionally with firms run by members of other religious groups.

8. Support efforts combating religious hate crimes and religious discrimination in your community.

9. Support local, national, and global interreligious organizations with your time, your ideas, and your material resources.

10. Pray that God may empower you to build interreligious community through your congregation.

Interreligious learning pushes the borders of all religious education. A practical need related to growing religious pluralism is building bridges within faith communities with interreligious families, as well as with those who live in the wider community. We now know that faith communities that support interreligious learning create spaces for deep conversations and for encounters to take place and for relationships to be transformed. They are sacred spaces which respond with compassion to the needs and concerns of their neighbors. They are places where we can begin to find God beyond the borders of our limited understandings about the Divine and share in the stories of our companions along the way as we form partnerships for the good of the world.

BIBLIOGRAPHY

Amin, El-Sayed M. "Kindness to a Non-Muslim Neighbor: Tips for Interaction." http://www.islamawareness.net/Neighbours/kindness.html.

Duraisingh, Christopher. "'The Multi-Colored Wisdom of God': A Pentecost Paradigm." *The Witness* (December 2001) 13–14.

Galloway, Kathy. "From the Holy City: Seeking the Heartlands." *Coracle* 4/29 (2007) 3–4.

Gyatso, Tenzin, The Fourteenth Dalai Lama. "First of Five Quotes This Week." One Million Acts of Kindness. http://www.onemillionactsofkindness.com/2015/12/first-of-five-quotes-this-week-3/.

————. *An Open Heart: Practicing Compassion in Everyday Life.* New York: Little, Brown, 2001.

Hollister, Juliet. The Temple of Understanding. http://templeofunderstanding.org/.

Kujawa-Holbrook, Sheryl A. *God Beyond Borders: Interreligious Learning Among Faith Communities.* Eugene, OR: Pickwick, 2014.

————. *A House of Prayer for All People: Congregations Building Multiracial Community.* Bethesda: Alban Institute, 2003.

Kujawa-Holbrook, Sheryl A., et al. *For One Great Peace: An Interfaith Peacemaking Guide,* 2013. Available for download from www.abrahamicfaithspeacemaking.com.

Parliament of the World's Religions. "A Call to our Guiding Institutions." Presented on the occasion of the 1999 Parliament of the World's Religions. Cape Town, South Africa, December 1999.

Patel, Eboo. "Acts of Faith: Interfaith Leadership in a Time of Religious Crisis." *Virginia Seminary Journal* (Fall 2009) 32–39.

Pew Research Center. "Religiously Mixed Couples: Cupid's Arrow Often Hits People of Different Faiths." Religion and Public Life, February 10, 2008. http://www.pewforum.org/2009/02/10/religiously-mixed-couples-cupids-arrow-often-hits-people-of-different-faiths/.

Selmanovic, Samir. *It's Really All About God: Reflections of a Muslim Atheist Jewish Christian.* San Francisco: Jossey-Bass, 2009.

Tutu, Desmond. Opening quote on the front page of The Tutu Foundation's website, http://www.tutufoundationuk.org/.

Williams, Betty. The Peace People. www.peacepeople.com.

Wuthnow, Robert. *Boundless Faith: The Global Reach of American Churches.* Berkeley: University of California Press, 2010.

ONLINE RESOURCES

Council for a Parliament of the World's Religions, www.cpwr.org. (Presently, the following site is active at https://parliamentofreligions.org.)

IslamOnline, www.islamonline.net.

Pew Forum, *Religion in American Culture,* www.religions.pewforum.org.

One Million Acts of Kindness, www.onemillionactsofkindness.org.

Appendix

Reflective Matrix: Spectrum of Reflective Practice in Seminary Teaching

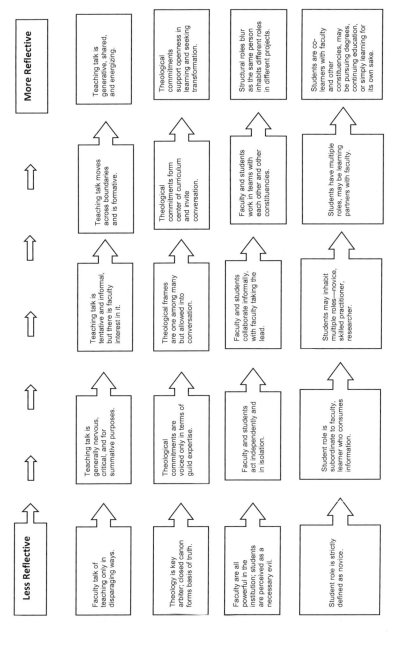

Less Reflective → More Reflective

Faculty talk of teaching only in disparaging ways. → Teaching talk is generally nervous, critical, and for summative purposes. → Teaching talk is tentative and informal, but there is faculty interest in it. → Teaching talk moves across boundaries and is formative. → Teaching talk is generative, shared, and energizing.

Theology is key arbiter; closed canon forms basis of truth. → Theological commitments are voiced only in terms of guild expertise. → Theological frames are one among many but allowed into conversation. → Theological commitments form center of curriculum and invite conversation. → Theological commitments support openness in learning and seeking transformation.

Faculty are all powerful in the institution; students are perceived as a necessary evil. → Faculty and students act independently and in isolation. → Faculty and students collaborate informally, with faculty taking the lead. → Faculty and students work in teams with each other and other constituencies. → Structural roles blur as the same person inhabits different roles in different projects.

Student role is strictly defined as novice. → Student role is subordinate to faculty; learner who consumes information. → Students may inhabit multiple roles—novice, skilled practitioner, researcher. → Students have multiple roles, may be learning partners with faculty. → Students are co-learners with faculty and other constituencies, may be pursuing degrees, continuing education, or simply learning for its own sake.

Reflective Matrix: Spectrum of Reflective Practice in Seminary Teaching (cont'd)

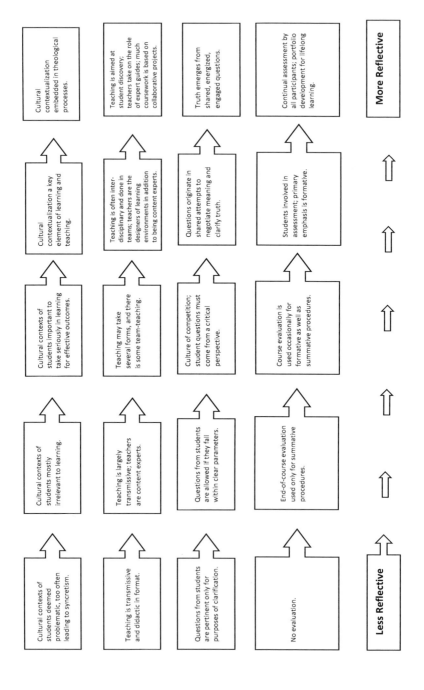

Less Reflective → → → → More Reflective

Cultural contexts of students deemed problematic, too often leading to syncretism.
→ Cultural contexts of students mostly irrelevant to learning.
→ Cultural contexts of students important to take seriously in learning for effective outcomes.
→ Cultural contextualization a key element of learning and teaching.
→ Cultural contextualization embedded in theological processes.

Teaching is transmissive and didactic in format.
→ Teaching is largely transmissive; teachers are content experts.
→ Teaching may take several forms, and there is some team-teaching.
→ Teaching is often inter-disciplinary and done in teams; teachers are the designers of learning environments in addition to being content experts.
→ Teaching is aimed at student discovery; teachers take on the role of expert guides; much coursework is based on collaborative projects.

Questions from students are pertinent only for purposes of clarification.
→ Questions from students are allowed if they fall within clear parameters.
→ Culture of competition; student questions must come from a critical perspective.
→ Questions originate in shared attempts to negotiate meaning and clarify truth.
→ Truth emerges from shared, energized, engaged questions.

No evaluation.
→ End-of-course evaluation used only for summative procedures.
→ Course evaluation is used occasionally for formative as well as summative procedures.
→ Students involved in assessment; primary emphasis is formative.
→ Continual assessment by all participants; portfolio development for lifelong learning.